FIRST TRIATHLONS

Personal Stories of Becoming a Triathlete

Gail Waesche Kislevitz

BREAKAWAY BOOKS
HALCOTTSVILLE, NEW YORK
2006

ISBN: 1-891369-64-4
ISBN-13: 978-1-891369-64-3
Library of Congress Control Number: 2006926645

Published by Breakaway Books
P.O. Box 24
Halcottsville, NY 12438
www.breakawaybooks.com

FIRST EDITION

CONTENTS

Droc, it's finally your turn.
Here's to all the great meals you prepare
for me when I return from my events.
I couldn't do it without your support and encouragement.

Acknowledgments

This book could not have been written without all the inspiring people who trusted me with their first triathlon stories. Throughout the interview process I laughed, cried, and was astounded, amazed and thrilled. Many thanks go to all my athletes for sharing their sometimes intimate, other time hilarious, and oftentimes heart-wrenching accounts.

I must acknowledge Lisa Swain for talking me into my first triathlon. She got me hooked and continues to be a loyal training partner. I always look forward to my Wednesday GBOs (Girls Bike Out) with Lisa and Linda as we pedal for hours on long training rides while discussing various topics such raising teenagers, raising husbands, night sweats, and the next race. As Lisa says, "It's not just biking; it's my therapy session."

I also want to acknowledge my proofreaders, who brought a sharp focus and fresh eyes to the copy. Every writer needs a good editor and my friends turned out to be the best. Their critiques were kind and on target.

Mike Llerandi and Amy Shigo were instrumental in opening doors to triathlon celebrities such as Dave Scott and Karen Smyers. Scott and Smyers were cordial, friendly, helpful, and acted more like old friends than first-time contacts who receive calls seeking interviews every day. I was a fan before speaking with them and now have their voice messages on my phone saved for infinity. My household is forbidden to erase the message, "Hi, Gail, Dave Scott here." I listen to it before my events for good luck.

The triathlon community as a whole—from race directors to event planners to participants—was more than helpful. In the book you'll read about how accepting and supportive the triathlon community is to first-timers, and I had the same experience every step of the way throughout my research and writing process.

My West Coast connection, Juliana Tsai, always came through for me with fascinating triathletes. She is the ultimate tri girl, a true ambassador for the sport. Gordon Bakoulis, runner extraordinaire, editor of *New York Runner,* and coach of Moving Comfort, a running team for women, also reached out to her contacts and I received many exuberant replies.

And finally, my family deserves some praise for putting up with all my late nights and weekends at the computer or on the phone doing interviews. My daughter, Anna, gave me weekly checkup calls, and my son, Elijah, who is living in China, would IM me late at night just as I was logging off to go to bed with a cheery, "Good morning, Mom! How's the book coming?" I think my husband will be just as happy as me to see the book finished so we can resume date nights and going to the movies.

I am sure there are many fascinating stories out there I missed. At every triathlon I meet someone who has an inspiring story. Since I can't capture every one of them, please do me a favor and at your next triathlon—or first—as you wait your turn for your wave, turn to the person next to you and just say hello. Show an interest. Open the door. I'm sure you'll get an earful.

Gail Waesche Kislevitz
July 2006

About the Author

Gail has run nineteen marathons and competes in triathlons. She maintains professional affiliations with North Jersey Masters Track and Field Club in New Jersey, New York Road Runners, where she has been an age-division Runner of the Year nominee, and has been a sponsored masters runner for Active Elite. She lives in Ridgewood, New Jersey, with her husband, Androc, and their two children. In September she completed her first half Ironman, thanks to all the advice she got while writing this book.

INTRODUCTION

During the summer of 1972 runners hailed Frank Shorter, America's first-ever gold medalist in the marathon, at the Munich Olympics. At that same Olympics, Mark Spitz became every swimmer's poster boy with his seven medals. Cyclists worshipped Greg Lemond long before Lance Armstrong became a household name. Every sport had its heroes and legends. Athletes identified themselves as runners, swimmers, cyclists, single event competitors. By the mid-1970s, a group of California athletes started experimenting with cross-training by stringing together two sports then three, and before long triathlon was created as a sport in and of itself.

In 1978, John Collins, a naval commander stationed in Hawaii, decided to hold a contest to decide who was the fittest athlete: a runner, cyclist or swimmer. The winner would be proclaimed an Iron Man (it was originally two words). The first-ever Hawaii Ironman contest drew fifteen entrants to the island of Oahu. To find out who won and whether it was the runner, cyclist, or swimmer, read the chapter on Gordon Haller.

Fast-forward thirty-seven years and on October 2005, more than seventeen hundred competitors endured the grueling 2.4-mile swim, 112-mile bike course, and 26.2-mile run at Kona. According to USA Triathlon, the national governing body of the sport, triathlon is the fastest growing sport in the United States with a 30 percent increase in the past five years. A profile of the average triathlete is a thirty-to-thirty-nine-year-old man or woman with a graduate degree and income of more than sixty thousand dollars. That salary will come in handy to pay for registration fees. It's an expensive sport compared with road racing. A sprint triathlon averages $70, an Olympic is around $150, and an Ironman will cost you an average of $500, not including travel fees and hotel expenses.

USAT has a current membership of seventy thousand, three times as many as in 2000. Another 225,000 people bought one-day memberships for events in 2005. It is estimated that nearly 500,000 people in the United States will do a triathlon in 2006. According to Tim Yount, senior vice president for marketing at USAT, people in their forties are the fastest-growing segment and of that group women are taking the lead. Reflecting these rapidly expanding numbers is the number of sanctioned triathlon events taking place in the U.S. In 2000 there were 686; in 2006 there are 1,800. The sport has come a long way since 1980, when Dave Scott won his first of six Hawaii Ironmans. He wore knee-high white tube socks, rode a thirty-pound bike, and his parents followed him on the course in their car just in case he needed anything. At the twentieth anniversary of the Hawaii Ironman, John Collins announced triathlon is no longer a hobby; it is a lifestyle.

What is the appeal? For a sprint triathlon (usually a 750-meter swim, 20-kilometer bike, and 5-kilometer run), it's the reality that almost anyone can complete the distance. Then the bar gets raised and the next distance becomes the challenge. (The Olympic triathlon is a 1.5K swim, 40K bike, and 10K run.) In triathlons, there's always room for improvement and you don't really have to master all three sports. The Ironman distance is another story. There's no faking that one. You're either ready or don't bother showing up. The consequences are too dire.

It conditions the entire body, not just the legs of a runner or cyclist. Sports doctors state that triathlon training can reduce the risk of injuries that runners and cyclist are prone to because of all the cross-training involved. It's also more social than solitary running and cycling. Sports marketers are quickly putting together family vacation packages centered on sports events like the Ironman Triathlon in Orlando which takes place on the grounds of Disney World. While Mom and Dad compete the kids are having breakfast with Mickey and everyone is happy.

Dave Scott has seen the evolution up close and personal. According to Scott, "At the shorter distances it's easier than a marathon and more forgiving on the body." He also credits women with taking on the sport full-throttle. "The women are really coming on strong," says Scott. "People are realizing triathlon is a very do-able sport and are enjoying them."

In *First Triathlons* you will meet amazing people who took up triathlon and loved it. Jody Llewellyn, a marathoner, decided to do a triathlon because it was less stressful on her body. Her first tri distance was a half Ironman and she lived to tell the tale, even though she completed the first half of the bike course with only one shoe. Jayne Williams, a self-described slow, fat triathlete, loved her first tri experience so much she wrote a book about it called *Slow Fat Triathlete* to encourage others like her to participate in the sport. Her narrative on trying to get into a wet suit for the first time will have you cramping over with laughter. Sister Madonna Buder started doing triathlons in her fifties. Now seventy-six, she's completed more than two hundred triathlons, including thirty-three Ironmans, and is the oldest female to finish the World Championships in Kona. "Life is never at a standstill and neither am I," says Sister Buder.

Triathlon is not limited to able-bodied athletes. Steve Nuccio, a below-the-knee amputee, finished the Hawaiian Ironman with five minutes to spare. "If I had known that, I would have slowed down," says Nuccio, a father of two and vice president at Merrill Lynch.

First-ever Ironman Gordon Haller gives his account of the very first triathlon in 1978. There were no course markers, aid stations, or information on what to expect. "We showered after the swim and didn't know anything about nutrition," laughs Haller, who goes back to compete at Kona. "I remember seeing a guy eating a bowl of chili between events."

What makes this book stand out from others is its ability—through first-hand accounts from all levels and sizes of athletes—to make the triathlon do-able. It's not about how to be the fastest or getting to the podium. It's about enjoying this unique sport and at the end of the day feeling proud of your accomplishments. By the time you finish this book you will be able to literally feel the athletes sprint, jump, fall, crawl, cry, scream and laugh across the finish line. Their accounts bring the triathlon to life.

The book also offers professional nutrition advice and coaching tips from world-class coaches like Chris Carmichael, cycle coach to Lance Armstrong; and Bart Yasso, race director at *Runner's World,* ultrarunner and triathlete. Bart's idea of fun is cycling across the United States, and not in a straight line, and then going for a long run back. Terry Laughlin, founder of the Total Immersion swim method, was my first choice for swim advice. Anyone who can combine the words *zen* and *swim* in one sentence and uses fish as a role model is definitely on to something. Dave Scott, "The Man," offers advice on how to pull it all together and enjoy doing it for life.

Whether you break out the old clunker or invest in a ten-thousand-dollar-bike; do the doggy paddle or stroke like Spitz; can barely put one foot in front of the other or are a lean running machine, triathlon has something to offer everyone at every distance, age and ability. It is the great unifier of sports.

DONNA ADAMOLI

DOB: 11-5-62
Residence: Chestnut Ridge, New York
Occupation: Doctor
First Triathlon: 1998 Wyckoff (New Jersey) Sprint Triathlon

Donna Adamoli is a doctor who practices what she preaches. When she gives her patients the talk on living a healthy lifestyle and including exercise into their weekly routine, she can back it up by telling tales of her triathlons. She rarely likes to talk about herself unless pushed to the wall—but then the stories of Escape from Alcatraz come out and inspire even coach potatoes to do something. Her athletic background includes being a competitive swimmer from age eight; switching to a competitive runner in high school; in college she was coached by the famous Joan Benoit Samuelson, America's first female Olympic marathoner from the 1984 Los Angeles games. Then she switched to triathlons. For now, she is content with the Olympic distance, but somewhere in Donna's future is a full Ironman.

"I started swimming at age eight and was on a YMCA swim team. Swimming was my first love. I never had a fear of water; swimming was just natural for me. I swam competitively till high school but then switched to track. I didn't want to spend my free time getting up early before school and then again after school for swim practice, plus I felt like

13

I needed a change. My sophomore year I joined the track team and eventually got a scholarship to Boston University for track and cross-country. I competed all four years at Boston. I swam only during a knee injury."

Her coach was Joan Benoit Samuelson, before she became famous for being the first American woman to win a gold medal in the marathon in the Olympics. Donna and some of her teammates at BU got tickets to attend the games, a highlight in her life.

"When I graduated college in 1985 I didn't race anymore but ran for fitness. It was hard to make the transition from being on top of the field to not winning. I admit it was my pride and I couldn't handle it. I didn't want slow times. I'm sure I missed out on a lot of fun races.

"Around that time I was considering getting into triathlon but also applied to medical school. I told myself if I didn't get into medical school I would train for an Ironman."

Adamoli did get into medical school, the University of Colorado. After her residency she moved to the East Coast and set up a practice. All through her medical school she ran for fitness but didn't race for years. A colleague at the hospital where she worked noticed she ran and suggested she look into doing a local triathlon.

"The Wyckoff Triathlon was only four weeks away when he told me about it. It sounded like something I could accomplish, so I decided to sign up. I didn't even own a bike at the time. I swam a few times at a pool to make sure I could still do it, and the night before I borrowed a bike which was too small for me.

"When I got to the event, there weren't even bike racks in the transition area. Bikes were just laid on the ground. I had never done open water swimming. When the gun went off, I plunged in and before I could catch my breath, people were swimming over me, under me, hitting me. It was dreadful and for the first time ever, I felt panicky in the water. I kept thinking of the other swimmers and if I felt like this, having grown up in the water, what must they be feeling? It was awful.

"I forced myself to calm down, pulled over to the side so I could have some space, regrouped, and just kept swimming. After I got out of the water I ran to transition and took my sweet time. I dried off with a towel, thought about combing my hair, and then began to notice that all the

14

women I passed in the water were now on their bikes and out on the course. I thought, *@#$%,* dropped my towel, and took off.

"The run was harder than I ever thought it would be. It took forever for my legs to work. When I finished I started packing up to go home. When I was walking to the car, I heard my name announced and it turns out I took third in my age group and went home with a big trophy. I was shocked."

As much as Adamoli enjoyed her first triathlon, she felt the commitment was too demanding for her schedule and didn't do another until the following year at Wyckoff. Up until 2004 she only did one a year, the Wyckoff Triathlon. But 2005 turned out to be a pivotal year for her. She had to miss the Wyckoff Triathlon to attend a family wedding. Wanting to continue her streak of doing one a year, she looked into other local events.

"I was so disappointed to miss Wyckoff. I looked forward to it every year, actually put aside a few weeks to train, although I still borrowed a bike, and now I had to miss it. I started asking around for another event to do and a friend told me about the Westchester Triathlon, which was an Olympic distance and a qualifier for Escape from Alcatraz. When he explained all this to me and was encouraging me to try to qualify, I didn't know what he was talking about. I never even considered doing Alcatraz. All I wanted to do was my one triathlon a year.

"He raised my curiosity so I went on the website for Escape from Alcatraz and it looked like crazy fun. Knowing it would be a long shot to qualify, I decided to give it a try."

Adamoli made it a goal to qualify for Alcatraz and trained hard all summer. She even bought a bike, and a wet suit for the cold waters of San Francisco Bay. She qualified by placing second in her age group at the Westchester Tri. The many new twists and turns of doing a competitive, scary, faraway triathlon kept her busy all winter and spring. She had to get used to swimming in a wet suit, get familiar with the gears on a new bike, even new logistics like taking her bike on the plane to California. But it all paid off in the end.

"By the time I flew to San Francisco, I felt confident that I had trained as hard as I could and was very prepared. My goal was not to just finish, but to place in my age group. The race logistics for Alcatraz can be overwhelming. There are mandatory meetings for all participants to learn about the important details of the swim: how to sight to shore, what landmarks to look for, how to deal with the cold water, and so on and so on.

"Race-day morning sixteen hundred participants boarded a huge ferry that took us out across the bay to Alcatraz Island. The ferry pulls up right alongside the famous prison and within five minutes, everyone was in the water. That sounds impossible, but it is amazing. The pros go off first and then wave after wave by age group everyone jumps in the water. If you hesitate, you get pushed. No time for panic attacks at this event. When I hit the water, the frigid cold stunned me. It was rough and choppy and I felt like I was in a freezing-cold washing machine getting tossed around. But as I settled in for the 1.5-mile swim and got acclimated, I looked up and saw the Golden Gate Bridge and the San Francisco skyline. It was very cool."

The biggest fear for the swimmers at Alcatraz is the fifty-five-degree water and being dragged off course. The current is so strong that it isn't uncommon for swimmers to find themselves being pulled closer and closer toward the bridge and open sea and not the shore. The bay is filled with volunteers on Jet Skis, kayaks, and boats who are allowed to pull swimmers out of the water and bring them back on course without being disqualified.

"I was very impressed with the safety concerns of the race directors. There were times when I felt totally alone out there and couldn't even see another swimmer but I knew if I needed help it was within reach. But for me the fear was not getting lost but being cold. I got hypothermia and started shaking uncontrollably and couldn't think. It was like my mind and body shut down and I couldn't move my fingers. But I kept trying to focus and just stay on course and before long it was over and I was out and running up to transition, which, by the way, is a three-quarter-mile run.

"I must have been a bit delirious when I got out of the water from the hypothermia because I swear I started pulling off my wet suit to get ready for T1 but a good friend of mine who was looking for me said I never did that; in fact, I looked a bit groggy and disoriented. My fingers were still numb and I had a hard time getting my shoes on.

"I was still freezing when I got on the bike but I knew when I hit the hills I would warm up. The eighteen-mile bike course is very scenic but also very challenging with lots of steep climbs and fast descents.

"As challenging as the bike course was, the eight-mile run was no picnic. Spectacularly beautiful, but tough. The course took us up steep hills, under the Golden Gate Bridge and up the Presidio headlands on narrow trails, onto Baker Beach and up the famous four-hundred-step sand ladder up Baker Beach that only the pros manage to run. Most of us walk the sand ladder.

"When I finished I had a great sense of accomplishment, made better by placing third in my age division."

Adamoli did Alcatraz again in 2006 and also placed third in her age division, taking nine minutes off her 2005 time. Since 2005 she does five triathlons a season, all sprints and Olympic distances. "The sport of triathlon is very addictive. It's like golf; you try it once and then you find yourself wanting to get better and better. There are so many components to doing a triathlon, it's tough to master them—which for me, is the constant challenge and why I like it so much. Biking is my weak link because I don't have the time to get out and ride enough. Plus I should hire a coach to teach me all the proper techniques. Running is my best event. I love running because it's all about the person, not the equipment. I don't have to rely on anything but myself to do well.

"But I do feel that my current schedule of five a season is making me crazy. It's too much and I need to back off for a while. Between my medical practice, my personal life, my dog and house, there isn't enough time to train the way I need to if I want to do an Ironman. Right now I am training eight hours a week but that isn't enough for an Ironman."

Adamoli is adamant with her patients about the important role of exercise in their lives. She hears all the excuses.

"When I ask my patients if they exercise, I get a thousand excuses as to why they can't. Then I ask them how many hours a week they spend watching TV and it hits a nerve. Some of that time can certainly go toward exercising. I recommend a minimum thirty minutes of exercise five days a week. You can do a lot in thirty minutes: go for a walk, a gym workout, play a game of tennis, go for a run, walk the dog, go for a bike ride, go for a swim. I tell my patients to just schedule it in like you would schedule a business meeting. It is that important. Every once in a while a patient will ask me in a challenging manner if I exercise. Then it's really fun to tell them about my triathlons. It certainly makes the point."

TOM BEGG

DOB: 8-14-64
Residence: Glen Rock, New Jersey
Occupation: Sales
First Triathlon: 1997 Harriman (New York) Sprint Triathlon

Tom Begg grew up in Waterbury, Connecticut, in a family that was very sports-oriented and competitive. His brother Bill ran his first marathon on a dare with no training. Dares and gutsy behavior seem to run in the Begg family. When not golfing with friends, Begg spent the vast majority of his time swimming in Long Island Sound.

Begg is a die-hard Bruce Springsteen, New York Jets, and New York Mets fan and remembers accidentally watching the first televised Hawaii Ironman. He was mesmerized by the passion and level of commitment and endurance he saw in the faces of the athletes. It stuck in his head as something that one day he would want to do.

A few years later, while on a golf outing with his brother, the marathoner, and a cyclist friend, they all made a friendly bet to see who would have the best time in a triathlon. It was a brutal experience, but it ended up being life changing; he decided he wanted to be a triathlete.

"Being the competitive kind of guy I am, I mentioned the Ironman to the group and we got talking about the sport and who is the better athlete, the runner, cyclist, or swimmer. I shot off my mouth about swimming being the superior sport in a triathlon and bet them I could kick their butts in a triathlon. My as-competitive brother felt that as a runner he would win and of course the biker had to uphold his sport so we placed a bet that day out on the golf course to do a triathlon and settle the argument once and for all. I remember leaving the golf course and reminding them about how anyone can ride a bike or run, but the winner will be the swimmer.

"We picked the Harriman Sprint Triathlon because it was the closest in distance to all of us and the date fit on all our calendars. We had thirty days before the event. This was going to be an adventure. I prayed they were going be nervous about the swim . . ."

Tom didn't take the bet too seriously because he was confident he would win. He already swam five days a week at his local YMCA and owned a mountain bike, but didn't bike or run once during the thirty days leading up to the event.

"The day of the race we met at Harriman at 5:15 in the morning. The first thing we did was start to brag about who would win. I had my mountain bike, the cyclist had a really decent bike, but my brother embarrassed all of us by bringing his son's Kmart knobby-tire bike. He also borrowed a wet suit that he didn't try on beforehand and almost drowned during the swim because it was too big and filled up with water.

"As we walked around getting registered and setting up for transition, I started to get nervous. I didn't check out the course beforehand and now I was hearing about all the killer hills. Hills? No one mentioned hills. I didn't train on hills. In fact, I didn't train at all on the bike. Now I got scared. I went from confident to *please don't let me die out there* in a matter of minutes. When other entrants heard we were all novices, they said we would either love it or hate it. That's the nature of triathlon.

"As I set up my transition area, I got even more nervous. There were so many people in the event and they all seemed to have amazing, high-tech equipment. They all looked pumped, like they had done this a hundred times already. I felt like I was the only newbie, along with my pals.

I began to realize this is serious business and I was out of my league.

"Everyone started out in the same wave and I jumped in hell-bent to go. Being a swimmer was a huge advantage because I wasn't afraid. And being a big guy I didn't mind getting hit or jostled and did my share of jockeying for position as well. I actually was having a great time in the water and had a good swim, fourteen minutes. As I got out of the water I was actually thinking, *This tri stuff is easy!*

"But it was all downhill from there. It didn't get easy; it got a heck of a lot harder. I soon realized the fun was over. Then I hit that 2.5-mile climb and reality hit. I went go into survival mode. I was dying on the bike but wouldn't submit to getting off and walking up the hill. *Why didn't I train? Why didn't I go over the course? Why am I here?* It was the longest seventeen miles of my life. All the people I passed in the water passed me on the bike. I wasn't feeling so cocky now.

"Back in transition I couldn't help notice that almost all the bikes were racked. Of course I had to see if any of my group had checked in and thank God I didn't see their bikes, which gave me some glimmer of hope that they were still out there sucking up that hill and I had the lead going into the run.

"Heading out on the run, I was exhausted, in pain, and could barely move my legs. I looked like a chicken pecking for grain. And I was also starving. I grabbed anything that was offered, water, oranges, GU, candy, a banana, anything. And to make matters worse, I ran in a heavy number 12 Joe Namath football jersey, just to be different. I wanted to make a statement but man did I suffer for it. I was sweating like a pig.

"At the 5K turnaround, I started back and saw my brother and the guys coming up the course. Although I was dying, I had to put on a smile like I was having a ball and enjoying myself. But as soon as they passed, and by the way they looked as miserable as I felt, I went back to looking dead and ragged. When I crossed the finish line there was nothing left in my tank; I couldn't even muster a fake sprint. I couldn't even take pleasure in the fact that I'd won the bet. All I could think of was I would never subject myself to this again. This was going to be my first and last triathlon.

"I found my brother and friends; we compared times, I boasted just a bit about winning the bet, and then it hit me. Without even realizing it, I was already planning my next triathlon and how I would train properly and beat my time. I went from never again to how to get better in less than ten minutes. When I got past the suffering stage, I realized I loved the whole atmosphere and the feeling of competing."

One month later Tom did another sprint triathlon. He continued to do his weekly swims but put in a little more time on the bike and run and managed to shave off some minutes. That first season he did a total of five triathlons.

"One of the reasons I love the triathlon is that I don't take myself seriously or worry about being last. I also discovered the Clydesdale Division, which was fabulous. Finally I found something where it paid off to be big-boned. At the West Point Triathlon, my last one of the season, I started to move up in placement. I continued to wear my football jersey for the run because I didn't care what anyone thought. My wife thought I was crazy, accused me of reliving my glory days."

In 1998 Tom jumped up to the half Ironman distance. He was happy just to finish as he hadn't put as much training into it. He still hadn't upgraded to a better bike and refused to buy a wet suit on principle. For the next seven years he developed a local reputation as the guy who shows up at triathlons without training. In 2005, as the popularity of the sport increased and more of his friends and neighbors were getting into it, he started a triathlon club. He and his friends Jamie Fisher, Tom Kramer, and Chris Hall founded the Glen Rock Triathlon Club with a noncompetitive focus and a low-stress approach to training. The first members were primarily women who wanted to get in shape. In its first year the club grew to sixty-one members, the average ages being thirty-five to forty, and 35 percent female, mostly moms with small children. Tom became the connecter, doing what he does best, which is encouraging people to try a tri and just enjoy it.

"I have to say that with the advent of the club I felt impelled to train and set a good example. I trained most of year with the members, getting up at 4:30 A.M. to bike with the group, running at the weekly workouts, and continuing to swim. It paid off and I took thirty minutes off my time and thirty pounds off my waistline at the 2005 Wyckoff Triathlon, the inaugural Glen Rock Tri Club outing."

His kids are all swimmers and have already participated in youth triathlons. His daughter Caitlin and son TJ, already competitive swimmers, joined Begg in his annual Swim Across America event (www.swim acrossamerica.org)—a one-, four-, and six-mile swim across Long Island Sound. The race is put on each year to raise money and awareness to help fight cancer. In 2005 the Begg family raised over sixty-five hundred dollars; the one-day event raised over a million dollars. Caitlin started doing the LI swim when she was just eight years old; TJ did the pool swim when he was five. Both kids are itching to do their first sprint triathlon.

"The beauty of training with a club is the constant camaraderie and support. I love going to the races with a group of friends and competing and cheering for them. I never realized what a difference it makes. I've been able to balance the responsibilities of my triathlon club and training with my family and work because I take such a low-key attitude toward it. To me, it's all about having fun."

RAY CAMPEAU

DOB: 10-15-61
Residence: Califon, New Jersey
Occupation: Entrepreneur
First Triathlon: 1982 Wyckoff (New Jersey) Sprint Triathlon

Ray Campeau took up triathlon in the early days of the sport and over the course of twenty years has competed in more than 250 events. He could be called the hardest-working triathlete in New Jersey. He is gutsy, tenacious, and pushes himself to the outer limits. When he doesn't meet his goal he gets mad and trains even harder. There is no middle ground when it comes to Ray Campeau. He's an all-or-nothing kind of guy. His passion for the sport is infectious and he has mentored many novices from their first sprint all the way to their first Ironman. His favorite event remains his first love, the Wyckoff Triathlon, where he still competes every year and is the host of the awards ceremony. But a bad hip is putting an end to Campeau's triathlon career. He plans on retiring from the sport that enriched his life, found him a wife, and gave him a room full of trophies. He now has a new goal that undoubtedly he will pursue with the same headstrong passion that got him to Kona twice: He wants to announce an Ironman race. Knowing Campeau, it won't be long till he has that bullhorn in hand announcing the start of the first wave: "All swimmers out of the water. The event is about to begin."

"I played all sports as a kid but swimming was my serious sport. Started at age six at the Hackensack YMCA. My mom threw me in the pool and I've been swimming competitively ever since. She's always been my role model. Even now, at eighty, she still swims in the masters division and wins her age group.

"My other sports as a kid were baseball and football. My sophomore year of high school we were the state champs in football. After high school I was a professional BMX racer. After I got bored with that I took up competitive cycling but that turned out to be too difficult and time consuming so I decided to go to college and swam on the team."

By age six Campeau was already showing his competitive spirit. He and his brother traveled the state for swim meets, and he quickly gained a reputation as one of the best swimmers in the state with a lot of promise. After college he went to work to support himself and help out his mom. He needed an outlet to stay active and involved in sports and discovered triathlons.

"One day I saw an ad for a triathlon sponsored by the Wyckoff YMCA. This was in 1982 and not many people knew what a triathlon was, including me. I read the description and it sounded easy. Heck, I was a good swimmer, I was a professional cyclist, and who can't run five miles? Sounded like a piece of cake and I signed up. I marked the date on my calendar and didn't give it much thought.

"I didn't train for the event and had never done open-water swimming. I just showed up on the day of the event. About 250 people entered, mostly guys. No wet suits were allowed and there were no bike racks. I just did what everyone else did. I saw guys getting buckets of water, so I did. I saw them placing their gear on a towel, so I did. I was totally clueless."

Despite being a great swimmer, Campeau was not prepared for a triathlon swim and got kicked, punched, dragged down, and panicked in the water.

"I could not believe how badly the swim was going. I panicked and started to hyperventilate. I didn't think I could finish. And to make it worse, I bragged to my mom, who came with me, that I'd be first out of the water. Well, I wasn't first, I barely made it out of the water in fiftieth place, huffing and puffing for my life.

"The bike didn't go so well either. I thought biking would be my strong point and that I'd pass everyone who passed me in the water, but it didn't happen. I was so spent after fighting through the water I had no energy left."

Campeau didn't like being passed. To this day it makes him angry. He started cursing and getting mad at himself but to no avail. No matter how hard he tried to catch up, he was just wasting more energy.

"By the time I started to run I was exhausted. Again, I was getting passed and it made me angrier. I managed to run the first mile and then gave up and had to walk the rest of the race. By the end of the triathlon I was angry and mad and disappointed. I hate losing and I lost big time. All the way home I vowed to get better and come back and win."

Despite his huge disappointment Campeau fell in love with triathlon. The combination of the three sports appealed to him, and since the sport was in its infancy he knew there would be time to get better and stronger and win. He joined a health club and started swimming regularly. He biked and ran with a schedule. A few weeks later he did another sprint and this time ran the whole distance, but was far from winning.

"I was getting better but I had to kick up the training. I was obsessed with winning my first triathlon. My next one, still at the sprint distance, included an ocean swim. I placed nineteenth overall and came home with a trophy. I still have that trophy. It was a great way to end my first season.

"The following year I started the season again with the Wyckoff Triathlon. I did three or four a season for the next several years, training hard and always improving. I started reading *Triathlon Magazine* and studied it cover-to cover. I read about the Hawaii Ironman and considered it for just a brief-second. At that time, the late 1980s, all you had to do to compete at Kona was call up and register. But I knew I wasn't ready for that just yet.

"A turning point for me was 1984 when I traveled to California for a triathlon called the Diamond Triathlon of the Stars. Dave Scott and all the big time Ironman guys were there. I finished fifty-second overall out of a thousand, and realized I could finally compete with the big guys. I decided to take my training to another notch and hired Mike Llerandi as my coach for ten dollars a week. I also joined a competitive masters swim team. My goal was to win more trophies and not be beaten. I wanted to win every event I entered. I was traveling around the country competing in nine events a season.

"In 1995 I made a jump to the half Ironman distance. Llerandi was still coaching me and decided I was ready. In fact, I thought it would be a piece of cake. To be honest, I didn't train in open water but didn't think it would matter. I'd be strong on the bike and run and probably place and come home with a trophy."

Once again, Campeau underestimated how difficult the open-water swim would be and panicked, swallowing water and having a bad experience. To make up for lost time he pushed too hard on the bike and then cramped on the run, having to walk.

"I was so mad at myself. I couldn't believe I blew it. I decided I needed to be better in the run so I signed up to run the 1995 New York City Marathon and finished in 3:30. That gave me the confidence to tackle a full Ironman."

At the time Campeau decided to train for a full Ironman, he was working two jobs and was already squeezed for training time. He decided to sell the bar he owned and dedicate more time to training. He also signed up for Ironman Canada.

"Training was torture but I stuck with it. It helped that I did the training with a group of friends and we'd meet on the weekends for long runs or bike rides. We all went to Canada together in August. I was scared out of my mind. The tri geeks were training all over the course days before the event but I lay low. The day before the race we did some warm-ups on the course. This was it, I was ready.

"The morning of the event I was pale and scared sitting in the middle of the pack waiting for the swim to go off. Then *bam*, kicking, punching, pushing all through the swim but I held my own and came out of the water in 1:03. The bike went well given it was a killer course. Halfway through I had to stop and go to the bathroom but I managed to have a good time. I started the run feeling good and finished in 11:15. My goal was to qualify for Kona but I missed it. All in all, I loved it and felt great."

By 1997 Campeau had enough triathlons under his belt to make some decisions. Should he go long or stick with the short distances? He decided to do both. He was racing just about every weekend, mostly short distances, and decided to do the Great Floridian Ironman.

"That race didn't go so well. I was doing fine till mile twenty-four of the marathon and passed out. I lay there for forty-five minutes and finally got up and crossed the finish line in 12:20. My big mistake was doing too many short-distance events and not putting in the training for the long ones. I learned a lot that day."

In 1998 Campeau decided to go to Kona. He signed up for the lottery and got in. Smarter and older, he was determined to make this his best race ever.

"I trained all summer. I didn't do any other events except Wyckoff. I wasn't going to make the same mistake I did in 1997 by doing too many events and not enough distance work. I trained with the same group of friends and worked really hard.

"When I got to Kona for the Ironman, it was one hundred degrees. I changed my goal from placing in the top ten of my age group to just finishing. It was the twentieth anniversary of the Ironman so it was a packed field. I played it smart, did everything as planned, and finished in 11:15, same exact time as Ironman Canada. I felt cursed."

Six months later Campeau decided to do the inaugural Lake Placid Ironman. Confident from Kona, he felt Lake Placid would be a piece of cake. During the run he cramped up and finished in 11:15. Cursed again.

In 2000 Campeau decided to re-create himself as an Ironman and hired a running coach. He raced almost every weekend, dropped weight, ran well, and felt strong. Nothing was going to stop him.

"I start the season with Wyckoff and push hard to win, which I do. I finally had bragging rights! Now I'm psyched to do Lake Placid again, six weeks away. I'm flying high and training like crazy. But things didn't go well at Lake Placid. My goal was to qualify for Kona but at mile six on the bike my legs cramped and I could not move. It felt as if someone took needles and stuck them all over my legs. I had to DNF."

Now he was mad again. The only way Campeau knows how to deal with defeat is to start winning again, so he entered just about every sprint triathlon he could find and started to win. He finished the season happy. He made plans to go to Lake Placid in 2001 but still had the cramping issues so he passed up the event which made him mad.

"In 2002 I re-invent myself again and hire a professional triathlete coach. He cuts me back from racing and we concentrate on training. I trained like this was my full time job. My goal is to do well at Placid and qualify for Kona.

"I woke up on race day haunted by fears of cramping again. I'm a mental mess. I want to qualify so badly it's driving me crazy. I start the swim and right around the first buoy I get kicked in the chest and can't breathe. It takes me three minutes to get going again and I am already freaking that I won't qualify.

"On the bike, I kick hard but start to cramp. I get off the bike and stretch but I am getting so mad. Nothing is going to stop me. I don't care what physical mess I end up in, I just want to qualify. I get back on the bike and hammer. I pass Heather Fuhr. I end up with my fastest bike time ever. Now I am hauling on the run and thinking only positive thoughts and hoping I didn't blow it on the bike. Every guy that passes me could be taking my spot at Kona so I don't let anyone pass me. I'm doing a 7:30 pace at mile fourteen when one of my training partners, Rob Isabelle, passes me. I yell to him, 'Don't take my spot!' and pick up the pace. For the next ten miles we play a cat-and-mouse game. But at mile twenty-four I start to cramp and have to stop and stretch. I slow down to a 9:30-mile pace. With half a mile to go I can see the stadium and just suck up all the pain and all the fatigue and go for broke. I finish in 10:12 and qualify. That day goes down in history for me. Not only did I qualify, I had the fastest bike time in my in age group, 5:14, a marathon time of 3:38, and was fifty-first overall, sixth in my age group."

Campeau was delirious. He couldn't believe he was going back to Kona to redeem himself. He had six weeks before Kona and worked on his nutrition plans to try to alleviate the cramps. His goal at Kona was to win a trophy, and to do that he needed to place top five in his age group and finish under 10:30.

"We arrive in Kona and the day of the event it is pouring rain with six-foot swells. Not a good day for an Ironman. Halfway through the swim I get seasick and start to throw up. I try not to worry about it and tell myself I'll make it up on the bike.

"I try to make up time on the bike but at mile eighty I start to cramp. I slow down and try to keep going despite the pain and cramping. No way I am stopping. I make it to transition but I'm sick and cramping and feeling like shit. I know I need a four-hour marathon to make my time so I head out.

"Although I'm running, everyone is passing me. At mile twelve I pull over and start to throw up. My friends are all passing me. My wife passes me and says, 'Hey Ray, having a bad day?' and keeps going. I start to run again but at mile twenty-one I start to get sick again. The medics come by but I wave them off. I think I can make it even though it's getting dark. At mile twenty-four I pass out and go down hard. The ambulance comes by and the medics recommend I don't continue. With two miles to go, I DNF."

Campeau made the right decision that day although it haunts him. He required six IVs just to sit up and feel normal. He took a year off from training, only doing Wyckoff to continue his streak. He continued to look for the cause of his cramping and along the way he found out he needed a hip replacement. The doctors told him he would never run again unless he got the new hip. He got a second opinion and the diagnosis was the same.

"Despite the diagnosis I think I can still do Lake Placid so I sign up for 2005 Lake Placid. I can barely move but so what. I'm used to pain. But it was too much and I DNFed at mile eighteen of the marathon. That was my last race."

Campeau managed to pull out another Wyckoff Triathlon in 2006, but walked most of the run. He wants to hold his Wyckoff streak until the twenty-fifth anniversary in 2007. In the meantime he gets therapy for his hip and can still bike and swim.

"I bike 130 miles a week, down from 250, and swim three days a week. I have my pride to uphold so I do what I can. My dream job is to announce an Ironman race. I don't care which one. I'm going to start sending my résumé around and see what happens. I love this sport and although I can't compete anymore I want to stay involved and see it grow."

FRANK CARINO

DOB: 10-8-64
Residence: Manhattan, New York
Occupation: Firefighter
First Triathlon: 1995 Sea Crest to Bay Sprint Triathlon

The son of a fire captain, Frank grew up in Great River. Long Island, and never intended to follow in his father's footsteps. After graduating from Hofstra he became an accountant, but his father never gave up on the dream that his two sons would become firefighters and signed them up for the civil service exam in 1987. Bored with his desk job, Carino entered the Randall's Island Fireman Academy, graduating in 1991. Being a firefighter suited him well. His athletic endeavors paralleled his development as a firefighter. He ran his first marathon in 1991 while at the academy and six months later ran his first New York City Marathon. He's run more than fifteen marathons with a PR of 2:57.

His buddies at the firehouse talked him into doing a triathlon. His first experience was horrible and he walked away thinking never again, *but Carino is gutsy, likes a challenge, loves a good adrenaline rush, and had to do one more to improve his miserable time. Soon he was hooked and spent his days off going on long bike rides and swimming.*

On September 11, 2001, his day off, he was training for his first half Ironman and returned from a twenty-mile ride at 8:45 A.M. He turned on the television to catch up on the news, and three minutes later watched a plane crash into One World Trade Center. He ran out the door to join his engine company. As Carino recalls, "I thought to myself, This could be the day I die. My life changed at that moment." *The memory of that day stays with him.*

"I never gave a thought to doing a triathlon. I got hooked on doing marathons and loved running the New York City Marathon every year as part of the FDNY New York City Marathon team. More than a hundred of us run it and on the day of the marathon we hire our own buses to the start and have our own VIP area. Afterward we rent an entire floor of a hotel near the finish and celebrate. It's one of the best days of the year for us.

"Some of my buddies at Engine 53 and Ladder 43 where I was assigned back in 1995 were triathletes and had signed up to do a sprint-distance triathlon in Long Island. They kept bugging me to join them, but I had no interest. They kept giving me crap about growing up on Long Island and that I had to do it, but the truth was I couldn't swim and hadn't been on a bike in a while. They wouldn't let up until I finally agreed to do it."

Being a marathoner, Carino never gave a thought to training for the triathlon. He owned a mountain bike but hadn't used it in a while and hadn't swum since he was a kid. As he said afterward, ignorance is bliss.

"I didn't train at all. I signed up and forgot about it till it was time to go. I was twenty-nine at the time and had better things on my mind than training for a stupid triathlon. Ten of us went that morning and in the car they gave me goggles since I didn't have a pair. Nor did I own a wet suit. I had no gear but my bike and helmet and the running shoes I was wearing.

"I lined up with my wave, hit the water, swam fifty yards, started to hyperventilate, and swam back to shore. I sat there resting and thinking how stupid this was and then I realized I'd have to drive back to the city with these guys who would be unmerciful if I didn't finish. I forced myself to get back in the water and swam from lifeguard to lifeguard, resting on the surfboards to gain control of my breathing before moving on to the next lifeguard. It was so pathetic. By the time I got out of the water I was so exhausted I could barely move. It was the most insane thing I ever did. All the people in my wave and the next wave were already finished. I was the last one out of the water. I was so waterlogged I felt like the Incredible Hulk and barely made it back to transition.

"The bike leg didn't go any better. Everyone passed me on their road bikes and I had a hard time catching up on my heavy mountain bike. Entering T2 my buddies were already finished and couldn't believe I still had to do the run. At least I passed people on the run and finally felt like I was doing something.

"The whole thing was a nightmare and I hated it. I swore I would never do another one as long as I lived. I didn't even make the results section in the local triathlon magazine afterward. It was a totally depressing experience."

Three years later Carino watched some friends compete in an Ironman event in California. Although he had no interest in doing an Ironman, he was impressed with the level of athleticism he saw, and the idea of doing a sprint distance again, the right way, started to take hold.

"When I returned home I decided to learn how to swim and joined a pool. I swam a lap, rested five minutes holding on to the edge, swam a few more, and rested. I did that till I worked up to half a mile. I signed up for a triathlon in Greenwich, Connecticut, in 1997 and this one went better. Having a better road bike and wearing a wet suit made a huge difference. Finishing eightieth out of five hundred also gave me the confidence that I could do this sport."

Carino was still not committed to doing triathlons, entering them sporadically each year, sometimes not doing any in a year, until July 2001, when he went to the Lake Placid Ironman to watch some friends compete.

"I was getting more and more inspired every time that I watched an Ironman. My swimming and biking had improved to the point I was feeling very confident and was gaining speed. I decided to go to the next level and signed up for a half Ironman in September 2001."

The morning of the terrorist attacks on the World Trade Center, Carino had the day off and was returning from a twenty-mile bike ride at 8:45. What he saw on the television stunned him; he couldn't move. His first call was to his brother, already on his way the towers, and the second to his father, retired in Florida.

He quickly joined a group of firefighters and headed down the FDR Drive, the billowing smoke just ahead of him. For the next twelve hours he desperately searched for ways to get people out of the buildings as they collapsed around him. The magnitude was incomprehensible. The most uplifting moment of the day was learning his engine and ladder Company had not lost a single man.

Although he had given up marathons, he knew he had to run the 2001 New York City Marathon to honor his fallen comrades. With no marathon training under his belt he started doing twenty-mile runs a few weeks before the November 5 date.

"This marathon was so important to me. I wanted to honor the guys who didn't make it back. Some of them were runners who were looking forward to the marathon. While running the 26.2 miles I thought about the friends I had lost. They died doing the job they loved and did it without question. I was so proud to have known them."

Carino didn't run the New York City Marathon again until 2004.

In 2002 he went back to Lake Placid in July to watch his friends compete and the day before the event swam the course just to see if he could do it—he was toying with the idea of doing an Ironman later that year in Ohio. Two days later he biked the Lake Placid course and bonked.

"I don't know what happened to me. I made it three-quarters of the way and collapsed. I called my girlfriend to pick me up and told her to bring a Big Gulp and a Snickers bar with her as I was famished and needed a quick sugar jolt. While I was waiting I found an old GU packet, ripped it open, and sucked it down without any water."

That September, Carino did his first Ironman in Ohio, the Pine Man, and finished fifth overall and first in his age division in 10:43. His girlfriend, now wife, went with him; her job was to provide the motivational music for Carino as he did the four loops on the run course.

"My favorite training song was 'A Town Called Malice' by a British group, the Jam. It pumps me up and I thought it would be good inspiration. Renee's job was to stand at the end of the loop and play it every time I passed by. We didn't think to put the song in a repeat format so she had to time the song to my estimated time of passing the designated spot. Renee played the song on the first loop of the run but I missed hearing it. She said I was running too slow—not maliciously or anything, but not what I wanted to hear.

"I still didn't know that much about training and probably could have done a better job of training but I was pleased. Just like a half marathon is not close to the expended energy and training required to complete a full marathon, a half Ironman doesn't come close to being as brutal as an Ironman. Let me put it this way: You know the exhausted burned-out feeling you get at mile eighteen of a marathon? That's how you feel *starting* the marathon at an Ironman. The tank is already on empty and you have to run 26.2 miles."

Since his first Ironman, Carino has gone on to do four more, including qualifying for Hawaii, which he completed in 2005. Now married with a new baby girl, his training has taken a step back.

"It's a little more difficult to train with my new family obligations but one of the benefits of being a firefighter is knowing when I have a full day off. I work twenty-four-hour shifts and have the next day off and I'll bike or swim or do a long run. Sometimes I bring my bike to work and afterward ride a few laps around Central Park before going home. My wife, Renee, is also a marathoner and triathlete so she understands about my training."

Carino doesn't think his athletic abilities help him much on the job. The one benefit he sees is that he recovers more quickly after fighting a fire than others.

"It doesn't matter if you are an Ironman or not. When the alarm goes off in the firehouse the adrenaline starts pumping, the heart starts racing, and your whole system speeds up. And no matter what great shape I am in, carrying seventy-five pounds of equipment up several flights of stairs is tough. Everyone is huffing and puffing, including me. Fighting fires is hard on the muscles and never gets easier; compared with that, training for a triathlon is a relief."

Carino doesn't see himself ever stopping triathlons. He has the drive and loves the sport. As long as he can get that adrenaline rush, he'll keep competing.

"I keep doing them to improve my time and get faster. It's the sense of accomplishment that keeps me going back for more. I also like the camaraderie of my buddies on my triathlon team at Asphalt Green. It's not anything spiritual or emotional; my goals are all performance-based.

"When I finish an event I'm happy. I always give 100 percent. Then on the way home I break it down and analyze every mile, every transition minute, and torture myself looking for where I could have done better, improved my time, been faster. I can't be content just doing it. It's sick. I make myself miserable all the way home.

"This year I have an Ironman picked out for September. That one will be very special because I'll be able to cross the finish line holding my little girl, Anna Rosemary, in my arms."

RICH DONNELLY

DOB: 12-15-62
Residence: Tuxedo Park, New York
Occupation: Copy editor, *Sports Illustrated*
First Triathlon: 1994 Pawling (New York) Sprint Triathlon

When Rich Donnelly was seventeen years old, he was the victim of a hit-and-run accident. He doesn't remember a thing about it since he immediately slipped into a coma. After he woke in the intensive care unit the next morning, he underwent the first of five surgeries to set the shattered fibula and tibia in his left leg and insert screws to set the bones. He had other scrapes and scratches that required stitches, had a broken collarbone, and required facial reconstruction surgery to repair his right eye socket.

Six months later when the cast was removed from his leg, it hadn't healed. Deciding against an experimental bone stimulating apparatus, he opted to have the doctor rebreak his leg and insert bone marrow from his left hip into the fibula along with a five-inch metal plate and five screws to hold the bone together.

Another six months passed before the final cast came off. The doctor told him he would always walk with a limp and he could forget the thought of ever participating in a sport that involved running. Nine years later Donnelly defied the doctor's expectations and ran his first marathon. The following year he completed his first triathlon. Since then, Donnelly has completed eight consecutive Ironman USA Lake Placid triathlons and eight marathons, along with countless other triathlons and road races of various distances.

Considering the obstacles he has overcome to compete in marathons and triathlons, it's no wonder Donnelly gains enormous personal fulfillment from his achievements. "Crossing the finish line at an Ironman is like no other feeling in the world," says Donnelly. "It's like a rock concert—and you're the rock star.

"Before the accident I played football, baseball, skied, ran around like any other active teenager. After the accident I was determined not to let my bad leg interfere with anything I wanted to do. My gait was off and I limped, but I managed to ski and stay active. I took up golf—an athletic endeavor I could do while walking. I favored my right leg, which probably threw off my hip alignment, but that wasn't a major deal. I was just glad to have a leg.

"I got married at twenty-seven and had a son, but after we divorced I wanted to spend as much time as possible with my son, Paul, so I got a baby jogger and started working out with him. We both enjoyed it, and it gave me a feeling of calm and peacefulness during a tough time in my life. After a few weeks the walks turned into jogs and the jogs turned into runs."

Donnelly decided to enter a 5K road race and was surprised when he didn't finish last. He entered more races, increased the distances, and seven months after his first 5K ran the 1993 New York City Marathon in 5:30.

"I admit there was some walking going on in that first marathon, but I finished it. I had a picture of myself pushing my son in his baby jogger printed on the front of my T-shirt with the words, YOU GO, PAULO! which I heard repeatedly for 26.2 miles. It carried me through. It was an incredible experience; I still get chills when I think about it.

"My friend's mom, Carmen Johnston, had done a couple of Ironman races, and I thought that she was a pretty amazing person for doing that. She knew I used to be a lifeguard, and she knew I was doing bike tours with Paul, so she encouraged me to do a triathlon. I had never thought about triathlons, but she planted the seed."

Donnelly considered a triathlon because he had already completed a marathon and swam when he was younger. By age twelve he was doing the mile swim at Boy Scout camp. He also took a swimming gym class in college—right after his final cast came off—for physical therapy and the three credits. Donnelly had to use crutches on the pool deck to get into and out of the water. Another deciding factor for him was that he was certain that he would find the same camaraderie he had found at running races and bike tours among the triathlon community.

"That college swim class actually taught me how to swim correctly, the right breathing techniques and the proper form for all four strokes. I rode a bike as a kid, the kind with the banana seat, but more recently I had gone on a few bike tours with my son so I knew I could do the bike leg as well as the swim and run. At the time my social life revolved around my running friends and going to races with my son. I wasn't into the bar scene and going clubbing. The idea of expanding my social friends to include a new group of triathletes was intriguing."

That's how he met his wife, Jean Palmieri Donnelly. For a couple of months before his first triathlon, Donnelly was training, but not with any real focus or schedule. No bricks, no transition training, just making better use of his time with more and longer bike rides, more and longer swims, more and longer runs—many with his son. He entered the event with no expectations other than to have fun—and finish.

"As much as I tried to be relaxed because I wasn't taking it all that seriously, I was nervous and anxious standing on the beach waiting for the start of the race. The buoys looked so far away, and the water—and the competition—looked rough. It was only a third-of-a-mile swim with thirty or so people in my wave, but it looked daunting. I decided to let the faster swimmers go out first, and then I followed along. I didn't even know drafting was legal in the swim leg.

"After the fear of the swim was over, everything else was a blast. I enjoyed myself immensely—I had a smile on my face during the whole race and tried to mimic everyone else's movements in the bike leg. I don't think I passed one person, but I learned about technique and etiquette. The run was a challenge, but I made it through. The whole day was just one big recreational romp for me, and it lit the spark to do more.

"The next season, 1995, I moved up to the half Ironman distance at the IQ Ironman Qualifier at Fairmount Park in Philadelphia. I didn't train that much and again, had no real structure to my workouts. My goal was just to finish, so I wasn't too worried. It was much harder than I thought it was going to be and I was out there for more than seven hours. I was amazed I wasn't last."

Donnelly continued to do triathlons, improving his times but still realizing his limitations. In 1998, while at the Dutchess County, New York, half marathon, he met Jean Palmieri. They struck up a conversation, found out they had a lot in common—they were both triathletes, both journalists, both survivors. They soon started dating and were married nearly a year to the day after they met.

"The next fall, while Jean was running the Newburgh-Beacon [New York] Bridge Run, a fellow spectator told me about a new Ironman event in Lake Placid, New York. I had always wanted to do an IM, but there were fewer Ironman events back then and I was on a waiting list to get into Ironman Canada. Jean encouraged me to go for it, so I applied and got in. My time was 14:01:29, still my best."

Since that first Ironman finish, Donnelly has kept coming back for more and has done eight Lake Placid Ironmans; he plans to keep going back every year for as long as "the body and the mind hold up." Donnelly, who usually finishes in the top 25 percent of most triathlons, is now a sponsored athlete, having been selected as a member of the Team Amino triathlon squad the past two years. Before that he was a member of the Degree Ironman team for three years.

"I really enjoy the sport. Triathlon—and Ironman—have become an integral part of my life. I have to admit every year when I finish the Ironman, I tell my wife and son and family, *Never again!* I'm so depleted and shot and can't imagine doing another one. But after a good night's sleep, by 9 the next morning I'm standing on line with all the other crazies registering for next year's race. The race sells out in a matter of hours now, and I wouldn't want to miss it for the world.

"And triathlon has become a family affair for us. Jean and I do about a dozen triathlons each year, and my son, now fifteen, did a few youth triathlons when he was younger. Jean, Paul, and my sister Mary and her family, Debbie and Missy, come up and volunteer at the Ironman. With them out there all day with me, getting up at 4 A.M. and volunteering at the race all day, and then meeting me at the finish line makes it worth all the effort. I look forward to the day we can all do one together."

The accident that mangled his leg and body at age seventeen left Donnelly with a legacy of issues. He has an odd gait, and favors his right leg in every activity. There isn't a lot of pain in the bad leg, but the seven-inch scar is a constant reminder of that fateful day. Donnelly, who describes his walk as more gimpy than limpy, also suffers from exercise-induced asthma, but fortunately nothing has kept him from getting to the start or finish lines.

"There's no way I should be doing what I do. The doctor told me it was a good thing that I got hit by a VW Beetle and not a Cadillac or I wouldn't be here. I know it could've been worse, a lot worse. Every time I see a wheelchair athlete or one on crutches or one with a prosthesis in a marathon or an Ironman, I realize just how lucky I am."

In addition to the twelve or so triathlons he does a year, Donnelly also participates in road races and bike tours. He goes back each year to do the Pawling sprint. That event has a special place in his heart, not only because it was his first but because his mother, Ella May, who was suffering from cancer and under hospice care, told him to go do the race instead of staying at her bedside. When he returned to tell his mom all about the race, the funeral directors were placing her into the hearse.

"I lost my mom that day. Every time I go back to do Pawling, I feel her spirit come alive. I say prayers in the transition zone and on the beach before the race. I think about her when I need some inspiration. Like many important things that have happened in my life, my mom and that race have become the fabric of my life."

JEAN PALMIERI DONNELLY

DOB: 8-10-60
Residence: Tuxedo Park, New York
Occupation: Executive editor, DNR, a menswear trade magazine
First Triathlon: 1995, Pawling (New York) Sprint Triathlon

In 1990 Jean weighed 215 pounds. She decided it was time to get in shape and started swimming. "At first I was embarrassed to go to the pool and be seen in a bathing suit. I couldn't even swim one lap," says Donnelly, now seventy-five pounds lighter. She never gave up and kept going back to the pool until she could swim a mile. Then she started running with the same dogged determination. As the weight came off, she noticed a lump in her breast. "It never showed up before because I was overweight. And I was only thirty-four at the time of my diagnosis," recalls Donnelly. In 1994 she underwent a lumpectomy and six weeks of daily radiation treatments. She has been in remission ever since. "Taking up sports saved my life," she says. "I'm not fast, but I savor every mile."

"I grew up in Greenwich Village in New York City; I was a real city girl. Our school's idea of 'physical education' was sending us out into the street at lunchtime and hoping we weren't hit by a car. I come from an Italian family and my mom was a great cook so I was a chubby girl growing up and just kept piling on the pounds. In my household it was always about the eating.

"My parents had a summer home in Wappingers Falls in upstate New York, which was my oasis. All summer long I swam, rode a bike, and did things other city girls didn't know how to do. My dad was a lifeguard so he made sure I learned how to swim correctly. Same with riding a bike; he didn't believe in training wheels so he ran alongside my two-wheeler until I was able to balance on my own.

"I went to New York University, so I never really left the city. I didn't do any sports in college; it just wasn't something that was part of my life."

Donnelly kept packing on the pounds and by the time she was twenty-eight years old she had 215 pounds on her five foot-four-inch frame.

"What made the lightbulb go off in my head that I was truly over-weight was attending a girlfriend's wedding and going for the bridesmaid dress fitting with the other girls. The attendant told me they would have to special-order my size-20 dress because they didn't stock 'that size' and I would have to pay extra to cover the material overrun. I was so embar-rassed I decided to do something about my weight.

"I started using the gym at my alma mater, NYU, and decided to start swimming. I got in a bathing suit but was so embarrassed to be seen in it I covered myself with a towel until I felt no one was looking and then jumped in the pool. I loved to swim in our lake but this was so different. I could barely swim one lap before I had to stop and catch my breath."

Donnelly is not a quitter and was so determined to lose the weight that she kept going back to the pool until she could comfortably swim a mile. She also altered her diet, eliminated the junk food, and paid atten-tion to portion control. With the combination of exercise, swimming a mile a day, and proper eating, she dropped seventy-five pounds. But an unexpected result of losing the weight was discovering a lump in her left breast during a routine self-examination.

"I was floored when I discovered that lump. I was only thirty-four years old and was in the best shape of my life. I didn't smoke or drink al-cohol and I was finally eating a healthful diet and exercising regularly. I immediately went to my gynecologist, who could feel the lump and scheduled a mammogram, but nothing showed up. Then I had a sono-gram but again, nothing showed up. My doctor sent me to a surgeon who performed a needle biopsy and finally, the cancer was detected and diagnosed. A lumpectomy was performed and a month later more surgery was done to clean the margins. I was very lucky. I didn't need chemotherapy but had six weeks of radiation, every day."

Donnelly continued swimming every morning during her radiation treatment. After her swim, she would get the radiation and then go to work.

"I was very thankful and extremely lucky the cancer was detected early and I attribute that to my exercise routine and losing the weight. I continued to swim every morning but it was getting boring. A friend suggested I look into triathlons, as NYU had a triathlon club with a coach, Scott Willett. My first thought was, *How ridiculous to think I could ever do a triathlon,* but I joined anyway. This turned out to be one of the best decisions I have ever made. Coach Scott was wonderful. He treated all of us the same, regardless of weight, size, experience, or training. It didn't matter to him whether you ran a twenty-minute 5K or took an hour. His enthusiasm and passion for the sport were contagious. He treated us all as if we were pros."

Donnelly came into the club with a strong swim background but had never run, and it had been years since she had been on a bike. But she embraced Coach Scott's philosophy of performing your best and not being judgmental or comparing results and times against others.

"The first time I got on the treadmill I had never run a step in my life. After a few seconds I wanted them to call the paramedics, I was so tired and panting for breath. But Scott was undaunted. Just told me to run at my own pace and not to worry.

"We were all training for the Pawling Triathlon, six months away. I still couldn't fathom the fact I would be doing a triathlon but Scott told me I could do it and I believed him. The event was near my childhood summer home, and that gave me some comfort. As the triathlon drew closer, I needed to gear up with some equipment. The only bike I owned was a three-speed Raleigh, which was sitting in the damp basement at the summer house, so I borrowed a 'racing bike' from another club member. We were advised to wear wet suits because the lake water would be cold in early June so I rented a 'real' wet suit, one meant for scuba divers and surfers. What did I know? I didn't even realize the difference between that and triathlon-specific suits."

Being part of a club was a huge advantage to Donnelly in many ways. She loved the camaraderie of the members, training together and being a part of a team. Scott took them up to the course a week prior to the event so they could see it and train on it.

"The borrowed bike had toe clips and gears, which I had never experienced before. I wobbled around the parking lot to get comfortable before we went out on the course and I'll never forget Scott's face when he saw me trying to maneuver that bike, since it was obvious that I didn't have a clue what I was doing. But Scott being Scott, he just nodded and said: 'Great. Let's go ride the course.' "

A week later, Donnelly and her teammates went back for the real event.

"I thought the swim was going to be a piece of cake but the water was very cold and I never swam in a wave before and I panicked. Heck, there weren't any lanes to guide me! And it was so frigid that I started hyperventilating. I ended up floating on my back for a few yards until I could calm myself down, but I completed that third-of-a-mile swim.

"After getting out of the water I spent a long time in T1. It seemed like an hour, but soon I was out on the bike beginning to feel better and I finally started to relax. The run was horrible, more like a three-mile walk actually, but there was Scott at the finish line, cheering me on and telling me to pick it up. You gotta love it. I felt like a pro. I had never done anything athletic before so this was a huge accomplishment. It was an amazing day and I was hooked."

It took Donnelly around two hours to do the sprint event but she didn't care. She was now a triathlete. She continues doing sprint- and Olympic-distance races, about twelve a season. She's also completed two half Ironman events but has no ambition to do a full Ironman.

"I'm not a natural runner so it is very difficult to do the run portion. No matter how hard I try, it's just not in me. I kick myself in the ankles, shuffle along, and watch everybody else pass me by. The run is torture for me but its part of the sport so I do it. I'm just a lot more comfortable in the water and on a bike.

"Triathlon has become a part of my life and luckily I share this passion with my husband. We both get a lot of satisfaction out of the accomplishment. And I don't ever want to get fat again. Triathlons keep me in shape. And if I am going to put in all the training to keep in shape, I might as well do the events. I met my husband through the sport. It's been good to me. It's my passion and I'll keep doing them as long as I can. There is no other feeling for me quite like crossing that finish line."

WENDY ELLIS

DOB: 10-6-60
Residence: Pensacola, Florida
Occupation: Title I pre-K physical education teacher
First Triathlon: 2000 Santa Rosa Island Sprint Triathlon

Wendy Ellis may not be the tallest or strongest triathlete, weighing in at 115 pounds for her five-foot-four-inch frame, but what she lacks in height and muscle she makes up for with heart. Growing up along the bayous of Louisiana, she was very active but never participated in organized sports. When she became an elementary school physical education teacher, she promised herself that she would stay in shape so she could keep up with her classes and do all the exercises and activities with them. Turning forty, she set a goal to do a triathlon. During the training phase, her niece Lindsey became interested in the idea of doing a triathlon with her. Little did either of them know that it would take five years to make this a reality. Why is this so special and why does Wendy really consider her second triathlon to be her first? Lindsey has cerebral palsy and is confined to a wheelchair. Lindsey's dream to complete a triathlon could not have been possible without a partner who shared her passion and without a ten-thousand-dollar grant from Balance Bar for the special equipment.

46

"I always loved being outdoors and playing sports, but not the organized type. I went to Catholic school and they didn't offer much in the way of team sports. At college I majored in physical education and became a teacher at an elementary school. I never wanted to be one of those gym teachers that stand on the sidelines and call out the drills and let the kids do all the work. I wanted to participate and set a good example. But somewhere in my thirties, my good examples started to slip and I noticed I was getting out of shape. I couldn't run a block without stopping."

Ellis decided it was time to do something about her own lack of physical fitness and joined a running club. Soon she was back in shape and ran a half marathon to prove it. But she wasn't crazy about distance running, so she set her sights on a triathlon.

"I was turning forty in October so I decided to pick a triathlon around then. I gave myself two months to train. I had a mountain bike but I borrowed a road bike from my brother to get a competitive edge. I wasn't about to invest in equipment like a new bike or a wet suit until I knew whether I liked the sport.

"I had no idea what to expect since I never even saw a triathlon before but I knew I had to train if I wanted to have a decent time. I made up my own schedule. I swam in the morning and alternated running and biking, doing two activities a day for five days a week. Toward the end of my training period, I threw in a few bricks, but looking back on my schedule I was flying blind. In fact, if truth be told I would have canceled the whole thing if I hadn't told everyone what I was doing. I just hoped for the best."

Ellis trained as best she could, practiced with GU and different fluids and was in the best shape she could be. The triathlon was right in her town, which eliminated the stress of travel and worrying about leaving anything at home. It was a sprint distance, and since most of her swimming had been done in a pool, she knew if she could just get through the Gulf waters, the rest would somehow fall into place.

"I slept pretty well, considering what I was about to do, but when I got up at 4:30 A.M., I got supernervous. I don't like the unexpected and the morning of the event, our perfect weather took a turn for the worse. It was windy and cold and there were whitecaps in the normally tranquil Gulf. I don't do cold well. I remember standing on the beach, shaking like a leaf, and thinking, *Man, this is going to be miserable.* I didn't want to get in the water and knew once I got in I wouldn't want to get out. There was a lot of kicking and pushing and jellyfish. The jellyfish were everywhere, even in my jog bra. I wished I had a wet suit on to protect me from the cold and the jellyfish, but I just kept going and persevered. Right after passing the first buoy, one woman in the water panicked and was yelling for help. Several of us tried to calm her down. I just wanted to put the swim behind me as fast as I could. My swim time was a little slower than I expected but I was so happy to get out of the water, I felt like the event was over. I didn't care what happened after that.

"Once on the bike I calmed down, although I was still pulling jellyfish out of my jog bra. There was a strong wind going out and I kept thinking it would feel good at my back once I reached the turnaround, but then the wind shifted and I had it in my face on the way back. Eighteen miles of headwind.

"The transition from bike to run was more difficult than I had imagined. My first few steps were like I didn't even have legs. I didn't expect it to be that hard. After a quarter mile my legs loosened up and I started passing people. My 5K run time was 25:00 so I was pleased with that.

"Crossing the finish line was the proudest I have ever felt of myself. I thought it was truly amazing. I couldn't wait to do another one."

Unfortunately, Ellis had to put her next triathlon on hold as she got injured shortly after in a road race. She overtrained for the race and ended up with a stress fracture that put her out of commission for a year. During that time, her niece, Lindsey, fourteen, brought up the idea of them doing a triathlon together. Ellis had pushed Lindsey in a few 5K races and Lindsey loved the thrill of participating in the events. When she brought up the idea of doing a triathlon, Ellis agreed to do her next one with Lindsey. That promise took another three years to fulfill.

"By the time I was healthy enough to start training it was already 2002. For the next two years I didn't focus on a triathlon and lost the momentum to do another one. After Lindsey first mentioned doing a triathlon together, I started to look at the logistics of how I was going to do this, and it became more daunting than I'd first thought. The list of special equipment I would need to purchase was beyond my financial means: a rubber boat big enough to hold Lindsey and light enough for me to pull through the water; the special-needs trailer to hold her while I biked; a new bike since I wasn't going to use my mountain bike and my brother's bike wouldn't do; and then the wheelchair to push her through the run. I was looking at anywhere from five to ten thousand dollars, and on a school teacher's salary, I didn't have that extra income to cover the expenses. One day while visiting Lindsey she mentioned that she had written Oprah Winfrey a letter. When I asked her what she wrote Oprah for, her response took me by surprise. She had written a letter asking for money to help us get the equipment to do a triathlon together. Until that moment I hadn't realized how much this dream meant to her. I felt as though I had let her down. She is so much a part of my life and so full of life, I wanted to do this for her. It's not her fault she was born with cerebral palsy. She wants to have as normal a life as she can. She wants to experience life. She never asks for anything and by gosh I was going to make this happen for her."

Ellis started looking for creative ways to come up with the money. In April, Ellis wrote to Balance Bar, which came through with a grant for ten thousand dollars. With that, they were on their way.

Lindsey lives in Baton Rouge and Ellis was in Pensacola, so most of the training was done by Ellis alone. The plan was to meet on weekends so they could practice both the bike and the swim. The swim would require Lindsey to lie on her back while Ellis pulled the boat with a harness attached to her waist. Ellis did most of the bike training in Pensacola, putting rocks and weights in an ice chest on the trailer to simulate Lindsey's weight, eighty-five pounds. But the training didn't go smoothly. Ellis got tendinitis from pulling the weight and had to stop for a few weeks. Three tropical storms and two hurricanes came through the area, cutting off most their weekend travel and training sessions.

In the meantime, Lindsey had to do her own preparation and training, working with her physical therapist to strengthen her abdominal muscles so she could sit upright in the trailer for extended time. And unknown to everyone but her aunt, Lindsey had planned a surprise ending of her own.

"The tropical storms and hurricanes put a real damper on my training. The roads were littered with debris and almost every time I would venture out on my bike I'd get a flat tire. I was getting discouraged. But I kept thinking, *Lindsey faces greater obstacles than this every day of her life,* and with those thoughts I'd overcome my frustrations and get back to training. My biggest concern was being ready and prepared by the time of the triathlon. I never did get to practice with Lindsey in the boat so my neighbor, Joann Mandato, graciously agreed to lie in the boat so I could get a feel for pulling it in the water with confidence. I still had to worry about how Lindsey would react. Her first time in the boat would be on race day. What if Lindsey got scared and panicked? Would the boat flip if the water got rough? All these realities were hitting me with just two weeks to go.

"The plan was for us to do the same triathlon I did for my first one, Santa Rosa Island Triathlon. But with a week to go, Hurricane Katrina came through, followed by Rita, so they canceled the Santa Rosa Triathlon. Things were not going our way. I had to make a decision to switch venues and we decided to do a triathlon in Destin, Florida, called the Destin Crab Trap. I called the race director to let him know my plans and that I was bringing a special-needs participant with me, but I never heard back. Without a definite confirmation, we left for Destin and were determined to go through with this."

The night before the event, Ellis was struggling with the enormity of what she was about to do. She couldn't afford any mishaps. The care and protection of Lindsey was forefront in her mind. "My training had been so sporadic, I had lingering doubts about my own ability to carry this off.

"The day of the event was a blessing. The weather was perfect, the water was like glass, and dolphins were jumping in the Gulf almost as if they were personally welcoming us. The race director greeted us and was pleased we were there. They were very encouraging and supportive. Our family and a lot of our friends were there to cheer us on. We wanted everyone to feel a part of this huge event in Lindsey's life.

"We went off in the last wave. Lindsey's dad placed her in the boat and she lay there with a huge smile on her face. She was great and didn't move or rock. I heard her yelling for me and encouraging me. Every once in a while I'd see her little head pop up as she'd try and see over the sides. The other swimmers, a mix of men and women in my wave, were all supportive and encouraging once they caught on to what was happening. I was worried that we would be in their way but everyone stayed out of our way. We were actually passing people. I could hear Lindsey giggling when I told her we were passing another swimmer.

"When we finished the swim, my brother, Lindsey's dad, met us at the beach and had a little cart with big wheels on it, kind of like a rickshaw, that he put her into so we could pull her through the sand to the transition area. At T1, he strapped her into the trailer, put on her helmet, and made sure she was comfortable. By now, word had spread about us and we attracted quite a supportive, cheering crowd. Lindsey was beaming.

"Once on the bike, I was lucky to get up to twelve miles an hour pulling the trailer. It was hard going. But Lindsey kept me amused. At eighteen, she's like any other teenage girl with hormones and wanted to see all the good-looking guys. I felt bad that most of the participants were way ahead of us and we were just about the only ones on the bike course.

"After the bike, the special-needs trailer transformed into a wheelchair jogger and off we went. During the run, we concentrated on the big surprise Lindsey had been keeping a secret all these months. Her plan was to 'walk' across the finish line. I kept her secret but told a few people before we left for the run so they would be ready with cameras to capture the surprise. Not even her parents or grandparents knew the treat they were in for. At first I felt badly that we were among the last ones on the course. I thought no one would be around to see her, but my friends back at transition started to spread the word that something amazing was going to happen so there was actually quite a crowd waiting for us.

"As planned, we got to the beginning of the finish-line chute and I stopped the jogger. I pulled Lindsey from her seat and she stood in front of me. With my arms tucked under her armpits supporting her body weight, she walked across the finish line, her little legs struggling but with the biggest smile on her face you have ever seen.

"There was not a dry eye anywhere. I watched a policeman standing at the finish line, tears rolling down his face, reach into his cruiser and pull out a camera to capture the moment. Much to my surprise and Lindsey's, a friend had seen to it that our theme song, 'Breakaway,' was playing as Lindsey walked the hundred yards to the finish. It was her time to shine and she brought down the house. It was a very humbling experience. All these huge, strong athletes were bawling. Even the overall winner asked to have his picture taken with her. When we crossed the finish line, the first thing she said was 'Can we do another one?' "

Wendy Ellis is a hero not only to her niece but to anyone who knows how difficult it is to complete a triathlon solo, and then realizes the effort she endured to make this dream come true for Lindsey.

JONI FOURNIER

DOB: 12-25-73
Residence: Watertown, Massachusetts
Occupation: Construction management
First Triathlon: 2003 Lions Spring Triathlon, Marlborough, Massachusetts

Joni was so enamored with triathlons that she signed up for an Ironman with only five sprint distances under her belt. She credits her friends in the triathlon community with getting her into—and through—Ironman Canada.

"I grew up in Bangor, Maine, and was definitely an outdoor girl. I played every team and individual sport I could. In high school I already knew I wanted to play Division 1 soccer in college so I joined the track team to build speed. I continued to play soccer at the University of Maine and after graduation moved to Boston and continued playing club soccer."

Fournier became frustrated with club soccer. She missed the level of competition she had experienced in college and concentrated more on her running. Working on the managerial side of the Big Dig, Boston's municipal government project to replace its elevated highway with an underground expressway, Fournier needed an outlet to alleviate the stress at the end of the day and decided to run a marathon.

"I chose the Bermuda Marathon and despite the fact that it is on a beautiful island the course is a hilly two loops around the island. My time wasn't great, 4:59, and it was painful and disappointing, but in some weird way I loved it and went on to run five more. After that I wanted a new experience and considered a triathlon. The first one I ever saw was Escape from Alcatraz and I thought the people were insane! I spoke to someone who had done Kona and thought he was even more insane. There is no way anyone would ever want to do that.

"In 2002 I joined an all-female triathlon team and took swim lessons. I trained with them for my first triathlon, which was absolutely wonderful. There was no intimidation factor; everyone was supportive and encouraging. I would recommend joining a team for anyone considering a triathlon."

Her first triathlon was a great success. It was an indoor pool swim and she did the backstroke, not in any hurry. Some of her teammates decided to train for Ironman Lake Placid and she went along to watch.

"Seeing my teammates finish their first Ironman was so inspiring. It reminded me of watching my first marathon and thinking, *I could do that!* I saw all different body types crossing the finish line and suddenly it seemed very do-able. Right then and there I decided to do an Ironman."

At this point, she had only done a few sprint triathlons. She decided to do Ironman Canada (IMC) because other teammates and friends were going to be doing it as well.

"As part of my training, I did two half Ironmans along with another sprint distance and then hired an online coach, Don Fink, to work out a schedule for me. For thirty weeks, he sent training schedules via e-mail every four weeks. To be honest, I've been training for this event my entire life. Between the years of competitive soccer and the marathons and the stress of my job, I had my base training already done. Everything is cumulative.

"Recounting my Ironman is challenging in one way but so easy in another sense. I thought for sure this would be routine for me, but it has proved to be a challenge. I feel I owe so many people recognition and so many details I want to share. My race report has to include the days leading up to the race.

"Tuesday morning, a friend came by at 5 A.M. to help me pack my trusty bike, which we did with ease considering the early-morning hour. That day I also got a beautiful arrangement of roses at work and a sweet package in the mail. I have some wonderful friends!

"By Tuesday night it was time to stop packing. My friend David came over shortly after 8 P.M. and took the role of keeping me calm, not an easy task. I owe him a huge thank-you and possibly a degree in sports psychology. Later that night I had a meltdown and David tried to say anything he could to ease my mind. Then he said, 'Fine, don't go.' All of a sudden everything was clear. This was *never* a thought in my head and I was doing this no matter what. David found the words to make me realize that. I am forever in debt for that statement. I was finally able to stop focusing on what I might leave behind in my packing and focus on more important things like what I was going to purchase at the finishers' tent the day after the race.

"I left for the airport shortly after 5 A.M. A good friend of ours somehow managed to get the airline to announce our names on the flight to wish us luck! We landed in Vancouver and went through customs. When I went to the oversized luggage area to pick up my bike, *there was no bike!* We had to make a connecting flight so there was no time to do much about it. I filed some paperwork and we headed off to our next flight. I was disappointed and nervous, but hopeful that it would somehow be there in Kelowna."

There was no bike waiting in Kelowna for Fournier. She filed more paperwork and kept her fingers crossed.

"I was freaking out but somehow calmer than expected. I suppose I went into the infamous Ironman survival mode. The next morning my friends and I went to the Bike Barn to see what I could do about getting a bike, just in case mine never showed. I will be forever indebted to Will and Gary at the Bike Barn. They were servicing probably all twenty-three hundred athletes, yet still went into *get Joni a bike* mode. By the next day they found a bike for me to ride."

Although Air Canada never confirmed they'd lost the bike, on Friday a driver delivered her bike to her hotel.

"I never thought I would be so happy to see my fifty-pound steel-frame bike. I returned the loaned one and brought my bike to my new best friends at the Bike Barn to be assembled in time to rack it by 3:45 P.M. Saturday.

"I was having some shoulder pain so I went for a pre-race massage.

The therapist informed me that I'd somehow managed to pull three ribs. I iced and iced and stretched and stretched and by Saturday it was still tender but much better. We did the underpants run, the Parade of Athletes and soaked in the atmosphere of Penticton.

Race Day

"I woke up at 1 A.M., but was able to fall back asleep and finally awoke around 3:45 A.M. I knew from the half Ironman that nutrition was going to be key, so I started forcing down my bagel with almond butter and started drinking my Amino Vital and water. About 5 A.M. I started the quiet walk in the dark with all the other athletes. It was pretty silent, but electrifying at the same time. You could see the focus in each face; most likely they too were doing a mental checklist of what they'd packed in their special-needs bags.

"After the special-needs drop I went to the body-marking area. I know I told everyone and their mother my race number, but that morning I stood there with a blank and then panicked. Was I in the right line? Did I give them the right number?"

Swim 2.4 Miles—1:21:01

"I have only been swimming for a short time, so this was certainly the most unknown to me during training, but my swim coach had prepared me well and my triathlon coach gave me a mantra to chant, *confidence and calm,* which I repeated over and over. What is it like to start swimming with about twenty-three hundred athletes? I loved it. Each person had a story and was making the same journey that day but for different reasons. I tried to think of these things when I got punched in the ear or felt hands at my toes as competitors tried to draft or swim over me. I ended up closer to the buoys at the first turn than I had expected and found myself in a sea of male competitors and just tried to find some space. About an hour into the swim I remember my mother telling me that my deceased Nana would be with me in Canada, but by no means for the swim since she was terrified of swimming so most likely would be cheering from the sidelines and would join me for the bike. I started talking to Nana, telling her she was swimming with me whether she liked it or not."

T1—6:43

"My first IM transition. Despite all my transition training, I triple- and quadruple-checked everything, applied sunscreen, and checked around again to make sure nothing got missed."

Bike 112 Miles—7:47:15

"I have heard so many things about this course, mostly about Richter and Yellow Lake and the bees on the descents. First goal for day: smile and enjoy it and take it as it comes. My second goal of the day was to finish healthy so I could stay up for the fireworks at midnight.

"We hit McLean Creek Road and all of a sudden it was tubular city. I was overwhelmed with how many flat tires people were having and found out later that tacks had been dropped on the road by nasty people who thought it funny for riders to get flat tires. Luckily all my friends stayed flat-free that day. At mile twelve I saw the most disturbing sight and it stuck with me the rest of the day. There is a sharp turn and as I approached there was a volunteer at the top telling us to move to the other side of the road because there was a rider down. I slowed to about ten miles per hour and as I turned the corner I saw the ambulance and the rider facedown, bleeding and not moving. I quickly gave a sign of the cross and said a small prayer. All the riders surrounding me shared words of concern and wished each other a safe ride.

"The first forty miles are effortless in comparison with what lies ahead. Turning right at Husky's was the milestone for the start of Richter Pass. I welcomed the climb because it was a nice change for the muscles and the spectators lining the course make you feel like Rocky. Using my granny gear, I spun up the hill and somehow found myself passing people, each of us offering words of encouragement. One guy was talking a little negative so I reminded him to look at the gorgeous view we paid for and continued on my way.

"As the saying goes, what goes up, must come down. However, the saying doesn't mention being white-knuckled on the way down or being blown around and scared to death. Next came the seven "rollers." I don't know about anyone else, but I was not rolling up any of those hills.

"By this point I was looking forward to the turnaround and my special-needs bag. I had a piece of beef jerky calling my name. After the out and back comes Yellow Lake. It's not as long as Richter Pass but where it comes in the race is the key: a thousand-foot climb at a 6 percent grade. Maybe

I was just biking at too casual a pace, but I enjoyed the climb. When I passed some guys playing music I threw my right arm into the air and started waving like I didn't have a care in the world and smiled.

"Now it was time for the scariest part of the day, the fast descent back into town. There were times I held my bike so tight between my knees and my hands, I was aching. I kept my eyes focused in front and tried to relax. I knew this was the place to make up time from all the climbing but I opted for the slower, safer route for my mental state. I wanted to finish the day in one piece."

T2—12:08

"I really took my time in T2. I used the restroom, changed my clothes, applied more sunscreen, and then stood there looking at the pile of all my stuff and for some reason just couldn't put it all together. Was I wearing my visor? Did I put on my sunscreen? Finally I got my act together and headed out."

Run 26.2 Miles—5:02:23

"I couldn't comprehend doing a marathon after all we had done that day, but I was delighted to be on my feet and in complete control of myself. No more legs and arms flailing about in fury to find open swim space, no more praying to the bike-flat gods; it was just me and my sneaks. Most importantly, I had my list of twenty-six names. At each mile I looked at my list and spent time with that one person, sometimes for a while, sometimes briefly, but each mile marker gave me something to look forward to.

"At the turnaround I stopped and went through my special-needs bag, and of course hit the restroom, my sixth time that day. I sipped some chicken soup for a nice salt fix and forced some gel down. I didn't want it but I could hear my coach and nutritionist saying, *Stick to your plan, no matter what.* I felt strong the second 13.1 miles. I walked a couple of miles, but my goal was to hit mile twenty and run the last 10K. I dedicated mile twenty to my coach. He and I have been through many months of training and he was the perfect motivation for that mile.

"I had a blast the last 10K. Loads of spectators were out and they love a smiling face, which I was sporting, and I made sure to thank every one of them. I ran down the last stretch of Main Street like I hadn't exercised all day, with legs feeling as light as feathers.

"At the finish chute, I heard, 'Joni Fournier from Watertown, Mass.,' and the rest is a blur. The light-headedness set in and I needed to sit down. Later on I met up with my friends and watched the last finishers come in. That evening, as I watched the fireworks, I noticed I still had my smile on from the morning. I loved every minute of this experience and can't wait for Ironman Wisconsin on September 10, 2006. *Bring it on!*"

Fournier is a USAT Level I Certified Coach and USATF Level I Certified Coach and sponsored by Team Amino Vital

What She Learned

"I had a wonderful experience at my first Ironman. I heeded the advice of friends, coaches, books, online forums, and from my own experiences along the way. I knew that eating breakfast on race morning was critical, no matter how my stomach felt. I needed the calories. I made the mistake of skipping breakfast at a half IM a few months prior and suffered the entire race.

"As I look back at the experience of my first Ironman, I learned a lot about myself and my inner strength. I also learned that I have an amazing support system of friends and family and I am glad that I gave them weekly updates on how my training was going. I think no matter what distance you train for, friends and family are excited to hear about your journey.

"There is only one thing I would change about my Ironman experience and that relates to priorities. For eleven months prior to IMC, I did volunteer work with an elderly gentleman by the name of Charles 'Tom' Cowen. I made weekly visits to his home and we did exercises to keep him mobile and work on his stability. Each month I gave him a copy of my training schedule and he always asked about the Ironman and made sure to say, 'Don't go doing that Ironman before I see you next time.' It became a comfortable routine for us.

"The day before I left for Canada, Mr. Cowen ended up in the hospital. I called him but he was a bit confused. I planned on visiting him before I left to keep my promise but in my last-minute frenzy I didn't go.

"When I returned from Canada, I was excited to see Mr. Cowen but he had passed away. He died on the exact day of Ironman Canada. I have no doubt he was with me on the course that day. If I could change anything, I wish I had taken a moment to recognize my priorities and found a way to go and visit him at the hospital before I left."

JACK FRIEND

DOB: 3-9-74
Residence: Chicago, Illinois
Occupation: Commercial real estate
First Triathlon: 1998 Huntington Beach (California) Sprint Triathlon

When I received an e-mail with an attachment from Jack Friend, someone I didn't know, I was almost going to delete it, but he had written "First Triathlons" in the subject heading so I clicked on it and commenced laughing myself sick. He is a self-described big boy who grew up in a family of big boys, all competitive athletes. More the football type than the lean runner, what Jack and his brothers share is a joie de vivre for anything related to sports. He has one of the goofiest stories about a first triathlon and he has no problem sharing it. Hopefully, first-timers will learn from his mistakes but also capture his effervescent spirit. He is moving his family to Romania to help organize and run a youth camp so maybe he'll have to start a triathlon there.

"I grew up in Huntington Beach surfing, swimming, and always active. At college I played football and basketball. I always liked organized sports. I consider myself a big guy, six foot three and 230 pounds of all muscle. With that build I'm not very good at distance events like running but I am good at coordination and bursts of speed.

"After I graduated from Wharton in 1996, I ran to stay in shape as I was sitting at a desk job all day. Not much, two to three miles a day. My

60

two younger brothers are also sports nuts and we are very competitive with each other, but in a fun way."

Friends and one of his brothers read the same inspiring book, *The World's Toughest Race,* and thought it would be awesome to do an extreme sport. They wanted to push themselves and see if they could do something like it. They decided on a triathlon.

"We knew about the Ironman and certainly weren't ready for anything like that. My brother-in-law had done a few so I asked him about doing one. It didn't seem that difficult. Heck, I ran a 5K once. Doesn't that count for something? My brother and I started looking for a sprint triathlon that we could do together."

On a Monday, Jack got a call from his brother, who had located a sprint triathlon in their hometown. What could be better? The only problem, which they didn't consider a problem, was that it was a week away.

"Monday, 6 P.M., I got a call from my younger brother, Jason, saying there is a sprint triathlon on Sunday in our hometown, Huntington Beach, California. We both considered ourselves to be in good shape and thought this would be a fun challenge. Jason went to University of San Diego so he was already caught up in the workout beach culture there. He was a workout maniac.

"It sounded so easy and we were in decent shape. It's a little swim, a little biking, and a run. What could be the big deal? It was most definitely a mental decision, not one based on our physical conditioning. Whatever our initial thought was going in, it was a disaster by the time we finished.

"I began my training on Tuesday: forty-five minutes on a stationary bike, thirty minutes on a treadmill. I did not own a bike so training options were limited. I did not practice swimming and just figured I would power through the swim since I once swam a mile at age thirteen. I was now twenty-three.

"Wednesday through Friday I did about the same training regimen of the stationary bike/treadmill combination. Saturday, I got the participant packet and read all the rules to make sure we had everything required for competing. It was 11:30 P.M. when we finally borrowed our second bike, a girl's model, for my brother, complete with a rain spoiler on the rear wheel. I rode an old mountain bike.

"To be honest, the rules never mentioned needing goggles or a bike helmet. After arriving Sunday morning at the event, they stated on the loudspeaker that helmets were required and the rule was accidentally left off the guidelines. This did not matter for anyone else because we were the only two people who did not show up with helmets. So we decided to swim and just try to ride out of the staging area without helmets. We found out the hard way that swimming in the ocean without goggles or a wet suit in cold water was very difficult. We both were so unprepared physically for the swim that it was the hardest thing I had ever done. When you closed your eyes to swim with your head down, your head would start to spin and you'd feel like you were going to pass out.

"Swimming with your head out of the water to see only made it hard to breathe. Given that both of us were former football players and weighed about 220 pounds each, mostly muscle in our legs, we tended to sink. I looked around for the junior lifesavers on surfboards just in case I needed to holler one over. Somehow we muscled our way through the swim and dragged ourselves out of the water, exhausted."

Back in transition, Jason and Jack got stopped by the volunteers because they didn't have helmets. But they weren't ones to quit:

"We waited for competitors to finish the bike section and lend us their helmets. At this point we were so far behind everyone it was like competing alone. It looked like we were out for a ride all by ourselves. The only downside to this is that we missed the group dynamics of being part of the ride.

"Back in transition, we stashed the bikes and started out for the run. By now I was really tired and couldn't understand why my legs wouldn't work. I couldn't get them to move. But slowly we caught up to some people in the run, but when we finished the event was about over. We were just about last. I went home and slept the rest of the day."

Despite being so ill prepared, Friend had fun and looked forward to his next triathlon. He moved to Chicago shortly after that, got married, and had a family, all of which put his triathlon plans on hold. In 2002, he decided to do Mrs. T's sprint triathlon and this time enlisted his wife, Laura. His training wasn't much more than his first experience: He swam a little, ran a little, and still had to borrow a bike. Laura swam in college so held her own on the course. They finished, had fun, and in 2003 decided to move up to the Olympic distance.

"A week before the event we found out Laura was pregnant. The doctor said it was all right to compete but if she felt fatigued to stop. I thought that was pretty lame advice. She's doing an Olympic-distance triathlon. Of course she's going to get tired!"

She took her time and finished in great shape.

"My wife and I have competed in the Chicago Triathlon for several years since and I have never forgotten my helmet or goggles since. By this time I learned to swim properly, bought a bike, a wet suit, and all the gear. And now that I've made this investment in triathlons, I'm moving to Romania."

Friend looks forward to introducing triathlons to his two boys when they get older. When he gets back from Romania in three years he plans to do a half Ironman. After all, he already has the gear.

What He Learned

"The training forces me to stay in shape. It's a great motivator. I mark my events on the calendar which makes it real and I don't back down from doing it. I like setting goals and then reaching them.

"I like the triathlon because it builds endurance, something I never had when playing sports like football. It's also good to get out and challenge yourself, do something you're not good at. With triathlons, my goal is to improve. I'm not competing against other people; I'm competing against myself and always try to do a little better each time."

SHAWNA GIBSON

DOB: 3-5-74
Residence: Fort Worth, Texas
Occupation: Marketing director, Benbrook Community Center/YMCA
First Triathlon: 2005 Athens (Texas) Sprint Triathlon

Shawna Gibson is a self-proclaimed obsessive-compulsive triathlete. In her first year as a triathlete she did six triathlon events: Shawna started out with the Houston full marathon, followed be a sprint distance, where she won her age division, followed a few weeks later by an Olympic distance, followed by a few more sprints, followed a few weeks later by a half Ironman, and ending the season with the Las Vegas Marathon in December of 2005. Two weeks prior to the Vegas Marathon, she was feeling tired and worn down, not unusual for someone keeping such an active training and racing schedule. However, with a history of cancer hanging on her family tree, she decided to go to her gynecologist for a checkup. The blood test came back positive for ovarian cancer. Gibson's response? Dang! Can I still run the Las Vegas Marathon?

"I wasn't terribly coordinated as a kid so I didn't participate in a lot of sports. I ran track in high school but most of my time was spent at home on the horse ranch my parents owned. There was a lot of work to do on the ranch, breaking horses, cleaning stalls, and anything else that was needed.

"I was not really college material, although I tried it, and I did not want to work on the ranch anymore. At nineteen, I moved to Fort Worth, Texas, trying to figure out what I wanted to be when I 'grew up.' I took a job as a nanny to make ends meet. I became a nanny for an amazing woman, a single mother of two children.

"I also worked part time at the YMCA of Metropolitan Fort Worth as an aerobics instructor and then was a certified Spinning instructor as well as a certified fitness and nutrition specialist. As years passed I ultimately moved up the ladder and became membership and marketing director for the Benbrook Community Center/YMCA.

"In March 2004 the BCC/YMCA put on a triathlon. I was the assistant race director. As I worked on the setup, I was intrigued with the race and all the components and thought it was very cool. In fact, I decided to enter it. Heck, I could run and everyone knows how to ride a bike and I could fake the swim, so the morning of the event I showed up with three hundred bagels for the post-race party and started to sign up to enter."

Unfortunately, she was not allowed her to enter. Same-day entries were not accepted. Besides, she was supposed to work the race, not do it.

"I was bummed not to be able to do it but I got to see it up close and thought it was pretty amazing. A few months later, a group of men showed up at the BCC/YMCA and went out for a long run from the entrance of the YMCA. This group, the Ridglea Master Swim Team, was using the BCC/YMCA while their facility was being repaired. I asked them if I could run with them because they seemed to know where to go, I always get lost, and they were very agreeable. They were better runners than I was but since I did not want to be dropped, it forced me to run faster. One of the guys was the masters swim coach and offered to teach me to swim. Pretty soon we had a schedule going of training runs and masters' swim practices."

What Gibson did not know was what joining Team Ridglea/Tri Ridglea was about to get her into. The team competes in many different sports, one of which was the Houston Marathon in January 2005. She had never even considered running a marathon but now she was an unofficial member of their team and decided to do it with them. She also did not realize they were not only marathoners but also triathletes.

"A few weeks before the marathon I fractured my ankle but was determined to still run. I went to a doctor who was a marathoner and very sympathetic to my plight. She showed me how to tape my ankle and said it would hurt like hell but I could do it if I was so bent on running it. She was right. It did hurt like hell and by mile eighteen, I was ready to quit but I saw so many wounded and pained marathoners lying on the side of the road I decided I was not going to be one of them and just sucked it up and kept going. I finished in 4:05 and was thrilled."

As soon as the marathon was over Gibson and her buddies started training for a sprint triathlon. She trained hard, doing bricks and masters swim workouts and continuing their long runs.

"Looking back, I really didn't train hard enough. It was very cold out and in T1, I took time to dry off, put on gloves, a hat, two jackets; you would think I also painted my toenails I took so long. It was over five minutes.

"The bike was fun, the run even better, and I picked off other runners one by one. Being on the bike, although I did borrow it, felt like being a kid again. I loved it and couldn't wait to do my next one."

A few weeks later, she did her own BCC/YMCA triathlon, the one she had watched a year before that had started her obsession with triathlon.

Her next event turned out to be a big mistake. She signed up for a sprint distance but ended up doing the Olympic distance through a twist of events.

"My friends and I were all set to drive to Galveston Friday night for the sprint triathlon but my grandmother had died and I stayed behind to attend her funeral, which was the next day, the same day as the sprint triathlon. I got a call Saturday night from my friends who surprised me with plane tickets to Galveston that night so I could enter the other triathlon event on Sunday.

"When I arrived in Galveston, they handed me my race packet when suddenly I realized they'd signed me up for the Olympic distance. They told me the sprint was full and they thought I could handle it. I had no idea what I was getting into. I didn't even have a wet suit or a bike with me."

She borrowed a wet suit, which was two sizes too small, and a bike she was not used to. The swim was in the ocean and she had only been in pools. Not to mention she had never swum a mile before.

"Not only was the water freakin' freezing but I was afraid of sharks showing up. I was so nervous, I convinced myself I was going to die in the water. When I finally got out my friends were there and I looked at them and said, 'That was the worst experience I have ever had. I hate swimming!'

"Thank God, the bike course was flat because I do not think I could have handled hills after the swim and never having gone more than fifteen miles on the bike before. By the time I got off the bike I was dead tired and had to run six miles. I just took my time—it was a flat course—and I finished exhausted but happy. In the end, I am glad I did it. Without training at all, I did an Olympic distance."

After that, she decided to do a half Ironman and upped the training. "We were already running eighteen miles so that wasn't a concern and the bike is a no-brainer but I was worried about the swim. A friend whom I worked with worked out a deal where I had to sell X amount of bikes and he would give me my first bike, a red five-thousand-dollar carbon-fiber Aegis T2 all decked out with the best of the best. I felt I had trained hard and well for the event but the one thing I did not train was reaching for water bottles. At this event, they had water stations where you could grab a water bottle. Right around mile twenty-five, I decided I wanted a fresh water bottle. Well, no one told me I should slow down before grabbing the bottle and I came in too fast and slammed into the curb, flew over the bike, and crashed.

"I was lying on the ground, dazed and confused, when the EMS volunteers reached me. I wanted to get up and check out my bike but they would not let me move. The more they held me down the more I wrestled to get up. I finally managed to get up and found my brand-new bike smashed on the ground. Nevertheless, it was still in one piece and so was I. EMS wanted to cart me off in the ambulance but I wouldn't have it and they could not force me. I got someone to help me hold my bike while I pushed the gears back in place and pounded out the bangs and dents. I didn't take the time to notice my brakes were gone. When I finally realized I had no brakes or big gears, the only thing I could do was spin in high gear for the last thirty-one miles. Thank God there were no hills."

Having to spin so long turned out to be a blessing—her legs were fresh for the run, and she had her best run time ever. Now she was ready to sign up for a full Ironman, a leap of faith, guts and determination considering it had been only seven months since she'd taken up the sport. She and her friends from Tri Ridglea registered for the September 2006 Ironman Wisconsin, a year away. With the Ironman indelibly marked on her calendar, she concentrated her training on the Las Vegas Marathon, three months away.

"I was feeling really tired after the half Ironman but kept training with the guys every weekend for long runs and continuing our weekly swim- and bike-training schedule for the Ironman. I have a history of cancer in my family and something just was not feeling right so I went to my gynecologist for a checkup and blood work. I clearly remember the phone call I received from the doctor with the bad news. I was driving in my car and got a phone call from the office asking me to come in to the office on Monday. I knew something was up and asked to speak with the doctor. I was not going to spend my weekend worried that I had cancer. She got on the line and confirmed that I had cancer. I told her since I had to have cancer I was hoping it was breast cancer so I could get a boob job but it turned out to be ovarian cancer, stage one. I was trying to make light of the situation and use humor to dispel my fears but I have to say I was shocked and struck with fear like I had never had before. I was thirty-two years old, not married, no kids yet, and I was facing a type of cancer with a huge fatality factor."

Gibson was lucky. Her cancer was detected very early, a rare opportunity in ovarian cancer patients. She had day surgery to remove a small piece of her ovary and had to undergo radiation five days a week for five weeks and chemotherapy in a pill form twice a day for six months.

"My first question to the doctor was whether I could still run the marathon ten days away, before I started the radiation treatment. She thought I was a nut and did not advise it. However, I was determined to run it and asked if it would hurt my chances for recovery if I did it. She could not confirm that it would but still advised against it. But I made up my mind and I was going to run it.

"I did not tell any of my friends that I had cancer, as I did not want to become the cancer poster girl and get that look of sympathy from everyone. I did not want to give my cancer a voice and have it dominate my life and become what identified me.

"I needed that marathon for my mental stability and ran it as if it was the last race of my life. I ran it in 3:44, missing a Boston Marathon qualifier by three minutes."

The day after the marathon, in December 2005, Gibson started her radiation treatments. She continued her Ironman training but by the second week, she was vomiting every morning and had no energy. She still didn't tell her training partners about her cancer even though she was constantly ribbed about being so slow. Finally one morning, feeling sick as a dog and lagging behind, she could not take the teasing and blurted out the truth. Her pals were shocked.

"I got a lot of grief for training for an Ironman during my treatments but I truly needed it. The training made me feel alive. My life sucked at the moment and I felt like crap but I was alive and wanted to live it to the fullest. I had big hopes for the future."

In March 2006, she went back to her first triathlon in Athens with big plans to do well. However, she spent the night before throwing up in the bathroom, weak and miserable.

"Every step of that sprint triathlon was hard work but at least I was doing something that made me feel alive and who I was. I was not going to let the cancer rob me of everything that was important to me. Having cancer sucks but I can make my life seem normal by doing what I do and keeping to my routine."

In June 2006, Gibson finished her treatments and is now in remission. She is building her immune system with lots of vitamins and waking up most days feeling alive and wonderful. She maintains a grueling weekly schedule that starts with a run on Monday morning, followed by an hour to an hour and a half of swim practice with drills. Tuesday and Thursday is the same routine with the addition of an evening bike ride of one and a half hours. Wednesday is a long run of up to eighteen miles. Friday is an easy day of a short run, and weekends are reserved for long morning runs up to twenty miles followed by a swim, followed by a four-hour-plus bike ride. Sunday is a six-hour-plus bike ride.

"Tri Ridglea has become a family to me. I do not have a husband or kids or close relatives or siblings. The family I was a nanny for all those years ago—Jake, Kate, Lisa Mullen, Grammy, and Uncle Bill—have adopted me. They are whom I call family.

"Without these folks, I would not be half the person I am today. I owe each of them so much. They believed in me when I didn't believe in myself. They are my world. Team Ridglea is just a group of average Joes. We are not elite, we are not professionals; we just are ordinary people trying to infect others with this extraordinary sport. We love being together and training together. Snickers Marathon Bars just sponsored me, a few of them were sponsored by Polar, and we are giddy over that. We are just a bunch of goofy people having fun. These folks inspire me and if I have to crawl across the finish line at the Ironman, I will. I will do it for all they have given me in life."

GORDON HALLER

DOB: 8-24-50
Residence: Centennial, Colorado
Occupation: Computer programmer
First Triathlon: 1978 Hawaii Ironman

Not many people can claim that their very first triathlon was the first Iron-man event in 1978. Fifteen people, to be exact, can make that claim, and the winner, Gordon Haller, will be forever known as the first Ironman. His story belongs in the annals of sports history and his accounts are often hilarious. It all started out with navy commander and sports enthusiast John Collins want-ing to prove who was the best athlete: a swimmer, cyclist, or runner. With no guidelines to go by, the event was organized in the living room of Collins's home on the island of Oahu, and fifteen men set out on a day in February that changed the world of sports forever.

"I grew up in Oregon and as far back as I can remember I was always running. In grade school I was the fastest kid in school. By junior high I wasn't the fastest but I had the most endurance, running ten-milers for fun. I was swimming by age six and riding my bike by age four. I was just very athletic and I just loved sports. I ran competitively in college at Pacific University, a small school in Oregon. I was also on the swim, track and cross-country, and wrestling teams. Sometimes I won and s records, other times I didn't. However, in 1969 I won something I really didn't want to win. As a freshman in college, I won a ticket to the US Army. My draft number was thirty-six, and I was on my way to Vietnam. Instead of going that route, I applied for Naval Officer Candidate School in Newport Rhode Island. Once accepted, I enlisted in the navy while still in school. A few months after I graduated college in 1972 I was a commissioned officer in the navy and my first base assignment was Hawaii, the beginning of a twenty-four year military career."

Haller was happy with his military assignment and settled into navy life in Hawaii. He didn't continue running much after college, thinking that part of his life was over. He had already run two marathons in his senior year in college and during OCS, and shifted his focus to lifting weights and building muscle mass.

"I got back into running when I was asked to join a civilian running team in Honolulu. My first race was a five-miler around Diamond Head. I won it and qualified for the team. The next event was a 140-mile relay race. I realized how much I missed running and quickly got back into my routine, upping the miles to 450 a month. In February 1973 I ran an unofficial marathon around the base while I was doing my laundry, a creditable 2:49.

"Since I didn't have a driver's license, I rode my bike everywhere, averaging three hundred miles a week. I also started swimming in the officers' club pool a few days a week."

Haller's idea of fun on his days off was to run fifteen miles in the morning, ride his bike a hundred miles, swim laps, and then run ten miles again at night. That year he ran four marathons in six weeks, winning the Maui Marathon twice, in 1973 and 1974. In late 1974, his tour in Hawaii was up and he was transferred to Long Beach, California, continuing his extreme training schedule.

"Maybe I overdid it a bit as I started to get injured. But the recovery powers of a twenty-four-year-old are pretty amazing and soon I was back ⟨...⟩ads. In 1975 I became part of the military pentathlon ⟨...⟩Allied Confederation of Reserved Officers (CIOR), a ⟨...⟩ that included throwing grenades, a swimming obstacle ⟨...⟩gues, orienteering, a running obstacle course, and shooting weapons. I competed for eight years, taking the world championship in 1981."

In November 1977 Haller ran the Marine Corps Marathon in 2:27, placing sixteenth overall and fourth military. The following month he started the Honolulu Marathon but had to drop out at mile six due to injuries. He pulled off to the side of the road to watch the rest of the marathon. Someone he knew approached him and said there was a new race that seemed like it was invented for him, something about a triathlon.

"About thirty people showed up at the home of Commander Collins, who had been doing multisports in San Diego but had never put together something like this. He suggested that the debate on who is the fittest athlete, the runner, cyclist, or swimmer, should be settled through a race combining the three existing long-distance competitions already on the island: the Waikiki Roughwater Swim (2.4 miles), the Around-Oahu Bike Race (115 miles, originally a two-day event), and the Honolulu Marathon (26.2 miles). Commander Collins calculated that, by shaving three miles off the course and riding counterclockwise around the island, the bike leg could start at the finish of the Waikiki Roughwater and end at the Aloha Tower, the traditional start of the Honolulu Marathon. Collins said, 'Whoever finishes first, we'll call *him* the Iron Man.'

"We all discussed the event, talked about it some more, had a couple more meetings, and finally decided on the three sports, the order and the course. We put the swim first because you can't really stop and rest during a swim. The idea was to get that one out of the way while the participants had the most energy so no one would drown from fatigue. The whole thing was a monumental task. We picked February 18, 1978, for the date of the first-ever triathlon. We drew up an agreement among us forming an organization called Ironman Triathlon Association, so that we couldn't sue each other if something bad happened. We all signed it and that was the start of the first official Ironman Triathlon.

"The race started at 7 A.M. and we were off and on our own. No traffic control, no support, no police, just us. We had volunteers on surfboards to guide us on the swim course as there were no buoys or markers on the course as we swam. Transition areas were unheard of so we just did our own thing coming out of the water. I took a shower and spent fifteen minutes getting ready for the bike. I had a road bike but did not have clip pedals yet. We did wear helmets, which were made of leather straps. Not very effective if there was a crash but it would hold the pieces together nicely. During the bike course I actually switched from a borrowed racing bike to my own commuter bike depending on what gears I needed and the elevation of the course. It rained a bit and I was glad I had my own bike at that point.

"I tied a bag of food onto my handlebars, some bananas, oranges, and chocolate chip cookies, and drank lots of fluids. Back in transition I took another shower, had a massage, did an interview with a reporter from the local paper, and then headed out for the marathon. My run time was 3:27 and I crossed the finish line, a piece of string pulled across the road, in 11:46:58, the first official Ironman. It was a great day and I think we all learned a lot. Heck, we officially discovered the sport and there were no precedents or rulebooks to follow. Most of the others knew very little about nutrition or training in multiple sports. I remember seeing some of the guys eating a bowl of chili or a hamburger in between events. One guy really didn't know how to swim and did the dog paddle for two miles. Another guy bought his bike the night before the event. We didn't know what we were getting into but we had fun.

"One of my co-workers at the Nautilus fitness center was Steve Epperly, a former modern pentathlete. He did a fantastic job organizing my support team, providing me with massage, food, and drink. His fiancée and my friend, Valley Ferrell, helped drive, made cookies, and was my official photographer."

That first year, out of the fifteen who started, twelve finished. Haller stayed at the finish, cheering each finisher across the line, as he does every time he participates. The last finisher arrived in well over twenty hours. The awards ceremony was held a week later at Collins's house; Haller was awarded a three-inch-tall trophy mounted on a piece of wood that had a logo and the words IRON MAN TRIATHLON WINNER. Back then, *Iron Man* was two separate words. They all agreed to do it again the next year.

In 1979, the race attracted fifty athletes but only fifteen started the race due to bad weather conditions. San Diego's Tom Warren, age thirty-five, won in 11:15:56. Haller took fourth as he competed with a severe sinus infection, but still had the fastest run, and the conditions were still bad with six-foot swells and forty-knot winds to contend with. The following year the number of entrants swelled to over one hundred due to *Sports Illustrated*'s eleven-page article on the sport. For the first time, ABC Sports televised the race in 1980. During the following year, hundreds of curious participants contacted Collins.

The year 1980 was pivotal for the Ironman competition. Collins retired from the Navy and "sold" the rights to the event to Valerie Silk, an owner of the Nautilus health club that had sponsored Haller the first two years. In 1981, Silk moved the site of the event from Oahu to Kona because it had grown so large she needed a less congested place to stage the event, and in 1982 moved the date from February to October. The original fifteen members of the Iron Man association were never informed until after the fact of Collins's sale to Silk, who formed the Hawaii Triathlon Corporation in 1981. Silk eventually sold the Ironman rights to the World Triathlon Corporation, which has run the event since. Haller has gone back to compete at the twentieth and twenty-fifth anniversaries of the event, where he finished in 14:21. He still stays in shape and works out two hours a day.

"I can't run distance as often anymore as I have knee problems now. My sixteen-year-old son, Ryan, is doing his first half Ironman soon and I will probably pace him. I still enjoy long bike rides with Ryan and my wife Beth, and have set some goals for myself: run a quarter mile in a minute, run a five-minute mile and a forty-minute 10K once more before I die."

Things He's Learned

"Almost anyone can do an Ironman though it might take awhile.

"Practice eating and drinking during a long event.

"Hydrate, hydrate, hydrate starting several days before the event.

"Taper a couple of weeks out.

"Schedule rest in your training program.

"Plan your race day carefully, use a checklist for equipment and clothing.

"Get enough sleep at least two days prior.

"Double-check your bike. It's the most likely thing to fail you.

"Practice changing flats.

"Wear your shoes enough to get your feet used to them.

"Don't let Ironman training interfere with your family and work, but know you will have to make some sacrifices in those areas for a while.

"Recover adequately after the race."

STEFANI JACKENTHAL

DOB: 8-4-66
Residence: Manhattan, New York
Occupation: Journalist
First Triathlon: 1996 Olympic-distance triathlon, Columbia, Maryland

The athletic history of triathletes can sometimes be a fascinating case of injuries, crashes, burnouts, and the journey back to recovery and renewal. Stefani Jackenthal has experienced it all. She was a nationally ranked professional cyclist when a bad crash ended that career. She tried a triathlon and hated it. Said she would never do that again! She gave it another try and went on to do two Ironmans. Jackenthal has run the triathlon gauntlet of getting seasick in the water, vomiting on the run, and passing out—and loved every minute of it. She is a survivor with true grit, determination, and a sense of humor. The perfect ingredients for a die-hard triathlete.

"I always loved sports. I played lacrosse in high school and college. After graduating, I moved to Manhattan and attended business school. That's when I started riding my bike with the New York Cycle Club (NYCC). It was a great way to work out while meeting single, athletic people. I joined their eleven-week progressive training program that taught us about gearing, technique, and nutrition while increasing the mileage each week. It culminates with a century ride (one hundred miles). Every Saturday morning we met in Central Park and rode out of the city

77

with the ride leaders giving us instruction throughout the day. Upon finishing graduate school, I treated myself to a bike tour through Scandinavia
with some of the people I'd met in the NYCC. One of the riders in our
group was an experienced bike racer who encouraged me to get my bike-
racing license. I had thought about it once, but dismissed the idea just as
quickly. But that trip gave me more confidence on my bike, and when he
planted the race seed in my brain it began to spin. I got my license when
I returned home, but it rained at my first race and I wimped out. I
watched the race instead and slunk home feeling demoralized."

Eventually Jackenthal started entering races and by 1992 was nationally
ranked. She went pro and spent the winters in Florida training and racing.
But in 1995 she experienced a bad crash that put an end to her racing career.

"After the crash I started swimming for rehab. But all the years of biking bulked up my legs and they sank like anvils. I never swam competitively, but thought I knew how to swim. I quickly found there was a big
difference between splashing around and swimming laps. I did get better,
although I zigzag with each stroke and have zero flexibility in my ankles,
so my kicking is pathetic. One swimming pal accused me of having meat
hooks at the end of my ankles.

"Some of the people I swam with were triathletes and they were training for an Olympic-distance triathlon in Columbia, Maryland. I thought
it sounded cool so I decided to go along—never considering starting out
slowly with a sprint distance. I thought I could get through the swim, I
knew I could bike, and I didn't think much about the run."

Jackenthal approached her first triathlon as a lark, a fun outing with
friends. Although she had no expectations of winning, her competitive nature kicked in and she toed the starting line ready to go hard. Wearing a
borrowed wet suit and using her heavy old race bike, she did not have to
invest in any gear—which made it even more appealing. What she did not
count on was cold water, the wrong type of bike, and just how long six
miles can seem.

"When I felt the frigid spring water I cringed. I hate being cold and
thought the wet suit would not only give me extra float, but would keep
me warm. But it was too tight in the neck and too baggy in the body, so

the cold water oozed through the opening of the arms and legs, giving me the shivers. To make matters worse, it was my first time swimming competitively in open water and I was petrified. I decided to tackle it up front and get it over with but I didn't anticipate getting kicked in the face, swum over, and pushed. I got hammered. I swam to the side to avoid the other swimmers but since I didn't know how to sight the markers, I swam a quarter mile off course. It was a miserable experience and I couldn't wait to get out of the water.

"Back at transition I couldn't get the wet suit off. I struggled with each leg and kept falling and was covered in grass by the time I got on my bike. My heart rate was sky-high; my breathing sounded like a locomotive, and the aerobars I had attached to my old clunky bike felt awkward—making steering scary. Still, I found momentary solace on my bike.

"When I finally relaxed, I enjoyed bike portion and was able to pass some of superstar swimmers who had crushed me in the water. But I couldn't believe I still had the run ahead of me. Oddly, my feet were still numb from the cold water when I reached the transition area and started running. I decided right then that triathlon was the dumbest sport in the world and I couldn't believe I'd decided to do one."

Jackenthal began her run tired, cold, and frustrated but quitting never entered her mind. Besides, how long could six miles really take to run?

"As I was running I kept thinking, *I will never do this again.* I just wanted it to be over and my grimace told all. Each step was an effort and running six miles seemed to take forever. I had nothing left by the end and as I limped across the finish line, I remember thinking that it was the hardest thing I had ever done."

Despite feeling out of place, tired, and beaten, she placed third in her age group. On the way home her thoughts quickly changed from *I'll never do this again* to *How can I get better?* She vowed to come back better trained and more prepared. But Jackenthal did not go right back to triathlons. She got into adventure racing—a team event involving trail running, trekking, mountain biking, kayaking, and rock climbing—and competed in places like China, Ecuador and Borneo, writing articles about her travel adventures for magazines and newspapers, and reporting for radio and TV. But she missed the solo nature of competing in triathlon and the camaraderie of her tri friends. She ventured back into triathlons in 1999.

The first thing she did was invest in a carbon triathlon bike. She trained harder, did more Olympic and half Ironman distances, and in July 2000 took on her first full Ironman at Lake Placid.

"I was inexperienced going into Placid—my first full Ironman, but the timing fit into my schedule and my friends were doing it. My nutrition was way off during the race and I bonked on the last loop of the bike from not drinking enough electrolytes. Then my quads felt like they had bullet holes in them during the run. Between my cheering friends and thick brain, I hung strong and surprised myself by qualifying for Kona—which was just a few months later in October.

"By the time I went to Hawaii, I was overtrained and a stressed-out mess. And it got worse. During the race, I got seasick in the choppy water and the wind was insane. There were frequent powerful gusts that blew racers off their bikes. I couldn't take my hands off the bars for fear of falling, so I didn't to drink much water—only the sports drink I had in my sippy cup on the handlebars. In hindsight I should have just stopped the bike and drank. But I didn't. By mile eighty my stomach was gurgly and I was vomiting.

"When I finished the bike I felt dizzy, but started the 26.2-mile run after a brief rest in the transition area. My legs felt dead. I slugged forward—each step taking its own special effort. I tried to drink, but each time I put a cup of water or energy drink to my lips I'd get sick.

"By the time I approached what I thought was mile fifteen, my head was swirling, my belly was swollen as though I was pregnant, and I was still vomiting. As I reached the water station tent, sporting a big red cross on its top, I realized I was in big trouble. It was mile thirteen—not fifteen. But I was sure, and would have paid money that I had already passed miles thirteen and fourteen. I needed help and stopped—momentarily. Slurring and spitting up, I explained my situation to a volunteer at the station. Though I tried to fight her suggestion to sit down and wait for the medics, I collapsed onto a folding chair and passed out.

"When I woke up—within a few minutes—I snapped to and remembered where I was. Without a word, I bolted out of the tent and shuffled away. An aide carrying an embarrassingly large red-and-white flag chased after me. She and the doctor—who had been called off the course to examine me—reached me at the same time.

"Following a brief exam of my pulse, eyes, and tongue for exhaustion, dehydration, and who knows what, he suggested I get into the van so he could take me to the finish line. It was a moment of truth. Taking a ride would have ended my misery, but I couldn't live with myself if I didn't finish. I didn't have anything on my calendar that day but to do the Hawaii Ironman and even if I needed to walk the entire course there was no way I was giving up. After a brief debate with the doctor, he agreed to let me continue with the warning that 'if you are going to fall down, just sit down and we'll come get you!'

"He explained that I needed to walk to let my body cool down as I was overheating like a car. I had consumed too much sugar and not enough water, so my body was unable to process to the nutrients sitting hostage in my bloated belly. He assured me that walking was the solution. So onward I walked."

Jackenthal's goal was to break eleven hours. Her race mantra was, *No glow sticks!*—meaning she wanted to finish before dark. She ended up walking miles thirteen to twenty, vomiting along the way. But miraculously her body started to restore itself and she picked up the pace—and ran the last six miles. Her time was 12:15.

"Crossing the finish line was monumental—it matured me as an athlete. The best thing I can say about doing an Ironman is that it definitely builds character. It was a huge challenge and very humbling—but oh, so personally rewarding."

SCOTT JOHNSON

Photo by Mark Taylor

DOB: 3-10-72
Residence: Wilmington, North Carolina
Occupation: Data analyst
First Triathlon: 2003 White Lake (North Carolina) Sprint Triathlon

Scott Johnson was born with cystic fibrosis, a genetic disease that fills the lungs with mucus and depletes lung capacity. Wanting to be a typical kid, not the sickly kid, he played soccer and skateboarded and wrestled in high school before the disease started to catch up with him.

"I made the most of what I could," says Johnson, thirty-four. "By the end of high school I tried to squeeze in all the sports I could like swimming and surfing because I knew my life had limitations."

By the time he was twenty he had to taper from all sports, except for surfing. "Surfing basically kept me alive both physically and emotionally during that time," says Scott. In 2001, at twenty-nine years old, he came down with bacterial pneumonia, which went undetected for three months because he thought it was a sinus infection. By the time he was admitted to the hospital in July, his lungs were scarred and he faced a certain death if he didn't get a new pair. "The doctors said my lungs were so bad, they basically fell out," says Johnson. He spent three months in the hospital, slipping in and out of comas, tethered to an oxygen tank. "I made a wish list of the things I wanted to do if I survived and on the top of the list was doing a triathlon."

In September 2001, he received his new lungs. He spent a year learning to walk again, as his leg muscles had atrophied during his hospital stay. Then he suffered a setback with a perforated colon. More surgery, but it was just a small annoyance in the way of his plan to do a triathlon. His doctors told him he was one of only three people in the world to survive a perforated colon after any kind of transplant.

"My stomach looked like I had a C-section from the colon surgery. I had scars from feeding tubes, scars from my ostomy, scars from the transplant surgery. My torso looked like a highway map. It took a year for me to fully recover from the transplant and the colon surgery. Once I recovered I started to tackle my list. I went surfing in Costa Rica with friends and hiked in the Rocky Mountains and the mountains in North Carolina. Then it was time to start planning for my first triathlon. A friend recommended the White Lake Triathlon, describing it as ideal for first-timers. Three months after my colon surgery I started training. It was hard to get motivated at first, especially with the running because I never could run before and didn't know how to breathe. And I guess I just didn't trust my lungs."

Johnson attended an introductory meeting for Team in Training at work with one of his best friends. "My friend Terry had done a few marathons with Team in Training and both of us really wanted to get into triathlons. We decided that this was probably the best way to do it.

"I decided to join because it was a good cause, my group was all first-timers, the training was very structured, and my coach, Matt, lived in my town so I felt I would get hands-on treatment. I had to raise nine hundred dollars but raised the bar and brought in twelve hundred. I knew that training for a triathlon would be like starting from scratch athletically, but I was up for the challenge. I had six months until the triathlon so I felt confident I had enough time to put into it.

"However, I didn't realize how far behind I had fallen in my athletic abilities and got intimidated. I fell behind in the training schedule and on top of that developed knee problems. I wasn't going to be a quitter and end up on a couch bemoaning my fate. God gave me a second chance at life and I was going to make the most of it.

"I went back to training and my coach worked with me diligently and soon I got my confidence back. I didn't want to invest a lot of money on equipment as I didn't know if I would do more triathlons, so I borrowed a mountain bike and put road tires on it. I already had a wet suit from my surfing, so the initial expense was nominal. In fact, it turned out I didn't need the wet suit because the lake was so warm.

"I loved the Team in Training approach to the triathlon. There was no elitism, no pecking order, just an overwhelming sense of encouragement. Everyone I met associated with the triathlon were the nicest people. No one, not even the elites, ever looked down on the newbies. They were quick to share tips and advice and encouragement. That is what I love about this sport.

"I kept my medical history to myself, not wanting to bring attention to it. My mom, my coach, and some of my tri friends were the only ones who knew what I had gone through to get to his point. My mom was, and still is, my biggest supporter and cheerleader. She never dreamed I would do something like this and she knew how important it was to me. We shared the sense of accomplishment this would bring to my life. I knew she would be waiting for me at the finish line.

"The night before the event I wasn't worried, although I didn't sleep much. I viewed it as a tune-up for bigger and better things in my life. The White Lake Triathlon in White Lake, North Carolina, is known for its warm-water lake swim, flat bike and run courses, and a relatively small field, five hundred for the sprint distance. There is a half Ironman the day before, which gets more participants and closes out within days of registration. Standing at the lake, getting ready for my wave, was fabulous. I went through a surge of mixed emotions, everything from being nervous, happy, couldn't believe I was finally doing it, and glad to be standing there. In those short minutes before my wave started, I reflected on the many steps that brought me to this point and realized it was that journey that mattered more to me than the actual event. My mom and my coach were there with me and I knew I would be fine.

"My wave was the last to go so I didn't feel a lot of pressure but as much I thought I could handle it, the mass start and all those bodies flying into the water at once was unnerving. I just took my time, gained my composure, and kept going.

"By the time I got out of the water and back to transition, most of the bikes were gone but I didn't care. It wasn't about time, just finishing. Even on the bike, I didn't rush. The bike course is two loops around the lake and after the first loop I was feeling really good so I pushed it the second loop.

"When I started the run I was still feeling fresh, but soon realized I had exerted too much energy on the bike and holy cow, was I tired. I fell into a group of fun people who, like me, just wanted to finish so we pulled each other along.

"The race just happened to be on Mother's Day and my mother was waiting for me at the end of the finish chute. When I crossed the line I hugged her and said 'Happy Mother's Day.' We both started crying because neither of us thought that I would ever do anything like that. My time was 1:58:23."

A month later Johnson did his first Olympic-distance triathlon in Pinehurst, North Carolina, one of the toughest Olympic-distance courses on the circuit, which he found out after he signed up. In that first year, he completed four sprint events and two Olympic distances. He also started investing in equipment, buying a road bike and a better wet suit.

The following year he went back to White Lake and did the half Ironman. "I really got bit by the bug. I was doing so many triathlons I didn't really have to train that hard, just do some maintenance drills between events. As I paid more attention to what I was doing, picking up tips along the way, my times began to drop. I started paying more attention to nutrition and really devoted myself to becoming a serious triathlete."

The epiphanic moment in Johnson's new athletic life came when he was watching the twenty-fifth anniversary of the Hawaii Ironman coverage on television in 2003. "I was totally mesmerized as I watched the participants and knew I had discovered my destiny and set my sights on the Ironman. My coach is about the only one who believed I could and would do it. I selected the 2005 New Zealand Ironman in March. Ironically the Ironman was scheduled a few days before my thirty-third birthday, which I wasn't supposed to live long enough to see."

According to his doctors, Johnson became the first lung transplant recipient to participate in an Ironman. Unfortunately he dropped out at mile eight of the marathon due to electrolyte depletion and a severely bruised knee from a bike wreck a few days prior. Because he had never ventured this far and put this much demand on his body, Johnson had no way of knowing the toll it would take. Technically, he still has cystic fibrosis, even though he has new lungs. The disease still affects his digestive system and he has to be very careful with his nutrition. People with cystic fibrosis sweat out salt twice as much as people without the disease so he has to monitor his salt levels very carefully during his events. He underestimated the need for salt pills and had to quit.

"Normally I pop salt pills like M&M's, but the race started out in cold temperatures so I didn't sweat much. By the time I realized I should have been taking them all along, it was too late. By mile eight, I was starting to black out so I quit. It's just a race and I wasn't going to put my health in jeopardy just to finish."

In November 2005 he tried a full Ironman again at the Florida Ironman. "It was a perfect day and I really thought this would be the one to cap my achievements. But I made one pivotal mistake that blew the day for me. I had a fantastic swim (1:11) and was on my way to a six-hour bike time. At mile one hundred I was going up the final high rise bridge and about ten feet from the top I decided to stand up out of the saddle and muscle my way up and over at a faster pace. I had already pushed my muscles to the max on the bike and hadn't really thought about how tired and worn out they were. I suddenly felt a sharp, blinding pain in my thigh like I had just been stabbed and when I sat back in the saddle I could only pedal with one leg. When I got to the bottom of the bridge I pulled over, got off my bike, and started massaging my thigh. I thought at the time that I had just pulled a muscle really bad. After all, I had plenty of time left. After a few minutes one of the paramedic cars saw me, pulled over, and one of the paramedics came over to check me out. When he pulled up my bike shorts to look at my thigh, he found a lump the size of a softball under my skin. I had partially torn two of my quad muscles. My first instinct was to continue, especially since I have developed a higher tolerance for pain, but the medical doctor, who knew my history, pulled me from the course. Basically, they saved me from myself. If I had continued I probably would have torn both of the muscles in half and never been able to compete again."

Johnson is signed up for the 2006 Florida Ironman and determined to finish. "When I first started doing triathlons it was purely for myself. Since then I have realized the effect and encouragement that it has on others with cystic fibrosis and now I run each of these races for them. A little girl in New Zealand named Amber, who has cystic fibrosis, summed it all up by saying, 'Lance Armstrong isn't my hero anymore, Scott is.'

On his refrigerator is a photograph of the spot on the bike course where he got his injury as a reminder of what not to do next time. He has teamed up with his original coach, Matt Clancy, and his best friend, Terry, is doing the race as well. He's back to training, starting his days in the darkness of the predawn dusk jumping in the pool, followed by some biking and later a run. "I do this because I always wanted to do it and couldn't. I feel lucky to be alive and have a lot of catching up to do. I want to live every day like it's a birthday party. Every day I thank my donor for this unselfish gift. Without it none of this would have ever happened. I thank my donor with every breath that I take and I hope that I have made that person proud with what I have accomplished. And to that person's family, I want them to know that their loved one is not gone but still lives on inside me with every swim stroke, pedal turn, and foot strike."

Scott's Advice for Beginners

"Realize that sometimes things go horribly wrong. It's how you react to those situations that defines you as a triathlete. Overcoming obstacles is what it's all about.

"Practice nutrition.

"Practice transitions.

"Nothing new on race day. I know that you might look really good in the new tri suit that you bought yesterday but if you haven't trained in it, then don't wear it on race day. The same goes for any kind of equipment, nutrition, amount of effort, et cetera. Sometimes it's unavoidable. I had to install and use a new bike computer one day before Ironman Florida. I got the same brand that I had previously just so it wouldn't be too foreign to me.

"Sleep is an important part of training.

"Don't spend a lot of money in the beginning until you decide if you want to continue competing in triathlon. This is not a cheap sport.

"An ultra-expensive, light, sexy-looking, carbon-fiber triathlon bike is only as good as the rider that is on top of it.

"Practice your weaknesses. People tend to concentrate on their strengths and suffer through their weakest disciplines.

"When talking to strangers at races, learn to lie convincingly about the amount of training that you do."

KIRSTEN KINCADE

DOB: 1-5-65
Residence: Franklin Lakes, New Jersey
Occupation: Mother, professional triathlete
First Triathlon: 2000 Wyckoff (New Jersey) Sprint Triathlon

Four seems to be a lucky number for Kirsten Kincade. Life is good for this forty-one-year-old mother of four kids, four-time Hawaii Ironman qualifier, and four-time International-distance World Championship qualifier. She is smart, a former Wall Street trader, funny, and at forty, a Triathlete Magazine *(June 2005) swimsuit model. Her athletic endeavors are an inspiration to family and friends. She also receives some negative comments about her lifestyle from those who don't know her well but nonetheless choose to judge her in a skeptical manner. No one would question her lifestyle and goals if she were a he. Kincade is an athlete; gender should not be an issue. She embraces the whole sport of triathlon—short and long—with the encouragement of her kids and husband. She trains effectively and efficiently, getting up at 5 A.M. for a long ride or run before the kids are out of bed.*

A star runner in high school and college, she started swimming for cross-training and then broke out the old Schwinn to prepare for her first triathlon. Everything seemed to be coming together, but marriage, a move to California, and the successive births of four kids put a hold on her new sport. When she finally did her first sprint triathlon in 2000, four months after the birth of her fourth child, there was no holding back. Two years later she completed the

2002 Hawaii Ironman.

She competes in ten to twelve events a season, finishing out the year with the world championships in Hawaii. In 2004, her ten-year-old daughter Nicole stole the headlines by completing her first sprint triathlon on the Wyckoff course, at Kirsten's side.

"I ran track and cross-county in high school and senior year I was the captain. I was good but not the best. When I ran cross-country at Smith College the coach took an interest in me and pushed me to be my best. I shaved four minutes off my time and became an All American. That big change proved to me that running is 50 percent mental. My coach changed the way I looked at myself as always being number two to being anything I wanted.

"The summer before I graduated college I had an internship on Wall Street for a brokerage firm. I ran in some of the Chase Corporate Challenge road races for the firm and did well. The traders on my floor all of a sudden took an interest in me and asked me to train with them. They were quite a competitive bunch. Some of them were Ironmen. At the end of the summer I was offered a full-time job upon graduation.

"When I started working I made friends with the triathletes on the floor and we trained together after work. They exposed me to what Ironman training was all about and I taught them everything I knew about running. It was great fun.

"I also swam and rode my old Schwinn for cross-training. The first time I went in the pool I couldn't swim three laps. But I watched the good swimmers, asked for advice and tips, and soon I was able to keep up and swim a mile. It's really all about the right rhythm and breathing. As I got better at swimming, the idea of doing a triathlon started to form."

After a few years of training with her Wall Street group Kincade was ready to compete in her first sprint triathlon. But marriage and a transfer to California put a hold on her plans. Despite the setback she kept training at a high level, always intent on fulfilling her dream. Thirteen years and four kids later she got her chance.

"Four and a half months after the birth of my last child, I entered my first sprint triathlon. I started running one week after delivery to get back in shape and swam and biked as much as I could with four kids at home. I was counting on my running for a strong finish, as I couldn't get enough training time in the pool and on the bike to get proficient in those events to make it worth saving a few seconds or minutes off my time.

"I was lucky enough to be a member of the club where the swim takes place and is also the center of all transitions so I actually got to swim, bike, and run the course before the event, a huge training benefit.

"I had no expectations going in to the triathlon. I was very nervous, especially for the swim. Seeing all the swimmers and the churning water was intimidating. First-timers tend to keep a safe distance from the edge of the water and have a certain look in their eye, a mix of fear and anxiety, and I was no different. I had that look.

"When the gun sounded, everyone rushed the water. I decided to swim to the side until I found my focus and rhythm. In order to concentrate, I counted slowly; one, two, three, and so forth as long as it took to get relaxed. As soon as I felt comfortable in the water, I found my groove and soon I was passing people. I was among the top ten females to come out of the water and the rest of the race went beautifully. I was comfortable on the bike and had the fastest women's run time. I won my age group and was fourth female overall. At that moment I fell in love with triathlon."

If it sounds like Kincade is competitive, she is. When she enters a race, it's to win or place. She is a serious competitor and keeps her ears and eyes open to everything on the course.

"The following year I went back to Wyckoff and finished second overall female. Later that season I did my first half Ironman in St. Croix. In 2002 I qualified for Hawaii at the Kona half Ironman. While I was in Kona I attended an Ironman camp and one of my instructors was Paula Newby-Fraser, which was very inspiring. She taught me the importance of pacing myself and not going all-out in every leg of the event. Runners tend to rush through each leg of the race instead of pacing each leg accordingly. She advised me to start thinking of myself as a triathlete and not a runner."

Kincade dedicated herself to being the best triathlete she could be. With the support of her husband, who was 100 percent behind her decision, she immersed herself in the art of triathlon as if studying for a master's degree.

"I couldn't have gotten to where I am today in this sport without my husband, Steve. He is a huge part of why I am able to do this. He takes the kids on weekends while I go for long runs or rides. In Hawaii, he manages the kids all day while I'm out on the course. I simply couldn't do this without him. He's also a great athlete in his own right and could probably do what I do if he wanted. But he is satisfied doing the Wyckoff Triathlon just to finish, not compete. An article about me cannot be complete without giving credit to him and my kids."

To learn more about the physical aspect of the sport and its impact on her muscles and overall physiology, Kincade made a trip to the legendary Boulder Sports Medicine Institute in Boulder, Colorado, and had a full range of performance tests done including VO_2 max, heart rate monitoring, blood analysis, and X-rays. She was fitted to her bike by the pros, ran on a treadmill for foot strike analysis, the whole enchilada of kinesiology, the study of human movement. To anyone serious about their athletic performance, this is like a trip to Disney World.

"I learned a lot about myself at the sports center. I always suffered with chronic hamstring injuries and couldn't locate the reason for it. The doctors at the center detected a slight curvature in my lower spine which throws off my pelvis and turned out to be the root of the problem. They adjusted the seat of my bike to compensate for it and the problem went away."

Kincade also attended the Chris Carmichael cycling camp in Santa Barbara, California, another eye-opening training experience.

"Their big mantra out there is *Stay in the zone* and *Build the engine.* Most of the camp attendants are cyclists with a few triathletes and overall the triathletes were viewed as harder working than the cyclists. I guess I wasn't building my engine properly because on a two-mile hill workout, Carmichael rode right next to me with his hand on my back and told me when to pick it up and when to hold back when I felt the urge to push harder. My inclination was to hammer, not stay in a zone. He kept repeating, 'Stay in the zone. Don't rush it.' That was some of the best advice I received, and I use it to this day.

"After more than fifteen years in the sport I consider myself a triathlete, no longer a runner who does triathlons. I have to say running is my strongest sport and the one I rely on to pull me through, but I still have to perform well at the other events."

With four kids, ages five to fourteen, Kincade gets up at 5 A.M. to get at least one training session done before the day starts. By the time they are home from school her training is over for the day and she shuttles them around to their various activities.

"The biggest reward I get out of this is the ability to set a good example for my kids about being motivated to reach for your dreams. They see the hard work and effort I put in to reach my dreams and I believe it has encouraged them to set goals and dreams of their own and work toward achieving them. When I come back after Ironman, I give talks to the local schools about the experience and the kids are very interested and want to know how they can get involved with the sport. Many of the kids I talk to have gone on to do youth division triathlons.

"I realize I am very fortunate to be able to do what I do and have the support of my husband and family. It's a real blessing and I respect it and am thankful for it. I plan to keep challenging myself as long as I can. It's what I do and with the help of my husband and kids, I will continue to be a dedicated mother, wife, and triathlete."

MIKE LLERANDI

DOB: 6-18-63
Residence: Ridgewood, New Jersey
Occupation: Software sales representative
First Triathlon: 1983 Splash Pedal Dash Sprint Triathlon, Schaumburg, Illinois

Mike Llerandi is always ready for an event. He's completed fifteen Ironman triathlons and over a hundred other races since he first fell in love with the sport in 1983. He trains seven days a week, fifty weeks a year, which keeps him in top form for his triathlon season, which starts in May and ends in October at Hawaii Ironman, where he has competed eight times. This Stanford graduate with the calculating mind of an engineer grew up with the sport, competing in the pro division for a couple of years in the late 1980s. In 1989 at the age of twenty-six he completed his first Hawaii Ironman, finishing in 9:22, a personal best until he beat that time at age forty-two. But Llerandi's real claim to fame is his ability to balance his triathlon life with work and a family. It helps that his wife, Alyson, is also a competitive triathlete and their three kids are already swimming and running. Llerandi is admired both on and off the course for his dedication to family and friends and his generosity in helping others train for their first tri.

"I basically grew up in a pool, swimming competitively since the age of six. My dad brought me and my sister Kitty to the park district pool in Schaumburg, Illinois, to sign us up for swimming lessons but the line was too long so he went to the shorter line and signed us up for the swim team. I competed all through my school years, ending up on the Stanford University swim team. That was a real eye-opener. I was an All American in high school but that paled in contrast with the credentials of the other guys on the team. However, shortly after my arrival I realized that I was burned out. I still remember the day I quit the team. I was riding my bike to practice, dreading it. The closer I got to campus, the more I slowed down. Just before I got to the pool, I turned around, pedaled home, and never went back. I was nervous to call my dad and tell him what I did, but when he asked me how I felt and I told him how relieved I was, he supported my decision. I felt I was missing out on my college life, shying away from parties and all the other adventures. Swimmers are the guys you see falling asleep in the library, not having any fun.

"I wanted to stay in shape after quitting the swim team so I started to run and went out with some buddies for three or four miles, no more. That summer I went home and took my usual job as a lifeguard at a public pool, which had hosted a triathlon the prior year. The sport was still in the closet for most people, and the few that were aware of it knew it through the *Sports Illustrated* article of 1979 that more or less introduced the sport to the public. I had heard of the Hawaii Ironman but didn't know others existed.

"I decided to give the triathlon a try. Only two hundred people entered. The swim was in the pool where I worked. I didn't train or do anything other than run to the pool and swim prior to the event. I borrowed my dad's bike and wore slip-on sneakers. The transition area was set up in the pool parking lot. For the swim, we went off twenty seconds apart and swam the lanes. I passed everyone in my lane, actually over and under most of the swimmers. Out of the pool, I ran to transition, jumped on the bike, and headed out onto the roads for the eighteen-mile course. The second transition area was located in another spot so we had to set up two transition areas. After the bike I headed out on the 10K run through town and finished. I had never run a 10K before but finished in 38:00. I finished second overall and loved it. I decided right then this was something I wanted to pursue."

Back at Stanford for his junior year, Llerandi started to look into triathlons. Very few people were putting the three sports together yet but his new roommate, Todd Watson, had competed in the USA Triathlon Bud Light series, which was the biggest sponsor back then. They were rooming in a fraternity on campus and picked a pledge who ran a 4:12 mile to train with them. Todd was a 34:00 10K guy who also ran, skied, played soccer, and swam. During that winter they did a triathlon together in Bakersfield, a longer distance than Llerandi's first one. Prize money was being offered, and it was rumored the pros would show up.

"The course was rolling hills, it was baking hot, and I didn't know what to expect. I had purchased a bike, but picked a hybrid since I wasn't ready yet to start making big investments in sport-specific equipment. I was sixth out of the water and feeling good until I hit the hills on the bike. At mile four I remember being passed by Scott Tinley like I was standing still. It just got worse because I also wasn't savvy enough to know about hydration and drinking and carbo-loading beforehand. By the time I started the run I was dehydrated and had to drop out at mile four. It was a very humbling experience. I had to take the sag wagon back to the start."

Llerandi didn't race again for a year. He spent his junior year training and learning about the sport and went back to Bakersfield the next year where he finished twenty-sixth overall out of six hundred. He concentrated on his running and did hill work throughout Palo Alto, increasing the distance. He also worked out with the water polo team. Continuing to train and compete at Stanford during the following year of graduate school, 1986, he ran the inaugural Big Sur International Marathon in 3:07.

"I wanted to break 3:00 for my first marathon but there were gale-force winds. After that race I thought about becoming a pure runner. Triathlons were fun but time consuming.

"After graduation I moved to Chicago to work for Arthur Andersen and ran on their team. My times were down to 32:00 for a 10K and 1:11 for a half marathon. I did two triathlons that year and with very little training did well. At the 1987 Chicago Olympic-distance triathlon in July, I finished sixty-sixth, close to where the pros were finishing. That got me thinking maybe I could be a triathlon pro. I was twenty-four years old, recently married, we had two incomes, and I felt if I was ever going to give this a try, now was the time."

Alyson, his bride of one year, agreed with Mike's plan to quit and become a professional triathlete. Other members of his family weren't so pleased. His grandmother commented about "the beautiful Stanford engineering degree" going to waste. But Llerandi never wastes anything: He put his engineering knowledge to work on his triathlon training, mapping out workouts, planning his strategy, and making his move on the pro circuit. They moved in with his folks to save money. His goal was to be as good as he could get and see where that led.

"I was very nervous about all this. I had no idea how good I was or could be. The night before my first pro race in Miami I felt so exposed, like doing something with blinders on and there was no safety net. I didn't want to disappoint my wife or my family.

"In my first two races as a pro, I crashed on my bike. The second crash was so bad, I broke my hand and had to drop out. My third race was in Little Rock, Arkansas. This race was a real turning point for me, especially since the first two events were miserable. I took third and qualified for Ironman Canada in August 1988, a little more than two months from the Arkansas race. I'd never considered doing that distance but now that the opportunity presented itself, I had to do it."

In 1988 there wasn't a lot of literature on how to train for an Ironman so Llerandi went back to the drawing board and, with his analytical approach, attacked his training like a term paper. With gradual increments of distance, he slowly built up his endurance. He gave himself tests. Ride eighty, run twelve. Ride one hundred, run twenty. He set up transition areas in the garage. He started taking supplements to build his energy reserves.

The Ironman was in British Columbia. He went by himself, staying for almost two weeks to adapt to the mountains, climate, and time zone. Typical of his analytical style, during the week prior to the race he reviewed the course over and over again. His longest distance was only an Olympic triathlon so he had a lot to make up for in a short period of time.

"I felt about as prepared as I could get. I was fourteenth out of the water, a good start with a race population of fourteen hundred. Once on the bike I knew I had to be disciplined and not get upset when people passed me. The competitor in me hates that. But I felt confident that if I kept a steady pace I would eventually pass them. I finished the bike in the top fifty but I was very nervous about the transition to the run. I took inventory of my body and everything was still working, but I felt like that scene in *Animal House* where the pledge is smoking pot for the first time and asks, 'I'm not going to freak out, am I?'

"Once my legs adjusted and I started passing people I felt comfortable and settled in, running the tenth-fastest marathon in the race and finishing fifteenth overall, qualifying for Hawaii in 1989."

After one year as a pro, Llerandi and his wife moved to California and he went back to work, giving up his full-time pro status.

"My life as a pro was very routine: eat, sleep, train. It's not all that exciting. After a year I felt confident that I could go back to work and keep training, just train smarter and harder. By learning to balance work, family, and sports, I became a better athlete."

At age twenty-six, Llerandi was on his way to his first Hawaii Ironman. Alyson was eight months pregnant with their first child so she missed the opportunity to join him. The 1989 Hawaii Ironman was dubbed the Iron War due to Dave Scott and Mark Allen's duel for first place the entire race, and Llerandi had a front-row seat to the epic battle.

"The conditions that day were perfect. Even though I ran my slowest marathon, 3:20, I finished seventy-fourth overall in 9:22:57, a personal best record that held till I beat that at age forty-two."

Now that he is a masters competitor, he is consistently ranked among the top ten Ironman triathletes in the world over forty, holding his own against the pros. With a full-time job, a wife who also competes and works full time, and three kids, two into their teenage years, he still approaches the sport, and his life, with the same analytical mind and remains committed and disciplined seven days a week. He's in bed by 9 P.M. most nights and up at 5 just about every morning.

"Consistency is the key to good training. You have to establish a schedule and stick to it. My daily schedule consists of swimming three times a week, Monday, Wednesday, Friday, in the water by 6 A.M. for an hour; Tuesday, Wednesday, and Thursday is cycling, either outdoors or indoors on a trainer. I run every night after getting home from work, except Friday. Friday night I don't do anything. On the weekends I do half of all my weekly training hours. I'll bike, run, bike again, run again for a total of seven hours, putting in 110 miles on the bike Saturday and 95 on Sunday, followed by a total of 35 miles running between the two days. It works for me, although there are times I've been called a stick in the mud with no social life."

All his schedules are laid out on a grid, which he keeps tweaking to perfection. Llerandi has his nutrition down after all these years as well. He has tested just about every conceivable supplement and food source, and is a big believer in E-Caps, a supplement company founded by a friend of his, who is also a sponsor. His caloric needs average eight hundred to twelve hundred calories an hour when he is training for an Ironman. He suggests that three hours is the maximum time allotted before supplements and more calories are needed to keep going or the body will start burning muscle tissue for fuel.

Based on Llerandi's years in the sport, he has a sense that most triathletes are runners first. There is an assumption that swimmers make the best triathletes—it is a big advantage, because it's the toughest event for most people, even swimmers. But Llerandi feels that instead of trying to figure out who has the advantage, concentrate on your strengths and weaknesses equally. He is still a solid swimmer, but cycling is his Achilles' heel so he doubles up on the biking during training. He also does track workouts and runs about forty to fifty miles a week.

"You can't be a purist in any of the three disciplines. No one sport will give you an edge. You have to be prepared in all three and pay particular attention to your weakness. The winner is the one who can successfully link them all together."

The winner is also the one who can balance triathlon training with a family. Llerandi always puts his wife and kids first, which is why he is up at 5 A.M. getting in training while the kids are still asleep. This is the life they have known since they were born. The family attends most of his Ironman events and have traveled to Hawaii more than once, a nice perk for the kids.

"Alyson and I want our kids to be athletes for life and keep a balance. Personally I won't push them to go for a sports scholarship. How could I when I walked away from mine? It takes so much away from other growth experiences. I want their focus for sports to be beyond college, beyond the regimen and routine of organized sports and do something they love for the passion. I'm sure they'll all want to do triathlons when they are ready for one but that will be their decision, not mine."

Llerandi is respected in the Ironman circles for being a consistently tough competitor who successfully keeps his goals in order: family first.

Advice from a Former Pro and Family Man

"Don't just train for triathlons—become a triathlete. Make a commitment to adopt a healthy lifestyle where multisport cross-training fits into your schedule. Never underestimate the amount of time required to train for a triathlon regardless of the distance. If you are not properly trained you won't have a good experience. Most first-timers make the mistake of working on their strengths and ignoring their weaknesses. Whatever your weakness is—and everyone has one, even the pros—make sure to double up on the training in that event.

"If you have a family, it's important not to neglect them during your training. Involve your spouse as much as possible and train together when practical. You'll need their support and encouragement at the end, when it counts, so include them in your training as much as possible."

JODY LLEWELLYN

DOB: 9-16-71
Residence: San Francisco, California
Occupation: Founder and CEO of skin care company
First Triathlon: 1999 Wildflower Half Ironman, San Antonio, California

Tackling a half Ironman as a first triathlon is not recommended and not the norm. But friends have come to expect the unexpected from Jody Llewellyn. Although she worked in a PR firm in New York City representing health care clients who sponsored high-profile sporting events such as the New York City Marathon, she didn't even own a pair of running shoes at the time and hadn't done anything truly athletic since she was in high school. Dig a little deeper into her formative years and you'll discover she was on her middle school and high school swim teams (best on the junior varsity team, worst on the varsity), and at age fifteen swam five miles around the perimeter of a lake in Vermont. Right after her college graduation, she did a three-month semester in Alaska, completing thirty days each of sea kayaking, wilderness trekking, and glacier- and ice-climbing expeditions. What she lacked in training she made up for in guts.

"Living in New York City right after college, I didn't believe I could be athletic and live in the city at the same time. After my swim feats as a teenager and my backcountry adventures in college, I didn't do anything athletic unless you consider drinking and smoking cigarettes an event.

The few times I did join a gym it was for the spa treatments."

When Llewellyn decided to head back to her home state of California, she packed up her belongings and drove cross-country to San Francisco at age twenty-six. She chose this city out of a desire to embrace a healthier lifestyle and reconnect to the outdoors alongside her urban lifestyle. The first time she attempted a three-mile run she almost died from exhaustion but she was determined to become athletic again.

"When I first arrived in San Francisco I found out there was a swim from Alcatraz Island and that appealed to me. For two years, I stared at that island thinking I could do it. But instead of signing up for a triathlon, I signed up with Team in Training in 1997 for a marathon. I knew it was going to take a force bigger than myself to get back in shape. I chose the marathon because I had always watched the New York City Marathon when I lived there and thought it was just so cool. And I chose Team in Training because my mom died of leukemia when I was in high school and I thought it was the perfect vehicle to honor her by getting my life back in shape and raising money to find a cure for the disease that ended her life.

"I arrived at the first training session a smidge hung over, with 'fashion' running shoes and all-cotton clothes. Not a good start. But I did quit smoking the night before. I stuck with the training, formed tight bonds with new friends in the process, and ran the Honolulu Marathon in December 1997 in 5:20."

Llewellyn kept running and ran her second marathon, the 1998 New York City Marathon. Earlier that year Llewellyn went to watch and cheer for friends doing the Wildflower Triathlon, one of California's most reputable and respected triathlons. It starts in a campground; most of the spectators and all of the participants camp out the night before the event.

"As I watched the triathlon, I kept thinking I could do it. Most of the participants didn't look any different from me. I knew I could relearn to swim, I could buy a bike, and I was about to run my second marathon, so I decided to set a goal to do the Wildflower Half Ironman Triathlon in 1999. The fact that Team in Training had also selected Wildflower as their first foray into triathlons was the deciding factor for me."

Llewellyn doesn't like to rush her events so she took four months off after running the New York City Marathon and did nothing. Starting from scratch again, she signed up for local 5K and 10K races to get back into running. She spent months researching bikes and finally decided on a pricey carbon-fiber Kestrel as her first racing bike, a decision she never regretted. The only thing she did regret was falling off five times and scratching the paint as she adapted to the clip pedals. Making a major investment in the bike was a conscious decision on her part to commit to doing triathlons. Besides, her last bike was a red Schwinn with streamers she rode in second grade; she felt entitled to invest in a good one.

"Training for my first triathlon was a blast. We had a very structured schedule that I taped to the fridge. The coaches built us up slowly, starting out with a ten-mile bike ride, with gradual increases to twenty, thirty, forty, and so on at our own pace. Two months before the event we were doing seventy-mile rides incorporating long, hilly climbs on the weekends. Since I bought such an expensive bike, I felt I had to live up to its image so I took my biking very seriously. (And lo and behold, I discovered in the process that I loved riding, thank goodness!) I didn't need to buy any other race gear because through the Team in Training fund-raising, if you raise the minimum of twenty-five hundred dollars you get a free wet suit and race jersey. In fact, everyone on the TNT team met the minimum and got a wetsuit. I was the highest fund-raiser, bringing in over eleven thousand dollars."

For Llewellyn, this was the perfect time to do her first triathlon. Her boyfriend at the time was also training for Wildflower on his way to his first Iroman race (and the inaugural TNT "Ironteam") later that summer, so finding the time to commit to training on weeknights and weekends was easy. Plus, she tremendously enjoyed the social camaraderie of these endurance sports training programs. She didn't know a soul until she signed up for the team, and was excited about being young, in shape, and having a ball. But why did she sign up for a half Ironman as her first triathlon, which breaks most of the rules?

"My coach felt that I could handle it because of my two marathons and my swimming history. My triathlon coach was also my marathon coach so he knew my ability level and thought an Olympic distance would not be challenging enough of a new goal. I knew I was biting off a huge endurance event so I was dedicated to the training, attending workouts every

Tuesday and Thursday evening, the weekend rides, and swim instruction. We only had one day off a week. It was so structured that if you followed the program you were guaranteed to finish. We practiced setting up transition areas, getting in and out of wet suits, entering the water, the transition from the bike to the run—everything we could possibly face in a triathlon, we practiced."

Packing for the weekend event created a new set of worries and anxiety for Llewellyn. She had to pack twice, one bag for camping and one for all the triathlon gear.

"My entire apartment was laid out in clothing. I went over my checklist fifteen times. The night before the event, as I lay in my camping tent with one of my teammates, I was nervous, excited, scared, prepared, and ready to go. Team in Training held a candlelight catered dinner the night before at the campground. The morning of the event we were up at 4 A.M. We all rode our bikes to the start and I began to set up my transition, making sure it was neat, planned out, and pretty. There was a lot of downtime because my heat didn't go off till 9 A.M. so I took an hour to set it up. I was so proud of it: perfect rows, folded towels, sunscreen, a bin of water to rinse my feet after the swim, a pre-peeled banana, Advil, BodyGlide, GU—it looked like I was setting up a pharmacy. I was so proud of my organized transition area that I asked another racer to take a photo of me posed beside it.

"My coach drummed into my head the importance of nutrition for such an event so I make sure I had enough foods and fluids, including the pre-peeled banana to eat in transition ready to go."

The legendary Wildflower Triathlon, referred to as the Woodstock of Triathlons, is a three-hour drive south of San Francisco in the middle of nowhere. The nearest motel is fifty miles away from the event. It typically gets about 7,500 participants and 30,000 spectators who all camp out for the weekend. Wildflower is known for its hilly and grueling course and its one topless aid station. For many triathletes it is a rite of passage.

As Llewellyn stood at the lake waiting for her wave, she cried.

"I was so emotional. There were more than a hundred women in my heat but I was geared up for the swim and decided to tackle it head-on. Among many discoveries during training was finding out that I was a decently strong swimmer. So I went in the thick of it, shoulder to shoulder, sprinted the first hundred yards to get away from the pack and then found my space and just went with it. We had practiced pushing people away and dealing with the panic so I was very prepared. The other thing we were told to do is peel the wet suit off as soon as we came out of the water, which of course we practiced. When I got out of the water my coach was there screaming and yelling for me. Back at transition I took my time drying off, stretching, standing in line for the bathroom, putting on my sunscreen, getting my bike shoes on. I didn't rush and although my time T1 time was fifteen minutes, I didn't care.

"Coming out of transition we were allowed to mount and bike before hitting the course because it was a long way to the 'bike out' exit. But I couldn't engage my left shoe. It kept sliding out of the clip. I got off the bike and checked it out and noticed the clipping mechanism was missing. I couldn't believe it! I went back to my transition area thinking maybe it fell off but it was nowhere to be found. (In the process of my mad shoe-clip-piece search, of course, I tore up my perfectly organized transition area!) Meanwhile my coach and friends were all calling from the sidelines, telling me to bike in my running shoes and get on with the race. So I got back on the bike with one running shoe and one biking shoe and off I went.

I knew it would be slightly uncomfortable and lopsided to bike fifty-six miles this way, but by mile eight and after the famous straight-out-of-transition climbs, I could feel strain in my quads. At mile ten, I saw my friends in their car at the top of a hill waving to me. At first I thought, *Oh how nice that they are here,* but then as I got closer I saw my missing bike shoe hanging out the window. I biked up to the car, they threw me my bike shoe, said they'd explain later, and off they went. I, of course, was thrilled to have my shoe and didn't even try to understand what just happened. (The mystery was solved later—turns out my tent-mate Nell Marshall and I had the exact same bike shoe size and style, and we had mixed our shoes. So when she emerged from the swim, she, too, had one shoe that did not clip in . . . and our friends spectating put two and two together!)"

The bike course seemed to go on forever and Llewellyn, in her angst not to get depleted, took a bite of a Balance Bar every twenty minutes, followed by a swish of Gatorade. By the time she finished the fifty-six miles she had consumed three bars and five bottles of Gatorade.

"I ate so much on the bike I'm probably the only person who gained weight during a half Ironman. I was now more than three hours into the event. Back at transition I stretched again, went to the bathroom again, changed my shoes, and started out for the 13.1-mile run. I was still pumped up, even though the transition area was half empty. I didn't let that bother me as my goal was to just finish.

"The run course is 75 percent trail running with two hills, each one mile long. The water stations along the course are theme-oriented, like the one staffed with students from Cal Poly San Luis Obispo who offer beer funnels to the runners or the Hawaii theme where the guys wore hula skirts and leis and the girls wore bikinis. Because of all the Gatorade I consumed, I needed to pee behind every bush. And then I started to feel nauseous as I was finishing the two-mile climb out of the so-called pit, a dry, hot, dusty, and particularly hilly part of the course. At the top of the hill, mile twelve, I took a sip of Gatorade at the aid station thinking it would help but it had the reverse effect. I started to hurl in front of the college students. For about twenty minutes I stood there getting sick to my stomach. With only a mile to go, I thought I would die.

"After emptying my stomach of all those honey yogurt peanut Balance Bars and quarts of Gatorade I actually felt like a million bucks and started to cruise the last downhill mile to the finish. A few yards from the finish I started to feel nauseas again but was able to hold it in till I crossed the finish line and then hurled again.

"I was so excited, I forgot about feeling sick and celebrated with my family, my coach, and the team, collected my medal, and headed back to transition to pack up. It was then that I started to feel a bit weak and friends were telling me I didn't look so good. I thought I was just punch-drunk happy but I couldn't stand up or untie my shoes so I was carted off the medical tent for observation. Four hours and two IVs later, I got to go home. I had become totally dehydrated from all the vomiting. I missed the banquet and all the partying."

In retrospect, Llewellyn says she was crazy to take on a half Ironman as her first triathlon distance. At the same, time it gave her the confidence to do more since she had already completed one of the hardest half Iron-man triathlons in California. She went on to do another half that season, as well as two Olympic-distance triathlons, for a total of four triathlons her first season, which included Escape from Alcatraz, finally realizing her dream to swim from Alcatraz.

Since 1999 she has gone back to compete in Wildflower four more times and, for the next six consecutive years, continued to do an average of four triathlons a season. She has done numerous Olympic and half Ironman distances. Her favorite local Olympic distance is Pacific Grove. Lots of great spectators, but the water is freezing and the swim is infamous for its course straight through kelp beds (Jody actually thinks this element makes it fun!). It's the bike course that she describes as a drop-dead gorgeous (and fast) stretch of California coastline. However, her favorite race experiences were ones that she could turn into vacations with her training friends—such as the three years they all went over to Kona to race in the (now defunct) Keauhou-Kona Half Ironman. In 2002 she did Ironman USA in Lake Placid, New York, an event she describes as taking over her life.

"After five years of racing and a particularly strong half Ironman race in Kona where I came in fifth in my age group, I decided over a celebratory mai tai that it was time to go for it and sign up for an Ironman for the following summer. I would be turning thirty, was again single, and thought if I was ever going to do one, now was the time. Between registration and race day, two significant events happened: I was hit by a car that autumn while riding my bike and fractured my wrist; and I met my now-husband just before the high-mileage training began. Thankfully, my coach Paul Lundgren and physical therapist at Presidio Sport and Medicine helped me view Ironman as a recovery goal, and my new romance thought that my training was 'cool!' But training for an Ironman can be a very selfish thing. I missed two weddings because I had to spend the weekends training, and I began to resent the amount of time it was taking. It was a goal that consumed my life (not that I wasn't having fun reaching new mileage heights of training and bonding with my training friends!). And just like déjà vu, after crossing the finish line I ended up in the medical tent from dehydration caused by getting sick from nutrition issues out on the bike and run courses. After Lake Placid I took a year off, and have kept it to fun Olympic-distance race goals since then.

"I came to the sport as a novice and basically learned it as the sport grew in popularity. (It is much harder to get into races these days!) What I love about being a triathlete is the mix of social camaraderie, athletic challenge, and adventure. I am proud of how I have grown as an athlete over the years, and the depth of impact these challenges and accomplishments add to the rest of my life. Though I have taken the last two seasons off from racing to get married (to my number one Ironman fan) and start my own business, the elements of swimming, biking, and running remain true passions, and I plan to return to the sport many times over my lifetime."

What She Learned After Her First Triathlon

"My biggest piece of advice? Relax and celebrate the night *before* the race—have that glass of wine—take your mind *off* the race, get a good night's sleep . . . and you'll wake up not fretful, but instead ready to go!

"I also have a triathlon ritual I started at Wildflower that I will pass on: Get a manicure-pedicure as close to the race as possible. It's relaxing, indulgent, and a great way to take your mind off of the race looming by sinking into the massage chair for an hour of trash-magazine-reading bliss. and, it's practical:(a) Short, lovely nails will make handling your wet suit easier and reduce the risk of puncturing the darn thing; (b) short, polished toes will reduce the risk of losing a toenail, and help you look chic when emerging from the water. Cheers!"

FRED MENDEZ

DOB: 12-8-65

Residence: San Francisco, California

Occupation: Director of community reinvestment, Silicon Valley Bank

First Triathlon: 2003 Escape from Alcatraz, San Francisco

Fred Mendez is a true California guy, who was born in San Jose and grew up on the peninsula. In college he was on the water polo and swim teams. After college he spent some time on the East Coast on Wall Street in New York City but got homesick and found his way back to San Francisco. He describes himself as that type of man who has enough testosterone to qualify him for coverage under the Americans with Disabilities Act. He'd done dozens of Alcatraz swims but never the triathlon. How much harder could it be to add a bike and run? Mendez found out the hard way.

"I was a competitive open-water swimmer and also played water polo in college, which is basically swimming for people with ADD. It was fun to mix up the two sports because, let's face it, swimming can get really boring. When I returned to San Francisco from the East Coast (my memory of that era has been erased), I joined the South End Row Club (or as it's casually known, SERC). SERC's been around for more than a hundred years and prides itself on being a club of mostly fat Scots that like to wear Speedos, swim in forty-six-degree water without wet suits, and hydrate afterward with at least eighteen-year-old Scotch. Once a week we take a boat to Alcatraz, jump off, and swim back. I've done it dozens of times.

"I was very happy with my swim routine and wasn't really looking to get into triathlons. But as any self-aware man or woman of any kind, anywhere, knows, men usually learn their lessons the hard way. That pretty much sums up the introduction to my first triathlon experience."

Mendez fell into the triathlon community through a member of SERC who started Thursday-night swims for triathletes to coach them on how to swim in the bay. Mendez volunteered to help manage "all of those type-A, easily distracted and overly competitive twenty- and thirty-year-olds." Before long, he got hooked into doing his first triathlon.

"The triathlon community is just a great group of people and also a great group to get in trouble with—and man, did they ever get me in trouble. They eventually talked me into getting a bike and doing the one thing I consider more painful than being castrated with an oyster fork . . . running.

"With quite a few Alcatraz swims under my belt, I thought it was a slam-dunk to do the Escape from Alcatraz as my first real race. After all, everyone says that it's the swim that makes the race so hard . . . and I've got that part down pat."

In 2003 Escape from Alcatraz was an open event. You didn't need to qualify and there wasn't a lottery. Mendez barely trained for the bike and run. He just knew the swim would be a piece of cake and the rest would fall in place.

"It must be a guy thing because I really did think this would be easy. Never gave a thought to training or how difficult it might be. I wasn't even nervous. I thought everyone else was an idiot, running around scared and nervous.

"A few minutes after the ferry pulled away from the dock in San Francisco and drifted into the bay, I made the horrible mistake of mentioning to the person next to me that I had done quite a few Alcatraz swims. Before I had a chance to finish the sentence, at least fifteen people surrounded me and frantically started asking questions about the swim, how to sight, how to figure out the tide, what kind of sharks are in the water, and if I know anyone who has died doing the swim. I realized how serious everyone else was taking this and my anxiety level jumped through the roof.

"We finally came to a drifting stop and the horn blew for the professional triathletes to start their race. From that point on, waves of age groupers jumped in groups of three out the door of the boat into the bay: One jumped to the left, one jumped straight forward, and another jumped to the right. (I imagined a group of tourists on Alcatraz doing the audio tour and hearing that nobody has ever survived a swim from Alcatraz, only to watch fourteen hundred people jump out of a perfectly good boat right in front of them.)

"A friend of mine was volunteering at the doorway and she wanted to take my picture right before I jumped, so I stopped and posed . . . but her flash didn't go off and she had to do it again . . . so I posed again . . . and then she said it was blurry and she would have to do it one last time. By the time this former friend took the damn picture, I was the third to last person to get off the boat!

"The water was very choppy, but the current wasn't strong yet so I knew what to do. I took a chance and swam in a straight line to the swim finish (the red roof of the St. Francis Yacht Club), hoping that I could swim fast enough and strong enough to beat the current before it pushed me out the Golden Gate. If you've never gone swimming in very choppy water, it's like swimming on a roller coaster . . . you know you're going to feel sick, but it's fun. I got completely spun around by a whitecap hitting my chest as I rotated from right stroke to left stroke, started laughing to myself, and promptly threw up in the water. Good times!"

As Mendez got out of the water, he was welcomed by hundreds of spectators yelling and screaming. The adrenaline rush of having such a large audience was incredible and he got pumped and excited. A volunteer handed him his transition bag (in this race, you give volunteers a small bag with running shoes so you can make the quarter-mile jog to the transition area without ripping up your feet), which he had carefully packed that morning. Thinking he was smarter than other more seasoned triathletes, he put his bike jersey and gloves in the bag as well as his running shoes so he could get a head start on the transition—but his plan backfired.

"Being a newbie, I hadn't realized that putting on clothes when you're wet, cold, and running is a battle and one you're going to lose. As I tried to pull on that jersey, it came alive and fought back. At the expense of fifty other athletes, the event photographer took approximately eleven photographs of me trying to run and put on a bike jersey at the same time. And these same photos were quickly circulated via e-mail throughout the tri community in San Francisco. More good times!"

Mendez was among the first two hundred out of the water. Visions of standing on the podium danced in his head until he started biking.

"Approximately fourteen hundred people did the race that year. Approximately two hundred were in front of me when I started the bike course and twelve hundred were about to pass me, including a heavyset older woman on an incredibly old, ill-kept, and creaky purple bicycle. You might be thinking that this happened because I got a flat, or my chain broke. Nope. I just plain sucked on the bike. My ego was absolutely destroyed. But that's when the race got to be fun. I started cheering people and they cheered back. I got to say hello to friends who were volunteering at the aid stations. I had a couple of really funny conversations with people on the bike as we weaved our way through the hilly neighborhoods of northwest San Francisco. I was having the time of my life and then it had to end in such an ugly way . . . with a run.

"A friend of mine calls the Escape from Alcatraz run course the 'Death Run.' It's not that bad once you get used to it, sort of like a bad girlfriend or a smelly old car. The hilly bike ride took a toll on my legs and everything hurt. Wearing the red-and-gold jersey of the Golden Gate Tri Club (my home team) increased the number of people who were cheering for me by a factor of a thousand, and it's the only way I was able to get through the run. As I crawled my way up the infamous Sand Ladder (I heard that Doug Flutie threw up there when he did the race a few years back), a smart-ass volunteer planted himself halfway up and was apologizing for the fact that the escalator was broken. If I had the energy, I would have smothered him in the sand until he couldn't breathe anymore . . . but I didn't, so he's still alive.

"Once I got to the top of the hill it hit me . . . *it's all downhill from here . . . really.* The realization that I was about to finish something that anyone in their right mind would spend a lifetime avoiding slowly sank in and I started to smile. It didn't make the pain go away but it made the pain matter less.

112

"As I ran through the last part of Crissy Field path and took the turn onto Marina Boulevard, I was astounded to see police barricades and people lined three- or four-deep all the way down the street, ringing the cowbells Clif Bar handed out, and screaming their lungs out. Just recalling this makes me emotional. I heard my name a few times, people cheering my club, but it was all washed into the background as I tried not to burst into tears. The support, the enthusiasm, and the sincere joy everyone was having in watching me finish was overwhelming. As I made the quick S-turn onto the Marina Green and down the finish chute, friends who had finished before me, volunteers from my club, even my ex-girlfriend were all there to give me high-fives as I ran the last hundred meters.

"Suddenly nothing hurt. It was as if I were floating across the finish line. And even if it was just for a moment, I was a triathlete."

Two weeks later he did an Olympic distance triathlon in San Jose and ended the season with his first half IM at Vineman in Windsor, California.

"There is no way I would have done these crazy things if it weren't for my friends in the triathlon community. They adopted me as a newbie and we clicked right away. We were all roughly the same age, young professionals working in the Bay Area, and found a great balance to our hectic work schedules through triathlons. Even though I didn't have a clue what I was getting myself into, I was willing to do it with them. I absolutely loved it."

One year later Mendez did his first Ironman in Brazil. He doesn't understand the logic of training for an entire miserable year, spending all that money on equipment and fees and travel and getting all excited for this incredible journey and transformation of a person's life, and then going to Idaho or Florida. His philosophy is to bask in the glory of the accomplishment as long as you can; whatever you do, don't rush back to work.

"Get out of town! Go to Germany, go anywhere that's different and unique. For me, that's part of the package. And again, my friends lied to me about how easy an Ironman would be since I already did a half. Actually their logic wasn't so off base. I added longer bike rides, at least a hundred miles every weekend, still did my Alcatraz swims, and threw in some long runs. The best part of all this was being able to eat whatever I wanted. I could go into a bar and down three hamburgers and still lose weight. That is awesome. For a goal like that I'll do one Ironman a year. It helps ease the pain to know I can happily eat eight meals a day.

"Aside from having a great time with my friends, Brazil didn't go so well. I hurt like I've never hurt before. I couldn't get my left knee to bend since mile eight of the run. But when I saw the finish line, the hurt disappeared and the emotion of finishing something that intimidated me just months before becomes overwhelming. Even if just for a moment, I am an Ironman."

Mendez planned to do another IM in 2005 but got hit by a car on a training ride. He considers himself lucky to be alive and took a year to recover from his injuries, which included a broken shoulder. He plans to do the Ironman-distance race at Roth, Germany, in 2007.

"The distance doesn't matter, your age doesn't matter, and how fast you are doesn't matter. The only thing that matters is having fun, and doing something that challenges you in a way that makes you proud of your accomplishments. I'm hooked."

Mendez's Advice

"Don't turn the purity of doing a triathlon into a science. Enjoy it for what it is and don't waste time dissecting each race into the minutiae of saving seconds. It's a hobby, not a job! The biggest lesson to learn is just to have fun. When you start worrying about the thirty seconds here and the ten seconds there you could have saved, you've lost more than time."

STEVE NUCCIO

DOB: 11-13-71
Residence: Evergreen, Colorado
Occupation: Financial adviser, Merrill Lynch
First Triathlon: 1999 MESP Huntington Beach (California) Sprint Triathlon

Growing up in Southern California, Steve Nuccio played basketball, football, soccer, baseball—just about every sport but swimming, biking, or running. He was enjoying his carefree college life at the University of California–Riverside when an auto accident his sophomore year in 1991 changed his life. He lost his right leg and became a below-knee amputee. Nuccio isn't one to dwell on the negative factors in life and pretty much rolls with the punches, even one as devastating as this. He did his first sprint triathlon in 1999 and with perseverance, a dedicated toughness, and a great sense of humor worked his way up from a sprint to a half Ironman and then to Kona for the 2003 Hawaii Ironman, finishing with just minutes to spare. He even qualified for the Boston Marathon at that Ironman, which he ran in 2005. He is a hero to everyone who knows him, especially his wife, Susie, young daughter, Charlotte, and son, Beckham.

"The day of the accident everything worked in my favor—well, everything after the crash. The man in the car we collided with saved my life by using a tourniquet to stop the bleeding. An ambulance just happened to come down the road a few minutes later and we were two miles from the best trauma center in the state. I was in the hospital for forty days while the doctors tried to save my leg but it had to come off. I went back to school the following September on crutches while my first prosthesis was being made. It was pretty tough emotionally. Then I got my first fake leg and it looked very robot-like, which garnered stares from everyone."

Nuccio had a lot of problems adjusting to the prosthesis due to the skin graft on his leg. Most doctors didn't want to perform another operation to remove the skin graft but he kept looking. He found a doctor who agreed to perform the operation in 1996, and that made a huge difference. He could finally be more active but despite constant adjustments, the prosthesis continues to be a challenge. In 1998 he married Susie, whom he met in 1996 while she was training for the Los Angeles Marathon.

"In October 1998 I went to an Ironman party for a colleague who had just completed the Hawaii Ironman in Kona and we were watching it on television. I had heard about an Ironman but didn't really know what it was. I can still remember how awesome I thought it was and that very day I said to myself, *I'd like to try that!*

"Soon afterward my wife and I bought mountain bikes but I had problems pedaling the bike with the prosthesis. After a few more adjustments I could manage so we decided to do a sprint-distance triathlon in 1999. My wife swam in high school so she was comfortable in the water but the first day at the pool I was thrilled just to make it to the other side. It took me about five weeks to get the breathing process down. And then there was the decision to swim with or without the prosthesis. I prefer not to use the fake leg because it feels as if I am dragging an anchor around with me.

"I had a different leg made for the bike that clipped into the pedal. I wasn't too concerned with the bike phase of the event but the run would be the worst out of the three. I used my every day leg for the run, but it was very heavy and clumsy so I was not looking forward to the 5K race.

"When we showed up the day of the race, the swim was canceled due to sewage so they changed it to a duathlon: run, bike, run. I couldn't believe it. The only event that doesn't hurt my leg was canceled and the one event I dreaded was doubled.

"I made it through the first run without too much pain. Transition was a bit awkward as I had both legs laid out so it took a bit longer to get set on the bike. Then I had to change legs for the second run, which as I suspected hurt like hell.

"When I finished I had a huge blister on the tibia of my residual limb, caused by the sweat inside the sleeve rubbing up and down inside the prosthesis. After that event I was back on crutches for a week. I was furious afterward but my wife had a great day. She finished early so her job was to get the car and my crutches.

"What kept me going at that event was the compliments and energy I received from the spectators and competitors. It was the first time I really exposed my disability to a crowd of strangers, and they were so supportive it made me feel great. Even the other athletes were telling me how I inspired them. It was an eye-opener for me to see that I actually motivate others. I never really thought about that. I never liked it when people stared at me because I thought they felt sorry for me. But after the triathlon I realized that a lot of people stare at me because they are taking it all in and are impressed with what I am accomplishing. Even tough teenagers will stare at me and say, 'Hey man, cool! Go for it!' It was a great lesson for me to learn.

"Determined to have a decent go at triathlon, I went back to the doctor and he adjusted the prosthesis so I wouldn't get any more blisters. Two months later I did another sprint triathlon in Redondo Beach. This was the first time I used the prosthesis for the swim and I was very nervous because I knew everyone was going to stare at me as I hobbled into the water when the gun went off. But now I realized they were staring in admiration and that made a huge difference to me. I actually felt empowered.

"I swam in my bike leg, hobbled to transition, and got on the bike. After the ride, I changed into my running leg by unscrewing the bike component and replacing it with a running foot that looked like a C. Kinda like playing with Transformers.

"The adjustments made to the running leg eliminated the blisters but it still wasn't comfortable. It hurts the most when I have to run downhill and all that pressure is put on the front of the socket. It's like running downhill on a pogo stick."

Nuccio gradually increased his triathlon distance. All along he learned not only how to improve in general triathlon skills but also how to improve his numerous apparatus changes. In 2002 he and Susie decided to do a full Ironman in May and started training in January but he crashed his bike, flipped over, broke his finger, and tore the cartilage in his right shoulder.

"That accident forced me to pull out of training for my first full Ironman. There wasn't much a one-legged man with one arm in a sling and the other hand with a broken finger could do. Susie went on and competed in that full Ironman and did very well. But what happened next cemented my decision to do Kona and only Kona. When Susie told people she had done a full Ironman, they would ask if it was the one in Hawaii. Then she would have to explain that she did Ironman California, which is the same distance, but not in Hawaii. People seemed to be unimpressed. I decided that if I was going to suffer through an Ironman, it may as well be Kona."

He started training in January 2003 for a half Ironman in April. By this time Nuccio and Susie had added a baby girl, Charlotte, to their family. He never let his daughter or Susie play second fiddle to his training. If there was ever a question of who was going to get his time and attention, it was always the family.

Somehow between his family and work, he got in his training for the bike and swim. Most of his running was done in a pool to ease the pain and discomfort from the prosthesis. He had never run more than six miles; the half IM would be his first time running thirteen miles, and it took its toll. "The run was insane and hurt like hell. It was a very emotional and painful accomplishment, but my family was there for me. I carried Charlotte over the finish line. Despite the pain, I felt blessed." He finished in 9:45.

He found out ten days later that he was selected through the physically challenged lottery to compete in Kona. "I was laughing and crying all at the same time. Laughing because I was ecstatic, crying because I knew how much it was going to hurt."

He now knew that he would have to do much better in order to finish before the course officially closed after seventeen hours. Doing the simple math and doubling 9:45—his best time—would mean a DNF.

Nuccio had six months to prepare for Kona. Although he had a strong base, he knew it was going to be a very difficult challenge. He had already dropped about twenty pounds preparing for the half, which meant he needed new prostheses and some serious adjustments. He got an online coach to help him with a training schedule, which included two to three hours of jogging in the pool three times a week. He opted to pool-jog instead of running on the road because the recovery time from the blisters, pain, and pressure on his leg was too long and not worth it.

"The online coach made training easier. I didn't have to work out the schedule; he did it for me. He was one of those obsessive types who lives for triathlon. I'm not like that. If I felt like missing a practice because I preferred to spend a romantic evening with my wife, I just changed the schedule."

The other issue Nuccio had to deal with was Susie being pregnant with their second child during his training. She was due about the time he was supposed to leave. They had to make the serious decision whether he would forfeit his shot at Kona and stay home with her or deal with taking care of a newborn in Hawaii.

"Life is filled with crazy events and I really thought this was my one shot at Kona so with Susie's blessing I decided I would compete. Eight days later she lost the baby. She was five months pregnant and had to go through the delivery. It was horrible and we were both grief-stricken. Susie insisted I continue my training and we were going to Kona. Actually, thirty people came with us. I had an awesome support group."

When Nuccio went to Hawaii, he really didn't think he would make the seventeen-hour cutoff time. Things were not going in his favor. One week before the race, Susie ran over his bike by accident.

"When I arrived in Kona I started thinking that even if things went perfect I didn't know if I could finish. I still didn't know if my bike could be fixed or if I'd have to borrow a bike for the race. Meanwhile everyone else was out on the road practicing while I sat at a Taco Bell eating and Susie broke down crying at times. But like a small miracle, my bike was fixed late Thursday night with hours to spare before the cutoff for racking bikes the night before the race started.

"Saturday morning was glorious. As I waded in the water, it was the most surreal moment of my life. I felt completely pain-free, calm, and at peace. All the issues I had dealt with in my life from losing my leg to losing the baby seemed to just vanish like they'd never happened. It was a beautiful moment, but when the gun went off I was rocked back to reality and jumped into the fray.

"The swim was awesome. I went right into the middle of the pack and started swimming. I didn't wear my prosthesis and truly enjoyed myself, looking down at all the tropical fish. It was very cool. My swim time was 1:16, not bad, and at least I wasn't the last one out of the water. When I got out of the water there were two aides assigned to me who helped me up a metal ramp to a place where I could sit down and put on my prosthesis so I could run to T1, where I put on my cycling leg."

Nuccio's leg was already beginning to hurt. It was covered in welts and throbbing. Things were falling apart way too early in the event.

"From the first minute I started to pedal my leg hurt more than it ever did before and I was facing a 112-mile ride. It was awful. Seven hours and thirty-two minutes of pain. I pulled over halfway into the ride and took it off to make sure I wasn't doing any permanent damage. By the time I finished the bike I was already pushing nine hours into the race, which meant I had to run a sub-eight-hour marathon to finish before the cutoff. I was going to finish regardless of my time, but I had my fingers crossed just in case."

Changing from his bike leg to his running leg, Nuccio noticed the welts on his leg had turned into oozing sores and needed to be cleaned. He sat in T2 and did some minor surgery, which consisted of scraping them down and cleansing them before putting on his running leg.

"I totally grossed out my assistants with that nasty procedure but it helped me get a better fit. But still, the pain was awful and my leg kept swelling. Within the first thirteen miles I had to take off the prosthesis four times just to make sure I wasn't inflicting serious damage. This may sound morbid but what kept me going was the reality that all the pain I felt that day wasn't as bad as the day I lost my leg, or the day we lost the baby. No physical pain compares with that. Those catastrophic events in my life helped to put my pain in perspective."

The other thing that kept Nuccio going was the necklace he wore that day. On one side was a photograph of Susie and Charlotte. On the other side were footprints of the baby, which the hospital had taken for records.

"That necklace kept me going. Every time I looked at it I realized I was lucky to be alive and lucky to have Charlotte and Susie in my life. Nothing else mattered, not the pain, the long hours, the thirteen miles still to go. Just at that moment, as if it were a sign, a guy in a wheelchair passed me and I felt so lucky to be standing, even if it was only on one leg. Everything in life is relative.

"At mile seventeen, I had to start using my crutches because my leg was hurting tremendously and my left knee was starting to go. Another man who was also in pain and as slow as me kept me company. At mile twenty-two, he said if we wanted to finish in time we needed to pick up the pace. I didn't think I could run so I started swinging my crutches harder to propel me faster. I decided to drop the crutches with one mile to go. Susie and Charlotte met me with less than two hundred yards to go. The last fifty yards I carried Charlotte and crossed the finish line with her in my arms. Everyone was in total meltdown. The crowd was going crazy, screaming chants for the last runner, blowing the conch shells, the hula girls swaying and fireworks going off.

"I wasn't actually the last finisher. A woman came in about three minutes behind me. If I had known that I would have slowed down and let her pass me. I also found out I qualified for the Boston Marathon. I needed a sub-eight-hour marathon time to qualify and I finished in 7:52. My overall time for the Ironman was 16:55. I had five minutes to spare. If I had known that I would have slowed down!"

As soon as he got back to his hotel he took an ice bath, which he credits for his speedy recovery. During the race he took electrolyte pills every fifteen minutes and a shot of gel every half hour. Nuccio couldn't wear his leg for a week, until it calmed down from the swelling.

In 2004 Nuccio and his family, with the addition of a son, moved to Colorado. In January 2005 he started training for the Boston Marathon, doing all his training in the pool.

"Boston was a cool experience because I went out early with the disabled runners, with a two-hour lead. I was the fastest in that group so for a while it appeared as if I was winning the race. I passed a drunk at a biker bar just before Wellesley who actually thought I was the lead runner. It was pretty cool. By the time I got to Wellesley, the halfway point, the elite women started passing me. Just so happens I was also the second-to-last finisher at Boston. Must be fate. The next day in the *Boston Globe* the front-page photograph was a shot of me and the two elite women at Wellesley."

His next goal is a race called the Triple Bypass, a 122-mile cycling race that covers three mountain passes in Colorado, in the summer of 2006. After that, Steve and Susie will do Ironman Wisconsin. He says he'll just do the swim and bike, but those who know him are already calling his bluff. He has no desire to do another full Ironman. In his affable way he asks, "What am I supposed to do, finish it five minutes faster? Will that make the experience any more fulfilling?" It beats him up too much and he doesn't need to prove himself.

"After Kona, I gave a few motivational talks to kids, which I called the Ironman Experience. I wear long pants and halfway through my speech I take my leg off. It usually blows them away.

"During the Ironman I figured out the meaning of life. It all boils down to this: Shit happens. Good and bad shit. It's how we deal with it that makes us who we are."

JOHN O'CONNOR

DOB: 1-31-72
Residence: Bradford, Massachusetts
Occupation: Electrical engineer
First Triathlon: 1998 Sharon (Massachusetts) Sprint Triathlon

John O'Connor has a low-key mild-mannered style that belies his strength, both emotional and physical. In high school he did the pole vault because no one else wanted to. In college, he was a walk-on for Boston University's track team and did well. But his freshman year a freak accident put him in a coma for six days. When he woke up he had to relearn everything, just like a baby. Nine months of rehabilitation plus speech and neurological therapy helped to put John back together again. Perhaps his own brush with death made him the perfect husband for his wife, Dottie, who was born with cystic fibrosis, received a double lung transplant, a few years later required a kidney transplant and was in a near-fatal car accident. John has run more than five marathons and two sprint triathlons while coping with the stressful ordeal of Dottie's illnesses. They both continue to run, bike, and swim and dream of doing a full Ironman together some day.

"I grew up on Long Island and in high school I was on the track team and did the pole vault because no one else wanted to. That was a good enough reason for me. I didn't like distance running; in fact running the pole-vaulting runway was long enough for me. My senior year we went to the Penn Relays and I did the 4x400 relay, which was a big deal. By the end of high school I was second in the county and set a few school records.

"At Boston University I was a walk-on because I never got around to telling them I did the pole vault and track. I was doing very well until the St. Valentine's meet in 1991, my freshman year. I was in midair, fourteen feet above the ground, veered off to the right-hand side, and landed on concrete on the left side of my head. I was in a coma for six days and have no memory of the accident."

John had to relearn how to do everything. He woke up with a sixth-grade mentality, slurred and slow speech, and neurological damage. He attended nine months of rehabilitation in New York. His doctors were ruling out college but John was determined to go back and started his sophomore year with a full course load. That was a bit much and he had a relapse, went home for a while, and returned with a smaller course schedule. He finally graduated January 1996.

"After I returned to college I picked up running again. I remember running Christmas night, 1994, with a friend who had just run the New York City Marathon. That got me interested in running one so when I woke up January 1, 1995, I made a resolution to run the Boston Marathon. That gave me a little more than three months to plan. I knew I didn't have time to run a qualifying marathon, so my father, a retired New York City police officer, got me a number to run with the Boston police team. I was just twenty-three at the time and thought I could do this. During my first training run I threw up twice. I ran the Boston Marathon with a woman who wanted to finish in 3:39 and believe it or not we finished in 3:38. Six months later I ran the New York City Marathon, a very cold, windy day. I wasn't prepared for that weather and got hypothermia. My hamstrings locked and I had to walk the last few miles. At mile twenty-five I looked up and saw my father, who yelled out, 'Why are you walking?' That was all I needed. I picked up the pace and ran across the finish line. Despite the weather and my injury, I was happy with my time, 3:53."

John has a way of looking at goals a bit differently. He sets a realistic goal and then he sets a "heaven" goal, one he hopes to attain. His heaven is always just a bit out of reach, but that makes him try even harder. In

1995 he reached heaven once, at Boston. After the New York City Marathon he didn't run another marathon until 2001.

"When more people began to run the marathon, I wanted a new challenge and started to look around for something new and different. The triathlon was uncharted waters back then and I wanted in. I selected one and went for it. I bought a bike and started biking. I invested in a Cannondale 800 and added aerobars. I bought Joe Friel's *Triathlon Training Bible* and learned about the sport from the ground up. I studied it diligently. I practiced swimming in a pool and in open water as much as I could. I have to admit I was pretty pathetic in the water. I was doing it for the fun of it so I did the worst training possible, concentrating on my strength, running, and pretty much ignoring everything else. I turned out to be a decent cyclist so that worked in my favor. I didn't have a set training schedule, just went out whenever I could catch a few hours here and there. I ran and biked during lunch but getting in the swim was a problem. I got up a few mornings early but not on a strict regimen. Dottie will remember better than me."

Dottie and John were in this together. Ever since their marriage they made a point to do everything together. She was excited for him, knew he could do it, but wanted him to have fun. The night before, he confided to her, "If I make it out of the water, the rest will be a piece of cake."

"The morning of the triathlon, I stood on the beach and thought, *I have no right to be here!* And to make it worse, I was in the first wave. I dove in and got clobbered. I tried to fake it, but couldn't. As much as I wanted to take this seriously, I was getting kicked in the head, my goggles fogged up, and I ended up treading water just to take a breather. Doing laps in a pool was nothing like this! The next two waves of swimmers all passed me by. I was so overwhelmed and it looked so far to the next buoy. Even the volunteers came by and asked if I was all right. I did every stroke I could think of: sidestroke, breaststroke, doggy-paddle, everything. In the meantime, Dottie was on the shore looking for me and thought I'd be out of the water by now and she was getting worried. When I finally got out of the water, relieved, I passed Dottie and waved. I ran as fast as I could just to get some distance from the water!"

John had practiced his transitions so he made up some time in T1 and got a good start on his bike. Coming back to T2, he did well in the run but was not thrilled with the hilly course.

"My legs were a little wobbly at first. It took me about a quarter mile before I could run smoothly and started passing people. When I crossed the finish line it felt great. Overwhelming. I got it behind me and overall I was a little disappointed in my swim. I knew right away I would do more."

John only did one triathlon that season and instead of doing more, concentrated on duathlons for the next few months, building up his biking and running but ignoring the swim.

"I can't really equate the feeling of finishing of my first triathlon with the finish of my first marathon. When I finished Boston I was totally spent and pushed myself beyond my limit. I felt like I was running in slow motion, watching a movie of myself finishing a marathon. It was a beautiful day and I will never forget that feeling of knowing that I accomplished an amazing feat. But finishing my first triathlon, I certainly wasn't exhausted. I was tired but didn't expend all my energy. Yes, I was proud of myself for trying a new sport but I was disappointed in the way I handled the swim and that left a bad feeling. I'm very hard on myself. Unless I feel I did my best, I can't accept it. I knew I could have done better that day."

John didn't do another triathlon till the next year, another sprint. He approached it same way but put more time in the pool to better his swim. His duathlon events paid off, and his biking and transition times fell. In 2001 Dottie got sick and was diagnosed with kidney failure. John focused all his time and energy on her. She needed a kidney transplant, and every day was touch and go. The stress on both of them was enormous. John went back to running as an escape from the emotional turmoil in their lives and ran another Boston Marathon in 2001 in 3:53. He wore a T-shirt that said RUNNING FOR MY WIFE on the back.

"I told Dottie we needed to keep fighting and tried to bring her into my training. It was a tough year. Our entire focus was on taking care of her. We never knew from day to day if she would get the transplant to save her life. In October 2002 she finally got her transplant. Life became good again."

With Dottie doing much better, John decided it was his time to do a full triathlon. It was always in the back of his mind and it became his focus when he could dedicate training time. In November 2002 he signed up for Florida Ironmanthe following year. That event closes within days of opening and he registered the first day it was available.

"I gave myself almost an entire year to train for my first Ironman. I took it very seriously and trained diligently. I swam, cycled, ran, took Spinning classes, and went to the gym, everything I could do to gear up for the event. All winter I got up at 5 A.M.to swim laps in the pool. In the spring I started swimming outdoors in a lake. I ran the Boston Marathon again in April in 3:25.

"Back home Dottie was doing much better but she still needed care. So my day was full. We've had our ups and downs but one of the best things about Dottie is that you can't keep her down."

John never got to do his full Ironman. The training got to be too much with everything else going on and his parents became concerned for him because his family has a history of a rare blood disorder that can cause cerebral hemorrhaging. Dottie was also training for a military-style obstacle course competition, her own way of coping with her illnesses, so John had her training to deal with as well his own. Dottie's competition was in early November, John's Ironman was also in November. One of the events had to be canceled and John decided to bow out and focus on Dottie. He built a replica of the obstacle course in their backyard, complete with a ten-foot wall for her to scale.

"Dottie's event was being followed by Bryant Gumble so it was a big deal. I realized that her event meant so much to her that I had to give up my training to support her. If I just wanted to finish my Ironman I could have done that, but I wanted to place. My heaven was to finish under ten hours and I would have needed to train so hard, Dottie's training would have suffered. It was a decision I made and I made it willingly. I can always train for another one."

John doesn't feel as if he gave up. He was in the best condition of his life, cycling 110 miles on Saturdays, running 50, and swimming laps. He went back to marathons and sprint-distance triathlons. He is shooting for Florida Ironman in 2007 and they are both training for a relay triathlon in Hyannis in 2006. He'll swim and bike, and they'll both run. But John and Dottie have one enormous and life-fulfilling gift that came out of her training for the obstacle course.

Dottie can't have children because of all the drugs she had to take for the double lung operation. She and John started looking into adoption before she got sick with the kidney problem. When that happened they put everything on hold. They had just started discussing it again when Dottie went to the WTF obstacle competition. She went down a month early to train on-site with her coach.

"She started telling her coach about our wish to adopt as soon as her event was over and he looked her straight in the eye and said, 'I might have a baby for you.'

"The coach knew of a woman in Dottie's competition who had a twenty-three-year-old niece who was pregnant with her second child and was considering adoption. He called and made arrangements for us to meet with the young woman. I flew down right away and we met the young woman, who was due the end of January. We all got along and agreed to start the adoption process. Two months later at the hospital while I was pacing the hall, Dottie was in the delivery room with her and cut the umbilical cord. We came home with our new son, Liam."

Dottie Lessard-O'Connor knows full well how lucky she is to be married to John. She feels John's story about his triathlon training is really a love story.

"He never talks about himself. He always stands in the shadows and lets me shine. I am so proud of him; he is truly a remarkable man. Although sometimes things will get fumbled in his head due to his accident and it gets him frustrated, he gets through it.

"John used his running and swimming training as an outlet while I was sick with the kidney disease. It must have been very difficult for him not knowing whether he was going to lose his wife on a day-to-day basis but he hid that from me, always strong for me and determined to make me laugh, fight, and focus on our future. I would not have made it through my kidney disease and transplant if it were not for him. He is the hero, not me.

"John is always the one who helps others push themselves farther. At one of my US Transplant Games, where I compete in the 5K, one of my team members who also had a kidney transplant was struggling in the race with about half a mile to go. John had already finished the race but turned around and jogged with the man, pulling him through. When they finished, the man hugged John and got teary-eyed, saying he will never forget the kindness John showed him.

"John's like that in any race he does. He always puts others first. At one of his triathlons, he helped a girl in T1 with her bike. He was already heading out when he saw she needed help and got off his bike and made sure she was fine before continuing on. That's John in a nutshell, completely unselfish.

"I hated that he canceled his Ironman for me but I was pretty sick and it took me longer to recover than we both expected. John has always put me first and now I try to do my part and put him first. He is shooting to do that Florida Triathlon next year and qualify for Kona. By the time Liam is five, in 2009, *I am determined* to watch my husband cross the line in Kona. I owe that to him.

"Our story is really about love and dedication to family first, something that all triathletes can relate to as they struggle with finding the proper balance of family, work, training, and time away from home. Some triathletes give their life to their sport but John gave his life to me first and now to Liam and we as a family will find the balance to get John to Kona. He certainly deserves it."

MICHAEL PICARELLA

DOB: 9-5-60
Residence: Exton, Pennsylvania
Occupation: Medical sales representative
First Triathlon: 2005 Olympic-distance St. Anthony's Triathlon, St. Petersburg, Florida

When Michael Picarella crossed the finish line of his first triathlon, he had good cause to celebrate. In February of 2004 he was diagnosed with an extremely rare and aggressive form of cancer that almost killed him. After visiting a doctor on a Monday for chronic fatigue, he was almost dead the following Tuesday from undiagnosed non-Hodgkin's lymphoma. A year and nine months later he fulfilled his vow of completing a triathlon. "I can't believe all the events that happened to me this past year," he says.

"I was always athletic and active in high school and college. I was lean and coordinated and chose sports where my slight build was a plus, like track and field and tennis. Definitely not the football type. After college, I didn't have time for recreational sports and started going to the gym to stay in shape. By my early thirties I was married with four kids, and even getting to the gym was beginning to become an effort. My pre-kids life, hitting the gym six nights a week, came to a screaming halt. My only exercise was chasing after the kids."

In the beginning of January 2004, Picarella was very tired. He attributed it to the frenzy of the holidays, the stress of starting a new job, and keeping up with his teenage children. He started to get night sweats but thought it was the heavy winter blankets. Then his wife started saying he didn't look well. Did he have the flu?

"I was exhausted all the time and not feeling well, flu-like symptoms," recalls Picarella. "On a Monday I went to the doctor for blood work. Even he commented on how miserable I looked. He called me the next day to go over the results of the blood work, which he described as being all over the place. More blood work was done to rule things out like Lyme disease and hepatitis. On Friday they performed a CAT scan of my chest and abdomen and found infractions, tiny scars, throughout my spleen. That called for more blood work. By Friday night I was admitted to the hospital. Saturday morning, another CAT scan, more infractions and now spots on my liver and pancreas."

By Sunday morning all hell broke out for Picarella. His white cell count was rapidly dropping. Now diagnosed with cancer, but not sure what type, he was fighting for his life. By Tuesday things were looking fatal. An emergency operation was performed to remove his spleen, which was already dead and rotted. The cancer had spread to his liver and pancreas.

"I was diagnosed with a very aggressive and rare type of non-Hodgkin's lymphoma, which is also noncurable, with a five-year survival rate of 50 percent. In twenty-one days my weight went from a normal 130 pounds to 170 pounds then down to 105 pounds. I didn't think I would survive, wouldn't live to see another summer with my kids."

Doctors started an immediate schedule of chemotherapy, five- to six-hour treatments, every three weeks for five months.

"I don't remember most of it. When I was released from the hospital I went home with a walker because I was so weak and had no stomach muscles as they were sliced through during the operation. The worst side effect was total fatigue. I was like a baby, totally relying on others for my every need."

During this same time, a close friend, Phil Ricco, who had four kids and was an avid triathlete, was going through similar treatments for brain cancer. They became closer, bonding through their fates. But Phil didn't make it.

"At the memorial service they spoke about his passion for triathlons and how proud he was to be an Ironman. It was very moving and his life was so inspirational I decided right there and then that I would do a triathlon to honor Phil."

Not an easy undertaking for someone who'd never swum or ridden a bike and had an aggressive form of cancer. But for Picarella, his life-threatening experience was also an eye-opener, like a light turning on within him.

"It really opened up my life in a way I had never experienced. I wanted to live life in the moment, in the here and now. I wanted to experience the rush of life and not worry about retirement plans or buying a bigger house. When you are faced with death, priorities change. I had a different outlook on life."

But how do you start training for a triathlon when you've just finished chemotherapy and your doctors are not thrilled with your decision? Picarella turned to Team in Training (TNT) for help. Not only would he receive professional training, but he liked the idea of raising money for the Leukemia and Lymphoma Society.

"I signed up in November 2004 for an April 2005 Olympic-distance triathlon. I knew I had made the right decision about TNT when the coach told me not to worry about time, just to relax and they'll get me through it. The first time I went to the pool to do laps, I couldn't even tread water because I had no stomach muscles. I needed a floaty. But with perseverance I was soon able to make it from one end to the other. Okay, so I was doing the doggy-paddle. It was still a huge step for me."

The Olympic-distance event, St. Anthony's Triathlon in St. Petersburg, Florida, April 24, 2005, drew more than 3,500 professional and amateur triathletes from around the country. Picarella would need all six months leading up to the event for his training. During training, he was also getting CAT scans every two months to make sure the cancer hadn't come back.

"There is an extremely high risk for this type of cancer to come back. In fact, my doctors talk about when it will come back, not if. I felt a sense of urgency to do this triathlon before the cancer came back. Focusing on my training gave me a goal to get through the mental trauma of when it would appear again. That fear was, and still is, so overwhelming that I needed a huge incentive to block it—and the triathlon was the perfect venue. I got e-mail instructions that included a workout schedule from my coach and on weekends we met as a group to do swim drills, long runs, or bike rides. There was always a lot of laughter when we were together sharing stories and confessing how awful or how good the training was going. The coaches really knew how to keep it fun.

"During the six months of training there were times I doubted I could pull this off, especially the swim. But with one month to go, it just all clicked. As for the fund-raising, we were required to raise four thousand dollars but I exceeded that goal and raised sixty-four hundred, mostly through a letter-writing campaign to family, friends, and co-workers. The fundraising also helped my mental attitude. I knew I couldn't let these people down after they gave me money to do the event."

With two weeks to go, Picarella felt nervous but ready. By now, his doctors had bought into his dream to complete the triathlon, but cautiously. The week before the event, he started his taper, which made him even more nervous.

"My entire family wanted to come to the triathlon. My wife, the kids, my brother, Mom and Dad, assorted in-laws, an uncle. They all came to Florida to watch. I couldn't sleep the night before, tossing and turning, lots of nervous energy. The alarm went off at 4:30. My mood was somber. I felt groggy with no sleep; the room was dark and quiet. I had told my family not to get up that early so I tiptoed out of the darkened room and met my teammates in the hotel lobby. We all had that same bleary-eyed look. Obviously no one slept.

"The excitement began to build as I started setting up my transition area, picked up my bib number and chip, and got the race number written on my arm and my age written on my calf. The first wave went off at 7 A.M. but mine didn't start till 9. I thought the two hours would drag by but it didn't. The only thing I didn't do right that morning was eat enough. I had breakfast at 7 A.M., but should have eaten more during the two hours I was waiting for my wave. A peanut butter sandwich would have hit the spot.

"As I watched the elites take off I got nervous about the swim. The water already resembled a whirlpool gone amok and bodies were pumping through it all over the place. I didn't know how I would survive just getting into the water. But then I remembered the advice of my coach who told me to just take my time, hang back, and stay to the outer edges. I wasn't there to set records, just to finish. So I did just that. Hung back, did the breaststroke, rolled over on my back, and tried to relax and find a rhythm to my panicked breathing. Rather quickly the swimmers spanned out; I found my niche and actually started passing people. I was so excited and happy I was waving to the support staff on kayaks. I also remembered another tip from my coach, not to worry about the swim. It's over before you know it and two more events are ahead of you so just relax and get through it. Sure enough, I was out of the water before I knew it.

"Now I was running back to transition and trying to take off my wet suit at the same time. We were told to peel off the wet suit before we got back to transition, which is really difficult and something I didn't practice. I tried pulling both arms out at once. One came out, the other didn't and I was wrestling with my wet suit while attempting to run and still trying to get the thing off. I started laughing, which didn't help my concentration. Back at transition I was trying to remember all the rules but first I had to find my bike. I forgot where it was and all of a sudden five thousand bikes looked the same. But I didn't panic because for me it wasn't about time.

"I finally got going on the bike but hit a monster headwind, which seemed to follow me the entire twenty-five-mile ride. I had to work harder than I ever did in training and could feel my quads burning. Back at transition, I knew the change from cycling to running was going to be tough, but because I had exerted so much energy on the bike it was brutal. My legs were exhausted. My running form was not pretty: butt hanging low, feet moving like they were stuck in cement, posture resembling a squat.

"But within the first mile my legs loosened up and I felt much better. I trained on hills back in Philadelphia but this course was totally flat so I actually gained speed and was finally enjoying myself. The temperature was delightful, low seventies, the neighborhood was beautiful, and I was having a grand old time waving to people and thanking the volunteers."

Picarella knew nothing would stop him now. He was two miles to his dream of crossing the finish line. But his lack of eating enough in the beginning caught up with him.

"Bam. I hit the wall at mile four. It felt as if I was back in chemo. Tired, dehydrated, couldn't move. I couldn't even visualize the last two miles. I dragged my feet along hoping I could make it. When I finally started to hear the crowd I knew I was close. Then I saw my coach, yelling and encouraging me, and then I saw my family and I got an adrenaline rush which I desperately needed, and I knew I was home free.

"I crossed the finish line in 3:18 and finally let my guard down. All the months of chemo, the near death, thinking of my kids and my wife without a dad or husband, I knew it was finally over. I had won and the tears wouldn't stop. My wife, Patty, joined me at the finish line and we hugged and cried and I thought of Phil and how proud I was to honor him. The euphoric feeling of finishing my first triathlon will stay with me forever."

Nine months from his last chemotherapy Picarella accomplished his dream. He says he is in the best shape of his life. Although his doctors still think his cancer will return, he doesn't dwell on it. He has other things to worry about, like living in the moment and making the most of his time with his wife and four kids. He's thinking about doing an Ironman, like Phil, and is already planning a hundred-mile bike ride to start getting in shape. He's also inspired by people like Lance Armstrong and Sarah Reinersten, who just completed the Hawaii Ironman with a prosthetic, the first woman ever to reach that milestone. Maybe he'll run a marathon. He was laid off from his job so he has the time.

"I am living proof that someone with a chronic illness like NHL can actively participate in physically challenging sports, push boundaries, and reach new personal milestones. I am amazed at how my life has changed and with the support of my family and friends, I wouldn't change a thing. So far, it's been a great ride and ironically my cancer has created some of the most memorable experiences."

Looking Back: Picarella's Training Tips

"I would have trained harder. For an Olympic distance I recommend long runs of ten miles and bike rides of thirty to forty miles. Adding more distance in training than the actual event makes it seem easier when you get to cut down on the day of the race. I also recommend eating a more sustainable breakfast and having some form of nourishment in the transition area, like a peanut butter sandwich, protein bar or GU, or even gummi bears. If I had eaten something on the bike or right after, I wouldn't have hit the wall."

DAVE PRUETZ

DOB: 8-30-63
Residence: Salt Lake City, Utah
Occupation: Director of sales/certified triathlon coach
First Triathlon: 2001 Sprint Yuba (Utah) Rock and Road Triathlon

Dave Pruetz has true grit. Literally. After falling twice at his first triathlon and having to pick gravel and sand out of his leg for days, he actually went back for more. In the beginning of his second season he graduated to an Olympic distance and closed out the season with his first half IM. Going into his third season he made the leap to an Ironman, an event he calls a bittersweet journey. His passion for the triathlon led him to a career change. He was accepted into the USA Triathlon coaching program and got certified at the US Olympic Training Center in Colorado Springs, a definite highlight in his life. He calls it the most rewarding career he could ever imagine. "Every time I see my athletes cross the finish line it is a very emotional moment. I know what they went through to get there and can appreciate their accomplishment. That's something you can't get from a desk job," says Pruetz.

"Growing up, I wasn't an athlete and didn't participate in any organized sports. I did play on the golf team my freshman year in high school but in the 1970s golf was still a geeky sport and very uncool, so I never thought it counted as a true sport. I had to hide my golf clubs when I

136

walked to school, worried that I'd be hassled by the real athletes like the football players.

"Despite my lack of team play in high school, I certainly wasn't a couch potato. I did the everyday active stuff kids do like riding bikes, swimming in the summer, a little bit of recreational tennis and basketball."

Pruetz continued to do his own thing through his college years. After college he started to put on weight and didn't like his overall appearance and being out of shape.

"I started running two miles a day, got into weight lifting, and decided to become a firefighter. I was living in California at the time and entered the firefighter academy. However, the job market was tight back then, three thousand applicants for two openings, so I decided to switch gears and try another career."

Pruetz stayed in shape, continued running, and started to race local 5Ks. He made a career move to Utah with his wife and baby and lived with his in-laws for a while until he got settled.

"My in-laws were great to take us in but unfortunately for me, they were basic meat-and-potatoes folk and I started to gain weight again. In nine months I put on twenty unwanted pounds. The good news is that my new job was with Weider health supplements and in order to learn about the supplements and vitamins I had to work out, get in shape, and basically practice what I preached. I loved the lifestyle so much I took it one more step and became certified as a personal trainer and started racing again."

Things were going well for Pruetz. He loved his job, loved working out, and was in the best shape of his life. His wife was the one who posed the question: *What's next?* That got him thinking.

"I had reached many of my personal goals. Was it really time to re-evaluate them? What did I want to do? That's when I saw an Ironman on television. I'd never heard of an Ironman and got totally absorbed watching the participants struggle through this inhuman, incomprehensible challenge. They highlighted a finisher who competed with one leg and I burst into tears watching his heroic efforts. The very next day I went out and started to train for a triathlon."

The enormity of Pruetz's gutsy new goal quickly became apparent when he couldn't swim one lap of the pool.

"I thought this was going to be a piece of cake. Heck, I was in great shape, was a personal trainer, how hard could it be? I jumped in, did one lap, and thought I would die. It took months to teach myself to swim correctly. Then it was on to the bike.

"That became an even greater challenge as I owned a mountain bike and had to learn all the techniques of biking. I developed my own training schedule, swimming and biking three days a week. As the triathlon date came closer, I got more nervous. I kept working on my form, which was horrible, and my endurance, which was worse. I was beginning to think this wasn't such a great idea after all."

Pruetz borrowed a wet suit that was too big for him and only tried it out once in a pool. He didn't have a clue about transitions, nutrition, or what to expect on race day. He also had to pack and travel to the event which added another layer of stress.

"I was so ignorant about this triathlon. I didn't know what to pack so I brought everything I owned. The day of the event I woke up with a churning stomach and wondered, *Will I survive?* Did I mention the howling winds outside? Nothing seemed to be going my way."

Pruetz's first mistake of the day was setting his bike up in the wrong area. He got yelled at and had to relocate all his laid-out gear. It was very nerve-racking and added to his stress. Finally in the right section, he did a quick study of the other participants and copied whatever they did. He certainly didn't want to get yelled at again for some unforeseen infraction.

"This was my first open-water swim and I had no idea what to expect. As the gun fired I began to swim, quickly realizing that the fifty-six-degree water was not nearly as delightful as the pool. The wind was still howling and there were whitecaps on the lake, not a pretty sight. Between a major brain freeze and attempting every swim stroke in the book, I finally struggled out of the water after thirty-five minutes. I was so tired coming out of the water that I couldn't explain to the volunteer wet suit strippers that I had zippers at the bottom of my borrowed wet suit. They proceeded to drag me about twenty-five yards across the parking lot until I could yell 'Zipper's at the bottom!'

"Once the wet suit was off I ran to T1 through a thicket of thorns, sticks, and rocks. By the time I got to transition I was ready to puke.

"I managed to get through T1, but not in the fastest of times, and hopped on my ten-year-old mountain bike and took off. But I was exhausted from the swim and the run to T1 and the overall stress was already taking its toll. I really didn't think I could finish. I was already on empty and had to bike 12 miles and run 3.1.

"About five miles into the bike course, I saw a group of riders sitting down on the ground. As I wondered why they were down, I hit the same patch of gravel that they hit and found myself down on the ground with them as well. After I plucked the embedded gravel out of my bloody knees and elbows, fixed my chain, and knocked the handlebars back in place, I proceeded to get back on my bike but when I put my bloody palms on the handlebars, I hit a new level of pain. I'd broken my fall with my hands and the impact had cut them to the bone. I couldn't put my palms on the bars without intense pain so I had to use my fingers, a very interesting way to ride.

"I continued on my way, not really enjoying myself. To make my mood even worse, when I approached T2, I heard someone say, 'Holy crap, that guy's on a mountain bike!' I wasn't sure if he was impressed with me or just amazed at how naive I was.

"Starting the run, I tripped on a railroad tie and went down in front of a few dozen spectators. I jumped up like I felt no pain, which I did, plucked more gravel out of my already open bloody wounds, brushed all the brown dirt off me, and continued on my way. I was not a pretty sight. Just about everyone passed me on the run.

"As I came through the finish line, I thought, *Well, at least I finished.* My wife was there and tried to cheer me up but all I wanted to do was go home. I felt beaten, battered, and disappointed. My wife wanted to stay for the awards ceremony but I thought that was a waste of time. There were twelve guys in my age group and I told my wife that I was probably dead last and headed off to the medical tent to have the gravel that was embedded in my skin and hairy legs attended to by the medics.

"As I sat there being doused in wound cleansers I heard them announce my age group . . . third goes to, second goes to, and first place goes to . . . What? Did they just say my name? I'll be damned, they did! Knowing what I went through, I feel sorry for what everyone else in my age-group must have endured. The moral of my first triathlon story is, *Don't ever give up!*"

Despite his dismal experience, two days later Pruetz was planning his next one. He did eight sprint triathlons that first season, always placing in his age division. Realizing he was good at the sport and finding a passion for it, he sold part of his antique car collection to buy better gear. His candy-apple-red, mint-condition 1965 Mustang went for eleven thousand dollars and enabled Pruetz to get a top-of-the-line bike and wet suit, all the right gear.

"In my second year, I moved up to the Olympic distance and finished with a half IM. I was getting better at training, realizing it was more about the quality of the training and not the quantity. I also volunteered at an Ironman, which got me hooked on doing one in the near future."

In 2003 he took the leap to an Ironman, which he describes as one of the most awesome experiences in his life, and got certified as a triathlon training coach. He started his business driving through neighborhoods in his mobile training van and going door to door seeking clients.

"Six years and about forty-five races from my first triathlon, I am now a USA Triathlon certified coach and the president of Utah's largest non-profit triathlon club. I have a thriving business with my wife, who is a massage therapist, and two awesome kids, an eight-year-old boy and a ten-year-old girl, who race in youth division triathlons. Life is good."

Pruetz's Advice to First-Timers:

"I tell my clients that getting into the sport of triathlon is like a journey and you'll learn a lot about yourself along the way. My biggest piece of advice is not to neglect your family while you take this journey. It's easy to get self-absorbed with the training and the mental preparation and ignore the people who are supporting you. I've seen lots of divorces in the triathlon community. Learn to balance your time well so that no one suffers along the way."

BOB SCOTT

DOB: 10-12-30
Residence: Naperville, Illinois
Occupation: personal trainer and coach
First Triathlon: 1981 Sprint triathlon, Racine Wisconsin

In 1981, triathlons were just getting their start. At age fifty, Scott did his first one and got hooked. Now seventy-five, he has completed eight Ironmans and sixty-four marathons. In October 2005, he set an age-group record at the Triathlon World Championships in Kona, Hawaii. He won his age division in 13:27, beating the old record by 1:45:20. Scott, who has completed eight Hawaii Ironmans, also holds the age-division record for seventy- to seventy-four-year-olds in 12:59:02. He was on the swim team in high school and college and played some soccer there too. He also picked up running after college and preferred to ride his bike to work as alternative transportation.

"My father was a professional soccer player in Scotland so maybe that's where all the good athletic genes came from. When I got out of college I wanted to stay involved with swimming, something I loved to do, so I got certified by the YMCA and taught swimming and lifesaving for years in high school pools and with the YMCA at night. During the day I was a mechanical engineer and at night I taught swimming.

"Then I got into running. At first, my running was recreational but then I got more serious. I have run Boston twenty-three times with a PR of 3:02 at Boston and a marathon PR of 2:53 in Milwaukee, 1983.

"It was the same with biking. At first I rode my bike to work as a means of transportation but then I started training seriously. I've always been interested in the lifestyle of an athlete so it motivated me to be around athletes and keep up with how they trained.

"When I moved to Racine in 1980, I met a group of die-hard runners and swimmers who took themselves very seriously. They started talking about the new sport of triathlon and we all decided to go do one that had been advertised in the local paper. There was only a few weeks to train so we just did a very few practice swims in the lake. For me, the swim was a lark. I didn't really need to train for that segment of the race. We did some brick workouts as well. At that time I already had a top-of-the-line road racing bike and compared with some of the old Schwinn bikes with rusty chains and poor gears that the other guys had, I thought I had it made on the bike as well. The distances weren't too challenging, a half-mile swim, a 40K bike, and a 10K run. I knew I could handle it.

"About four hundred people of all ages showed up that morning on the shores of Lake Michigan. My most vivid memory of that first triathlon was the cold water. It was very, very cold, in the fifties. I waded in the water to get used it but when the gun went off, I put my face in the water to start my swim and got a shock. It was so cold I couldn't breathe for a few seconds. It literally took my breath away. Everyone was doing the breaststroke because they didn't want to feel the cold water on their faces. Some people were already yelling for help. No one wore a wet suit, we didn't know any better.

"When I got out of the water my only thought was I never wanted to do that again. When I got on my bike I couldn't move my jaw for the first three miles because my body was so cold. Fortunately everything else worked fine.

"I don't remember much about the transition from bike to running; I probably just put on my running shoes and headed out very casually. We didn't know anything about nutrition back then, we didn't have gels or GU or water bottles with special hydration fluids. And there were no rules either. People were drafting on their bikes, riding in packs, and even at the swim, some people were in the water and some were on the beach at the start. It didn't matter. Nowadays everyone has to be either on the beach or in the water.

"It was exciting and to my surprise I won my age division. I truly believe the bike was my secret weapon. I still have that bike."

Scott went back the following year to do the same triathlon, and was very thankful that the water was warmer. His customized bike, which cost him a hundred dollars back in 1978, was still his secret weapon. For the next twenty years he competed in three to five triathlons a year, most at the Olympic or Ironman distance, and raced two marathons a year, Boston in the spring and a fall marathon.

"My first Hawaii Ironman was in 1997 when I was sixty-seven. It was a very tough race for me. I was undertrained and had great expectations. A bad combination. When I was at the exposition the day before, I met a massage therapist from Chicago. We talked and he told me how stiff I would feel coming off the bike and if I wanted, he would give me a massage at T2. Sounded like a good idea. And he was right, I was stiff so I went looking for the guy and he gave me a massage. But all the time I was lying on the table I kept thinking to myself, *Man, time is ticking away. What I am doing here?* I blew twenty minutes getting that darn massage. So when I headed out for the run I thought I had surely blown any chance of placing or winning. Plus I was terribly dehydrated. Didn't drink much at all except plain water and that doesn't count for much. You need the electrolytes in a long hot race. When I finished the run I ended up in the medical tent with an IV in my arm. Three, to be exact.

"When I got out of the medical tent, I packed up my belongings and headed back to the hotel. The next day I met a guy who had also done the race and he told me I placed fifth, good for an award in my age group. I couldn't believe it."

Scott runs fifty to sixty miles a week. When he is training for a triathlon he adds 250 to 300 miles of biking and four sessions of swimming. "I never thought I could run a marathon, and I did. I never thought I could do an Ironman and I did," says Scott, who firmly believes anything is possible if you train correctly and do it in gradual increments of time and distance. His secret to success is never taking his events for granted. "Every time I finish an event I say, *Great, I can still do it!* It makes me feel healthy."

In 2000, Scott retired from his day job and became a full-time personal trainer. "I get a lot of satisfaction from helping others train for events, and it actually helps my own training."

Over the course of his own competitions and now as a trainer, Scott has come up with his own philosophy about triathlons.

"Everyone respects the swim, even very good swimmers. I always advise my first-timers to swim to the side so they don't get beat up by over-aggressive athletes. No sport-specific athlete has a big advantage in a triathlon. It's the mind-set that matters. Tour de France cyclists don't run well. Swimmers don't necessarily bike well. It takes experience to do a triathlon well. Having said that, most tri experts will say you win the Iron-man on the run. A good runner can make up quite a few minutes from the other stages.

"I've heard the saying that triathletes are burned-out runners, but I've also seen burned-out swimmers and bikers, especially the younger kids who get beat up by coaches who overtrain them. The key is not to get burned out in the first place. I am a big believer in taking a day off fre-quently. Always follow a hard training day with an easy day."

Doctors have been studying Scott to see what makes him able to com-pete at the level he does at age seventy-five. He thinks it is due to his low body weight and large bones. He is a big advocate of eating and hydrating well. He breaks down his advice on the following:

"Nutrition: I ask what people eat, what they like, what their food weak-nesses are. I try to get a feel for how they live. You need 60 to 70 percent carbohydrates, 20 percent fat, and the rest in protein to be able to compete well. I ask them to write down what they eat in a week and then I break it down into calories consumed. It's all right to indulge in a minor way. One cookie, not the whole bag. One scoop of ice cream, not the entire pint.

"Drinking: I don't see anything wrong with a glass of wine or a beer once in a while. Personally, I don't drink.

"Eating: Once you move up to the half Ironman distance you must eat to sustain the high level of energy output. Cut up a peanut butter sand-wich and stick it in your bike pouch and nibble on it during the bike ride or race. You'll be glad you did once you start the run.

"It's been my experience that most people get hooked after their first triathlon. It's usually the expense of racing fees and equipment and the time required to train that keeps others away. As for me, I love my life; I think I'm finally getting it right."

Scott has put together a list of things that he teaches to his first-time triathletes:

"If you are in shape and have trained, a triathlon is 90 percent psychological and 10 percent effort.

"Don't worry about the other participants. Do your first triathlon for experience, the second one for time.

"If you are not a competitive swimmer, hang back in the swim. You'll get beat up if you try to go out with the fast swimmers. Swim to the side at your pace and avoid the crowd.

"Practice transitions. Lay your gear out on the ground beside the bike, stand off about twenty-five yards, run to the spot, get it on and run back to the starting point, then repeat and take time to complete measurements. Drill it into the brain."

Other concerns he hears from his clients are about open-water swimming and getting lost. "Transitions are of some concern and most first-timers spend far too much time in transition. There is also concern about having to fix flat tires. Many don't have a clue how to do this. Practice, practice, practice!

"Running in the heat of the day with leg muscles tired from the long bike ride is another concern. Better conditioning is the answer. There is also fear generated by overexcitement or breathing problems that require an inhaler to allow adequate breathing. How does one carry an inhaler?

"The greatest concern first-timers *should* have is whether they are properly prepared for the event and know how much to eat and drink to stay strong. Do they know how to pace themselves to keep from running out of gas before the finish? The longer the triathlon distance, the more these factors need to be understood."

AMY SHIGO

DOB: 6-9-67
Residence: Ridgewood, New Jersey
Occupation: Television producer
First Triathlon: 1992 Harriman (New York) Sprint Triathlon

Amy has such an engaging personality that after spending an hour with her, you want to be her new best friend. She has a great laugh and is warm and interesting; she has befriended and been befriended by some of the world's best triathletes, even though she considers herself slow. Her Team Psycho teammates say she has what it takes, Psycho Karma, to compete. At races pros, elites, and age-groupers consider her a friend.

Shigo grew up in Bethlehem, Pennsylvania, in the shadow of her big brother—the town's celebrity football player. She was an active kid, trying various team sports, an equestrian, and a sports fan. And like many young girls Shigo had body image issues, always wanting to be smaller. After working her way up the television production ladder at ESPN and the NHL, she took a job with the women's production company Oxygen, and one special assignment in 2001 changed her life. She was sent to Hawaii to interview triathletes at an International Triathlon Union race, specifically profiling Karen Smyers. A few weeks later she visited Smyers in New Hampshire at Team Psycho Weekend, Smyers's triathlon team's annual "sufferfest." Shigo was so moved and impressed with the people she met that she signed up for Ironman Canada with

146

only one sprint triathlon under her belt. Within one year she'd transformed from sports producer to Ironman athlete.

In an article she wrote about her first Ironman experience, she said: "I've heard that one new thought, idea, or suggestion can forever alter your life and lead you down a different path. It's a simple premise, but I found it to be true." Amy Shigo is a woman who got inside the world of triathlon by being an outsider.

"We are a football family. Everyone loved the game, and my brother was a standout in high school and college football. I was an active kid, always a sports fan, and played on various teams. I tried to participate on the swim team but couldn't stand the smell of chlorine. My first day of junior high school I met the football coach and he asked if I was John Shigo's little sister. I was thrilled to get the recognition in a new school setting and said yes. Then he said, 'It's a shame you aren't a boy.' He didn't say it to be rude or mean; it was just a fact. John was the star. I love my brother and in high school kept a picture of him in my locker. But it took me another twenty years before I would also become the family athlete."

After college Shigo went to work in the television industry, but sports was her passion. Perhaps there was some foreshadowing in her friend's invitation to participate in a triathlon in Harriman, New York, in 1991.

"I didn't know anything about triathlons but it sounded like fun. How hard could it be? A little swim, a little biking, and a run. No problem. I had no access to a pool so I would sneak into the pool at the Tarrytown Hilton and did some laps. I ran here and there and rode my old rusty Schwinn a few days. I truly had no idea what I was getting myself into.

"My parents drove up to watch and did what comes naturally: They set up a tailgate party. As I set my bike up in transition I saw bikes I never knew existed. I had no wet suit, no gear, nothing but my bike, helmet, sneakers, and shorts. When I went down to the water I was shocked to see so many people. Now I started to get a little nervous. I had never swum in a pack before, and when I went into the water with my wave I started getting pummeled. This wasn't like swimming in the Hilton where all I had to contend with was getting caught and kids in floaties. I was getting hit, kicked, and punched. I started to do the backstroke halfway, wondering how to get out of this.

147

"After I survived the water I went to transition, slipped on my shorts, and took off on the bike. Thinking back on it, I don't remember ever putting air in those tires, didn't own a pump, and didn't have a water bottle cage.

"By the time I got on the run course, people were packing their cars and driving home. I survived and my family was waiting for me at the finish so we celebrated and had another tailgate party."

Shigo didn't do another one for eight years. She worked for ESPN and the NHL. Her job was demanding and she had little time for anything else.

"I traveled a lot and wasn't getting any exercise. During a vacation in Vancouver I saw a sign for the Vancouver Marathon and half marathon. It appealed to me and I decided to train for the half marathon the following year, 1998. It was my first race ever and I did it to reduce my thighs. I thought if I ran a half marathon I would have thighs that could crack walnuts. I'm not a runner but I really wanted to do this. I ran twelve-minute miles and finished the half in 2:36."

Shigo loved the experience and ran another one in Budapest a few months later in 2:21. She went on to run the Steamtown Marathon in Pennsylvania, finishing in five and a half hours.

"I am pretty sure a walker passed me as I was running. I remember the guy next to me saying, 'The Kenyan that won this thing is home showering by now.' But it didn't bother me; I was in awe of myself that I was doing it."

Shigo moved to Ridgewood in 1999 and was hired by Oxygen, covering women's sports. An assignment to cover an International Triathlon Union race in Kona changed her life. Her main focus was Karen Smyers, who was attempting to make the inaugural Olympic triathlon team in 2000. She was a Princeton graduate, mother of two kids, and cancer survivor; she'd been hit by a truck while training and was doing the Ironman.

"We did the interview in her hotel in Kona as she scrambled for her morning coffee, stepping over her daughter's toys, just so normal. She didn't come across as superhuman or superwoman, but relaxed, funny and humble. I had a great interview but needed more training footage so Karen invited me to New Hampshire a few weeks later to something called Team Psycho Weekend (TPW), her triathlon team's yearly training getaway. Something about that name really appealed to me."

Shigo flew to New Hampshire and met with Karen and the team members. She found them to be smart and funny, a tight group of athletes who loved to trash-talk one another and were very dedicated to training. Their routine was simple: three workouts a day, three meals a day, lots of naps and beer.

"My crew and I shot during the day, and at night I spoke with various members about why they race, which were their favorite races, how they handled life and training, and most importantly—how a 'normal' person might tackle an Ironman. Like most triathletes that I have met, the members of Team Psycho were more than willing to hand out advice and take a newcomer into the fold. Even though months before I had declared that I would never run another marathon, I left Team Psycho Weekend saying—I'm going to do Ironman Canada (IMC) 2001!

"I guess I was somewhat naive, but I rode that positive feeling from TPW into the summer: purchasing a tri bike, two pairs of running shoes, BodyGlide, a wet suit, and registering for Ironman Canada over the internet. There were several people that questioned what I was doing, but my enthusiasm and blind determination usually won them over. The moment I got the e-mail saying that I got into IMC I screamed—'I got in!! I'm going to do an Ironman!' And then I screamed again—'Oh my God, I got in . . . I'm going to do an Ironman.'

"I devoted a year to IMC, rationalizing that since I was single I could afford to be so selfish with my time and that once it was accomplished— that would be that. I hired a coach and started training. I once thought that this type of training would be impossible to fit into an already busy schedule, but it seemed to fold perfectly into my life and I became a time management wiz. I also found that I slept better, ate better, and handled stress better. I trained at home in New Jersey and while I was on the road for work. After all, goggles and running shoes are easy to pack. I ran in Prague and Zurich and Freiburg, Germany. I swam in Florida, Vermont, and California. I can honestly say that I loved every moment of it. That spring I returned to Team Psycho Weekend, this time as a participant. Even though I was a newbie, they were so accepting of me."

With a schedule and help from her coach, Shigo buckled down and did a sprint triathlon in June, followed by a half Ironman later in June, two months before IMC. This type of training is not recommended by anyone but somehow Shigo stayed injury-free and loved every minute of it.

"My mom, Martha, came with me to Ironman Canada. She was my cheerleader. The atmosphere at an Ironman is incredible, but your first Ironman is beyond special—it is magical. I was so happy to have my mom be a part of it and she loved every minute of it. Lots of fit guys were all over and although I told her no one uses the word *hunk* anymore, she used it freely day in and day out.

"I set three goals for my Ironman: finish, finish with a smile, and finish in under fifteen hours. My friends from Team Psycho were very helpful and gave me lots of tips. The day of the event as I was packing my gear I found a note tucked inside my T1 bag from one of them offering the final piece of advice. He wrote, 'It will be a long day. Bad things might happen. Enjoy every minute as it will be over before you know it.'

"At an Ironman the participants get to prepare two special-needs bags, which are placed halfway through the bike and run. It contains anything we need or might want to put in to make us feel better mentally or physically. I decided to use my bags to create a happy space to cheer me up if I needed it. I put in photos of my niece and nephew, Pringles potato chips, anything that would make me happy."

Shigo's Ironman experience was one of the happiest days of her life. Things did go wrong but she never doubted she would finish. Her mindset was not, *Can I do this?* but *Why am I doing this?*

"The swim was bearable but I got the dry heaves afterward. When I got on my bike I relaxed, enjoying the scenery. I passed a few riders with flat tires and was glad I wasn't one of them. I passed a few more with flat tires. Something seemed wrong. Then I heard a sound I had never heard before . . . *swoosh* . . . I had a flat tire. This was a tack attack, a rotten prank by locals who come out on the bike course the night before and throw tacks on the road. They blend in with the black macadam so you don't see them. I fixed my flat but two minutes later got another one."

Lucky for Shigo, a race official car came by and changed her tire. They had been alerted about the tack attack and went out on the course helping the stranded riders. Then another bad thing happened at mile fifty-six. When she reached for her bottle behind her, she didn't see the wasp that was sitting on top of it until it was too late. The wasp bit the inside of her lip before she could spit it out; her lip swelled up like a balloon.

"I had to ride eighteen more miles to get to the medical tent. I looked like a freak going in with my huge swollen lip. I iced it for fifteen minutes and started to feel way too comfortable just sitting there and knew I had to get out of there and back on the course.

"I finally made it through the bike and headed out for the run. Another piece of advice I received was to just get out of town as fast as I could before settling down and making my plans for the run. Mentally it was good to get clear of the finish-line scene and seeing some of the athletes already coming in. I saw my mom in the bleachers and waved to her on my way out. One of the spectators called out, 'Have a great marathon!' and it hit me hard that I was about to run 26.2 miles after swimming 1 mile and riding 112. I really didn't need to hear that.

"With twelve miles to go, I met Greg Sylvester, a sixty-year-old retired schoolteacher who wanted company. We stayed together, encouraged each other, and kept each other laughing. By now it was dark and we had our glow sticks on. As we got near the finish I realized I could break fifteen hours, and with Greg's blessing, I sprinted ahead and crossed in 14:59:20.

It was amazing to cross the finish line. I could hear my mom screaming my name, I even saw her cane waving in the air. The fact that she had been sitting there since before 5 A.M. made me proud for her as well. When I finally got to her, my new medal around my neck, she looked tan and proud—and then she said, 'What took you so long?' I told her all about the tacks and the bees during our long walk back to the hotel. I didn't sleep well that night and when I woke up I said to my mom—"I'm an Ironman"—I feel like an Ironman too! She groaned. Johnny, my brother, was the first person I called. When I saw him later on at his annual pig roast he kept telling everyone about my Ironman, the length of the race, everything. He was so proud of me. Funny how things work out."

It's been almost five years since Shigo started down this path. She truly believes anyone can do an Ironman if you have the time to train and have the right mind-set. Since Ironman Canada in 2001 she has done three more Ironman competitions.

"People ask me why I do triathlons, especially an Ironman. The best answer I can give is that it is very empowering. The happiest times in my life thus far have been training for and competing in the Ironman. I officially became a member of Team Psycho in 2002. At a recent event I had on my Team Psycho race singlet and was on the course forever. Although my teammates had finished long before me they cheered me, high-fived me, and made me feel like Sally Field . . . *You like me!* And I love them all right back.

"If there is the smallest inkling in your mind that you want to do one, go for it. Yes, it's hard, and yes it is a huge commitment, but if you want it bad enough, you can do it. I've been passed by a man swimming two miles with one arm. I've been passed on the run by a seventy-six-year-old nun. I've been passed on the bike by a man with one leg. They don't discourage me; they inspire me. I didn't grow up an athlete but I am one now. For me it's not about time, it's about enjoying the day. That, and being able to say I am an Ironman!"

KAREN SMYERS

DOB: 9-1-61
Residence: Lincoln, Massachusetts
Occupation: Professional triathlete, mother, wife, triathlete coach
First Triathlon: 1984 Harvard Women's Sprint Triathlon

Karen Smyers won the 1995 Hawaii Ironman. Since her first triathlon in 1984 she has competed at the top of her profession despite numerous life-threatening setbacks such as a severed hamstring in 1997, being hit by an eighteen-wheeler truck while on a training ride in 1998, and her diagnosis of thyroid cancer in 1999. Her roots for triathlon success started at Princeton University, her 1983 alma mater, where she was a decorated swimmer, placing in the Eastern Swimming Championships, and also ran track. A natural athlete, she isn't happy unless she is moving around, active, and involved in sports. These days she can add chasing around her two kids to her weekly training schedule of running thirty to thirty-five miles a week, biking one to two hundred miles a week, and swimming six miles a week. At forty-five she is still at the top of her game. She is married to a fellow triathlete, Michael King.

"I was a sports fanatic growing up. By age eight I was already swimming in the town league, playing baseball, tennis, any sport that came by and was in season. I can clearly remember a moment in time when I was twelve years old and sitting on my bike holding my tennis racket and baseball glove and thinking, *If I can always have my sports equipment with me it won't ever get better than this.* By age twelve, I was swimming year-round. In junior high I did gymnastics, track, and started a field hockey team. In high school I was still swimming and doing gymnastics and tennis, and by college I concentrated mainly on swimming and track."

Despite being All Eastern in swimming, Smyers feels she never reached her ability because she burned the candle at both ends with training hard, studying, and staying out too late partying.

"I don't regret a thing; it was a wonderful time in my life. After Princeton, I moved to Boston with two roommates, one was a runner and the other a swimmer. I joined a running club, the Irish American track club. I didn't think I'd be able to keep up my swimming and I knew I had to have a sport in my life so I decided to learn more about running and build up distance. I did go to a pool just to keep in swimming shape and keep the weight off.

"When my roommate did her first triathlon in 1983, she came home with prize money and I thought that was pretty cool. I did have a vague idea of what a triathlon was as someone back in Princeton was training for the Hawaii Ironman. When I heard what the event entailed I remember thinking that was totally insane. After finding out there were shorter distances, the idea of a triathlon really appealed to me. I was already running and swimming, and since I didn't own a car I was biking to and from work and on the weekends. Putting all three sports together seemed like the perfect niche for me."

Smyers didn't train for her first triathlon. No brick workouts, no transition training, nothing. She felt the time she already spent riding, swimming, and running would be sufficient.

"I was in good shape so I didn't really give it a thought. But the night before the event my bike got stolen so I ended up borrowing my roommate's bike. It was a decent bike but not great. The swim leg was in the Harvard pool and I felt very comfortable. The bike course was two loops around Storrow-Memorial Drive. I remember being on the bike and spinning like crazy because someone had told me to keep the bike in a high gear so I wouldn't tire my legs for the run. But I felt like I was going nowhere and all of a sudden my roommate passes me, mashing her gears and going all-out fast. I quickly started using more gears and caught up to her just as we got off the bikes. The run was weird. I actually started laughing because I couldn't control my legs. They felt like deadwood and wouldn't cooperate. But after about a mile they kicked in and the initial discomfort phased out. There were probably about a hundred women in the event and I won. It was mostly first-timers. In this particular event the distances worked in my favor because I was one of the first out of the pool and the bike and run were short enough that I didn't lose my edge. I had such a great time at that first event I couldn't wait for the next one. I was definitely hooked."

Four weeks later Smyers did her second triathlon, moving up to an Olympic distance.

"That event really opened my eyes. What a difference a few extra miles made. I was on the bike course forever, being passed by ladies in their sixties with baskets on their bikes. I quickly realized success in this sport at the longer distances was not something that came easily, like my first sprint distance. I was still treating triathlons like a hobby and didn't mind when I lost or didn't do well. That first season I did six triathlons. At one event I won a Bianci bicycle, which was huge for me because I now had a better bike.

"At the last race of that season, in 1984, I entered another Olympic event. I was still checking the amateur box on the application but when I checked the overall results afterward I realized if I had checked the pro box I would have taken second place and won several hundred dollars. Back then you didn't have to qualify to be a pro. You just checked that box. From that moment on I decided to check the pro box and race as a professional."

Smyers was still working full time and not seriously training yet for triathlons. In 1985, she entered the Bay State Triathlon, which offered big prize money and was organized by the race director of the Boston Marathon, Dave McGillivray. The distance was her longest yet, a one-mile swim, forty miles on the bike, and a ten-mile run. Elite names in the marathon, such Alison Roe, entered the event. Coming off the bike she was able to catch and pass Alison Roe and ended up winning.

"That event was a big turning point for me. I realized I could be good in this sport if I really trained. To test myself further, I went on to the nationals next and got killed. That planted seeds of doubt as to how good I really was. Maybe I was just the local favorite? I just wasn't sure. The next big break through for me was in 1989 when the World Championships were announced. I made it my goal to place on the team. My company was having some problems and put the employees on half-time schedules so I had more time to train hard, especially on the bike segment. I trained on my own, winging it for the most part. There were no training books, online coaching, nothing but our own common sense."

Smyers made the team and traveled to Avignon, France for the event. She had her best bike time ever, finishing fourth overall in the championships. When she returned to work, her company decided to go bankrupt and she decided to become a professional triathlete.

"The first thing I did as a pro was look for sponsors. New Balance was my first sponsor. Then Trek signed me up as well. I'm still with Trek. They're a great company. I didn't have any plans to do a full Ironman. I still thought that was for crazy people, but seeing it firsthand in 1991 gave me a new perspective, that it wasn't just a survival race of misfits and sufferers but a real race of amazing athletes. I was amazed and started to think how to train for something like that. The whole ambience of the race also appealed to me. I started to think that as a professional, I needed to do it."

At that time, there were very few Ironman event locations: Hawaii, Japan, Germany, and New Zealand. Participants had to qualify to race at Hawaii, and Karen's husband and friends decided to try to qualify. She told her husband that if he qualified, she would race Hawaii as well. He surprised her when he got a slot so she had to live up to her word and managed to qualify at Mrs. T's Triathlon in Chicago.

"My first Ironman was very scary. I was very respectful of the distance and conditions. Looking back, I probably didn't read enough about it or prepare enough. And six days prior, instead of beginning to taper, I did a very difficult Olympic-distance triathlon in St. Thomas. I didn't know about nutrition and didn't eat enough. I ate on the bike but not during the run. By mile eight I was out of gas and didn't know how I would ever finish. At the next aid station, I saw a Coke and grabbed it. It gave me an instant energy boost and I could run for half a mile before I had to walk again. At the next station I grabbed another Coke and kept doing this till I felt I had enough energy to resume running. That year I finished in fourth place. It was definitely the hardest thing I ever did. I told myself never again. But it didn't take long for the pain to wear off and the satisfaction and feeling of euphoria to take over. It was very cool and I knew I could do better. It would be false advertising to describe it as fun but it is one of the biggest challenges you'll ever do."

Smyers went back in 1994 and placed second, and then won in 1995. That same year she won the Triathlon World Championships.

"To win in 1995 I knew I had to beat Paula Newby-Fraser (eight-time World Triathlon Champion). During the run, Paula had a twelve-minute lead on me. As I started to close the gap she stopped taking the time to fuel herself at aid stations the way she normally does and eventually started to suffer from lack of calories and fluids. I managed to pass her with half a mile to go in the race. It turned out to be my day.

"In 1996, I planned to go back and win and prove my first place wasn't a fluke. I came off the bike one minute behind Paula but she had a three-minute penalty for drafting so I actually got out on the run before her which was a huge advantage. But this time, I made the nutrition mistakes and ended up having to walk early on in the marathon. Paula and Natasha Badmann went on to have a really great duel on the run and Paula ultimately won her eighth Hawaii Ironman that day. I managed to get my stomach back in order and finished third."

Smyers was planning on going back to Hawaii in 1997 but a fluke accident in June of that year ended those plans. While she was removing a storm window at her house the glass shattered, severing her hamstring. The injury required several months of rehabilitation to heal properly. She decided to take the time away from training to conceive, and gave birth to her first child, Jenna. A few months later she started training again but while out on a bike ride she was sideswiped by an eighteen-wheeler truck. That left her with six broken ribs, a lung contusion, and a separated shoulder.

In September 1999 she went to see her doctor for what she thought was swollen glands. When the diagnosis came back, Smyers was told she may have thryoid cancer but needed a biopsy to confirm it. Her doctor told her it would be okay to postpone the biopsy until after the Ironman since it was a slow-growing cancer and the delay wouldn't make a difference in the outcome.

"The Ironman needs total concentration and I would rather deal with one thing at a time, so I decided to wait on the biopsy. I had a great race and finished second and I remember thinking after the race, *How could I have cancer and race this well?* I decided to do one more race, a draft-legal event in Mexico, to end the season before the biopsy but a woman crashed right in front of me and I toppled over and broke my collarbone."

Two days later, the biopsy turned up positive for papillary carcinoma, thyroid cancer. In December 1999, Smyers had a total thyroidectomy. Although the season ended on a down note, she was voted the 1999 USOC Triathlete of the Year for her comeback performances that year. She set her sights on recovering from her collarbone and surgery in time to participate in the Olympic Trials just five months later, putting off her radioactive iodine treatment in the hope that she could make the first-ever Olympic triathlon team.

"I wanted to be part of the first-ever US Olympic triathlon team at the 2000 Sydney Olympics. Already a sixteen-year veteran in the sport, I wanted this very badly. I started training for the trials in January but the broken collarbone was still healing and I didn't have complete range of motion. By early March things were beginning to feel back in place and I was on track. I was one of about twenty women competing for three spots. At the first race in Sydney, one woman qualified. Then it was down to two spots at the second race in Dallas. I gave it my best shot but finished seventh. It was very disappointing but at the same time, I was so appreciative of having had the opportunity to try. It was very therapeutic to have something that motivating for me to make me sail through what could have been a difficult time emotionally."

Although she didn't make the Olympic team, she was voted the 1999 Olympic Committee Female Triathlete of the Year. Later that summer, as she prepared for her radioactive iodine treatment, a scan revealed enlarged lymph nodes that required a second surgery. She had that surgery in August 2000 and followed it up with a radioactive iodine treatment a couple of weeks later.

In 2001, she returned to Hawaii and placed fifth at age forty. She also won her seventh national title at the Olympic distance. In 2002, she had hoped to be taking time off for maternity leave but as the months went by and she hadn't conceived, she decided to start training for the Ironman once again. She found out she was pregnant just three weeks before race day. Excited to finally be pregnant, she put her thoughts of racing aside until two weeks later, when she miscarried.

"I was going to Hawaii anyway as my husband was racing and we had already made our plans, so I asked my doctor if it would be okay if I still raced. It sounds callous maybe, but I knew that the best way to heal is to move forward. I had done most of the training before finding out I was pregnant and thought it would be better to do the race rather than sit on the sidelines and feel sorry that I wasn't pregnant *and* I wasn't racing. I did well through the swim and bike but had some real problems on the run. I actually stopped for a medical consultation for about an hour before finally continuing. It was a pretty emotional few weeks."

Smyers got pregnant the following year and son Casey was born in January 2004. She returned to Hawaii nine months later and finished in nineteenth place. In 2005, at age forty-four, she finished in ninth place.

"I'm just taking it year by year. I still have goals and in 2006 would like to finish Hawaii in the top five. Despite everything that has happened to me I feel I lead a charmed life. I plan to keep competing for as long as the body will hold up. I'm not sure I'm comfortable being called 'the legendary' Karen Smyers. I'm not that old yet!"

MAGDALENA STOVICKOVA

DOB: 2-24-75
Residence: Upper Saddle River, New Jersey
Occupation: Professional triathlete, swim coach, Wyckoff YMCA
First Triathlon: Slovakia, 1991

Magdalena "Maggie" Stovickova was born in Communist-controlled Czechoslovakia. A promising swimmer, by age eight she was tapped to attend a state school for sports. Under the control of a grueling coach, she had two-and-a-half-hour practices before and after classes, logging ten to twelve miles in the pool a day. By the time she was a teenager she was a twenty-time champion on the Slovakia national swim team, despite poor conditions at the pools and a lack of decent equipment. For years, she had to repair her one pair of goggles and swimsuit because she could not afford new ones—and even if she could, the quality was horrible. At sixteen she switched her sports major to triathlon and became a seven-time Slovakia triathlon champion. In 1998, she came to the United States to work at a summer youth camp in Monsey, New York, an event that changed her life. A family invited her to live with them, an opportunity she jumped at even though it meant being away from her parents and two brothers. After a long hiatus away from serious competing, she found her competitive spark and in 2001 fulfilled a lifelong dream of going to Kona for the Big One. But for Maggie, the day was filled with disappointments. However, nothing keeps her down for long and with her "suck it up" attitude she'll find her way back to Kona and won't quit till she crosses the finish line. Nothing less.

"Growing up in a Communist country teaches you to be tough. All the kids were athletic because we were outside playing all the time, kicking balls, climbing trees, running, biking, whatever we could do to amuse ourselves. If you are not an athlete, you are a nobody. Athletes get to travel and be someone special, someone to be admired.

"When I was selected to go to sports school in the fifth grade, I had no idea what I was getting myself into. The coaches were good, but so strict and rigid. If you looked at them the wrong way it was not unusual to get punished. We had to be respectful and there was no time for fooling around. We had to do what we were asked to do. Practice came before anything, even classes. If we were sick with fever or cramps or stomach ache, we still had to practice. There was no such thing as an excuse. The attitude of the coaches was, *Suck it up and go.* And because my country was so poor, our equipment was miserable. I had one pair of goggles for four years, which kept leaking. I had to repair them with bicycle tire tubes. The swimsuits were made of a harsh material that left me bloody where it cut into my thighs, neck, and chest. After a while the material would separate and fall apart at the seams. My mother could not afford to buy me new ones all the time so she would patch my suits until they were threadbare. And when I got a new one she always bought it too big so I would grow into it and have it for a few years.

"At school, we practiced two hours in the morning and two hours in the afternoon. I liked it in the beginning but when I started traveling and it got more serious I didn't like it so much. I traveled alone, without my own coaches, and I missed my family. I had two passports, my personal passport and my professional sports travel passport. The coaches always kept the professional passports at all times. And my family never got to see me compete as they were not allowed to travel.

"When I was training for the nationals my team practiced with the East Germans. I thought my coach gave us harsh drills but this coach was brutal. We had to swim fifteen miles in practice per day. When I was six-teen I was hoping for the Olympics but never tried out as I realized I needed to be more talented to qualify. I was talented but not enough to compete at the international level. When my coach told me to lose weight, I kept losing and my times suffered. I challenged myself to do the best I was capable of but I couldn't make it to the next level.

"At that time I was struggling with what to do with my swimming career when a group of men I knew from school asked me to do a triathlon with them. Like me, they had started out as swimmers but switched their major to triathlon. I was not worried about the one-mile swim, I knew how to bike so no problem there, but running? No way. I was not a runner.

"I borrowed a man's road bike that had a pair of homemade aerobars and took it out for a twenty-minute ride a week before the race. I also went out for one twenty-minute run and thought I was overtraining so I stopped.

"My first triathlon was a total joke. Of course, the swim was a breeze and I was the first one out of the water. Then I got on the bike and headed out onto the street and all the cars started honking at me. Turns out I was going the wrong way. There were no markers on the road and I was in the lead so I had no one to follow. I had to wait for the traffic to pass, carry my bike across the road divider, and when I started to ride again, the chain came off. I was able to get it back on and then tried to catch up, staying in the aerobar position for the entire twenty miles. I cruised into transition so fast that when I put on the brakes, I fell off the bike right in front of everyone. My swimsuit was ripped, I was cut and bloodied up and down my thigh, and I thought I had ruined the bike. I sat there crying when the man who owned the bike came over. I thought he was going to yell at me but instead he said, 'Shut up, stop crying and start running.'

"So I started to run but the cuts on my thigh were hurting. As I passed an aid station I grabbed a cup of what I thought was water and poured it on my wounds but it wasn't water. It was some sweet, sticky fluid that made the cuts hurt worse. But I kept going and won the race."

With that one event, Maggie was hooked on triathlon. Two weeks later she competed in the Hungarian National Triathlon Championships, an Olympic distance, the first time she'd ever run a 10K. After that, she switched her major at her sports school from swimming to triathlon.

"I loved the variety of training for a triathlon. It was so much more interesting than swimming laps five hours a day. It was also a lot more social than swimming. You can't talk when you swim but I can talk with my partners when biking or running. And I loved training outdoors as opposed to being inside in a pool all day. That was so new to me. I still have beautiful memories of running in deep snow through pristine fields in the woods."

After high school, Maggie wanted to go to college and study economics but less than 15 percent of the student population in Slovakia goes on to college and she did not make the cut. At eighteen, she was out of school and on her own. In 1992 she competed in the Junior European Triathlon Championships and placed fifth overall. In 1993, the country split and she was thrilled to be able to compete for a free Slovakia. The very first time she competed in a major race for her country she collapsed just two hundred yards from the finish line. Diagnosed with bronchitis, strep, and anemia from overtraining, her body was depleted of just about everything. For weeks she went for iron shots, and in about six weeks she was able to win the next event.

In 1994 she went to college and studied physical education and triathlon. Mentally she was learning everything about the sport but physically she was burned out and gave up competing.

"There was too much pressure on me to always be the best. The pressure just got too much and I quit. Plus I had no money and no sponsors and my equipment was old and useless.

"In 1998 I came to the United States for the first time to work in a youth summer camp in Monsey, New York, as a camp counselor and absolutely loved it. But I could not believe how spoiled some of the children were. They threw food away that I know would feed many people in some very poor countries. They talked back to the counselors and were rude and disrespectful. I was shocked.

"I got my master's degree in 1999 and came back to the camp. I was offered a job by a family at the camp to be their housekeeper and au pair, and never went back to Slovakia. They became my family."

Maggie enrolled in a local college to better her English and understanding of America. She made friends easily and fell in with a group of triathletes who convinced her to enter the Wyckoff Sprint Triathlon in

June of 2000, where she finished first overall.

"When I showed up at the triathlon I couldn't believe all the expensive bikes. I thought I was going to get blown away but it turned out that most of the bikers didn't really ride well, they just owned expensive bikes. I had such a good time that day. There was no pressure at all, something new for me. And I couldn't believe people did it for fun, not to compete or win. That was crazy!"

With her competitive spirit back in full force, Maggie took to the triathlon events like a cat out of the bag. She loved training with her tri friends, who spoke about going to Hawaii. That triggered a memory of being back in the Czechoslovakia in 1991 and sitting in a small room with her triathlete mates all huddled around a tiny black-and-white television set watching a taped copy of the Hawaii Ironman. She had been captured by the event and vowed to go to Hawaii some day. And here she was, ten years later, actually discussing the likelihood of making that dream come true.

"I started doing every triathlon at every distance I could get to. I doubled up on my biking and running, my weakest link. In July 2001 I went to Lake Placid, hoping to qualify for Kona, and had a fabulous day, finishing in 10:35, thirteenth female overall and fourth in my age group. It was the best race of my life. It was a perfect day and everything just clicked."

But things didn't work out as well at Kona. She didn't recover as quickly as she hoped from Lake Placid and with only two and a half months to go, she didn't get in as much training as she planned, especially the running. Then tragedy struck with the 9/11 terrorist attacks on the World Trade Center. Her boyfriend, a New York City fireman, who was planning on going to Hawaii with Maggie, was working at Ground Zero 24/7, looking for remains. Depressed and stressed, he stayed home while Maggie went to Kona.

"I left for Kona in a very bad state. I was very worried for Steve and missed him terribly. He was supposed to me my anchor and my crew and now I had no one. Basically, my heart wasn't in it. I was lonely and miserable."

Despite a heavy heart and a nagging leg injury, Maggie had a good start, seventh out of the water. During the bike, an old IT band injury kicked in and she hit the wall. By mile seventy she was in tears and kept calling out her mom's name into the wind. Finishing the bike in just under six hours and already falling apart, she still had a full marathon ahead of her.

"I was crying as I started the run but I recalled my former coaches from Slovakia telling me to shut up and just suck it up and I dug deeper and pulled myself together. I hit the wall again at mile eleven, and by mile fifteen I was down on the ground. The medical crew came over to me and asked if I wanted to be pulled from the course, but I was not going to quit. I just sat there and focused and tried to visualize the last eleven miles. A friend came by and offered support and encouragement. I started talking to myself, saying, 'Come on, you can do it, just get up. It's like being back in the pool doing a four-hour session and you have one more hour to go. You've been in this place before now get up.'

"By the strength of my mind, I managed to pull myself up and walked and ran the last eleven miles. Another female competitor who was also struggling came alongside and we made a pact to pull each other through this. When she hit the wall or started to walk, I talked her through it and she did the same for me. Slowly we moved forward until we could see the finish line. In one swooping movement, we grabbed each other's hands and held them high as we crossed the finish line."

After Kona, Maggie became depressed and wanted to give up triathlon altogether. She didn't run or train for four months. But after seeking advice from her tri buddies who had been in similar situations, she relaxed a bit, took care of her injuries, and refreshed her mind and body. For the next three years she competed in local sprint- and Olympic-distance events but did not train so much. For her, the event became her relaxation with no pressure to perform or meet expectations. And in that relaxed state of just enjoying herself, she usually won.

"What I love most about competing here in the United States is the support from other competitors. When I was competing in Slovakia it would be unusual for another athlete to stop and help out a struggling competitor, like the woman at Kona did for me. Here in America it's like we are all in it together and when one suffers we all know the feeling and try to help. In Eastern Europe it was so much more cutthroat. You competed to win and nothing else was acceptable."

In 2002 she took a full-time job as the youth swim coach at the Wyckoff YMCA in New Jersey. During her first season as coach she scheduled three workouts starting at 5 A.M. for eleven-to-eighteen-year olds, a regimen that was met with some resistance from parents.

"The kids have no idea how easy they have it over here. They think I am tough but they don't know what tough is. If they lose goggles, their parents buy them another pair. They have at least three or four swimsuits at one time. They have cell phones, iPods, credit cards, and their parents drive them everywhere."

But her drive and drills have paid off as many of her swimmers qualify for the YMCA Nationals every year and she has lots of youths training for the Junior Olympics. Maggie is also training for the Olympics. Her new goal is to make the Slovakia 2008 Olympic Triathlon team. To prepare, she is swimming almost every day, bikes up to three hundred miles a week, and runs thirty-five miles a week. It's not uncommon for Maggie to load up her car and drive to Lake Placid for the weekend, seven hours away, and bike two hundred miles.

"I know I need to concentrate more on my running, my least favorite part of the triathlon. As much as I enjoy all three disciplines, swimming is my world. I have to force myself to get out and run."

She maintains a strict diet that includes lots of fruit, vegetables, low-fat cheese, and yogurt but enjoys an occasional chocolate, cookie, or candy bar. During events or endurance training she snacks on pretzels, granola, or fruits, salty stuff like beef jerky, even chips. She still gets a kick out of the American obsession with exercise as a way to just keep fit or—as one mother told her—so she can eat desserts. Along with swimming, biking and running she goes to EAPI (Elite Athletic Performance Institute) in Ramsey, where they help build core strength, running technique, and recovery, and use ART (active release technique) to treat her injuries.

In 2005 Maggie got her green card so she can travel to Slovakia and visit with her mother and brothers more often. She wakes up thankful for every day and appreciates this second phase of her life made possible by her American family—but also values the strong work ethic and heritage of her native country. It's a perfect blend. Life is good for Maggie Stovickova.

What She Has Learned, Mistakes She Has Made:

"Never give up your dreams. If you want something really badly you can get it.

"Practice all aspects of the race, especially transition. My first big international race I was the first female out of the water, way ahead of the other women. It took me almost five minutes to take the wet suit off. I worked so hard to be able to swim fast. I just needed a little practice to be able to take the wet suit off much faster.

"Don't use brand-new sneakers for a race. It takes a very long time to heal those blisters.

"Take care of your equipment. At one of my first races as I was running out of water I just threw my goggles and cap away. I never found them afterward.

"Practice drinking on the bike with a water bottle. At a national championship I started biking and tried to drink. It was on a bumpy road and I lost my water bottle. A guy I passed had a flat tire and gave me his water; otherwise I would not be able to finish the race in that heat.

"Practice putting your helmet on. When I first started racing triathlons I put my helmet on and did not know how to buckle it. I rode for a while with an unbuckled helmet. Not very safe or smart.

"Memorize the transition area and where your bike is racked. At one of my first international races I ran to transition after the swim and could not find my bike. Then I started out the wrong exit. I lost valuable time because I didn't memorize the exits and entrances."

CATHY STRAHLE

DOB: 9-7-52
Residence: Ridgewood, New Jersey
First Triathlon: June 2004 Wyckoff (New Jersey) Sprint Triathlon

No one said it would be easy. Not her doctors, her family, her friends. But everyone agreed if anyone could do it, she could. Cathy Strahle made a lifelong dream come true when she crossed the finish line of her first triathlon. "I had no business doing this, but it was so much fun," reflects Strahle. "I love sports. I knew in my heart it was just a matter of time before I did this."

Growing up in Shrewsbury, New Jersey, Strahle was always on the move. She was a competitive cyclist and played basketball on her high school team. One of her first bike races was called the Beer and Bike Race: the course went from bar to bar, from Sea Bright to Belmar, New Jersey. She also played softball and kept active with that sport all her life.

After college, Strahle worked as a special-needs teacher, married Tom Strahle, and with their three kids—all under the age of four—moved to Ridgewood, New Jersey. "I kept waiting for the time when I had the time to train for a triathlon but it never came."

Putting on some extra pounds after the birth of her fourth child in 1992, Strahle got serious about losing weight and getting back in shape. She made a promise to herself to lose the weight and do a triathlon before turning fifty. As much as she was dedicated to that goal, setbacks set in, mainly three ACL (anterior cruciate ligament) knee surgeries. The only form of exercise she could do was a Spinning class at her gym.

"I became a Spinning maniac, going to classes four times a week. At one class I met a man who was training for the Wyckoff Triathlon and a lightbulb went on in my head: *I can already bike so all I need to do is learn to swim and run.*"

Like a dog with a bone, Strahle would not let go of her dream. Not when confronted with foot issues that stemmed from the knee surgery and required orthotics; not when having to shell out money for a new bike, her first in thirty years; and not when she had to put on a bathing suit and a wet suit and learn to swim all over again, this time with her head in the water. And not even after she found out she was allergic to the chlorine in the pool, leaving her lethargic and sleepy the rest of the day. Strahle held steadfast to her dream.

"I didn't want to leave anything to chance so in February, I did the bike course twice. I dragged my husband, Tom, along and he wasn't real happy with that as it was freezing. But after the second time I felt comfortable with the course and the hills. All those Spinning classes really paid off but I still needed more time on the bike to practice with my clip pedals and reaching for the water bottle without falling off.

"I did my laps at the pool and even learned to swim with my head in the water, which I didn't do as a kid. Although I felt comfortable with the swim and bike, I knew that running would be my Achilles' heel. I was prepared to walk the five miles if that is what I needed to do to finish."

On the morning of the triathlon, Cathy and Tom were at the site by 5:30 A.M. Setting up her transition area was a new experience but she found everyone helpful and supportive.

"The transition area is an art form in itself. I didn't know how to juggle all my equipment. It was quite a scene. When we were called to the lake to start the swim event, I was very nervous. I held back as my wave was called, not wanting to get crushed in the frenzy of two hundred women all starting together. Once I found my rhythm, I was fine and finished the half-mile swim in a respectable twenty-one minutes."

On the bike, where she felt most comfortable, Strahle was an animal.

She took off fast and never looked back, finishing the seventeen-mile course in 59:40. But the run, her nemesis, was still to come.

"I walked the first few miles, wondering when 'it' would kick in. Unfortunately it never did. Over the course I only managed to run about two miles, finishing in just over two and a half hours. Even my good leg went bad that day. As I crossed the finish line, I was so sore the only thing I could think to say was, 'Can I stop now?' "

She found her husband who was more excited than she was at her triumph. By the time she got home to her family she had her sights set on the next triathlon.

"Everything was new to me at Wyckoff. Now I can go all-out and not hold back. It took me thirty years to get out of shape and now I am determined to get back in shape. I don't crave Milky Ways anymore. I want fresh vegetables and fruit. At the age of fifty-one, I am starting over, a work in progress."

Strahle did another sprint triathlon the following month with her nephew. Her swim was better, and since the bike course was shorter than Wyckoff, just eleven miles, she went all-out, averaging twenty miles per hour. She thought the three-mile run would be easier because it was shorter but her legs were beat after pushing so hard on the bike.

"I blew past my nephew on the bike but he flew by me on the run. Those three miles seemed to go forever. But I must have improved because I took second place in my age division. After that race I started to think that maybe, just maybe, I could try for a half Ironman. I knew the swim wouldn't be an issue, the biking would not be a problem, even 56 miles, as long as the course was flat, and I was prepared to walk the 13.1 miles if I had to."

Strahle set her sights on a new half Ironman in New Jersey, the Devil Man, the following May. She hired a trainer who worked on her core muscles to build strength. She taught her how to taper and how to know when you've pushed just enough, not too much. She instructed her to get used to sitting on the bike for three hours or more. Her last words of advice were how to put it all together mentally.

"She told me to think of the swim as a warm-up, use the bike as my strength and just get through the run any way I could. I didn't know if I could do this but I was surely going to try. And the biggest thing I had going for me was a wonderful support system in Tom and the kids. All you really need is someone to believe in you and you can make anything happen."

Strahle drove to the event in South Jersey alone, without Tom or the kids. She needed to focus totally on herself and the task at hand and decided it was best to leave them behind. The morning of the event she felt calm and together.

"The water was cold but I had my wet suit on. The first thing I noticed was that the swimmers, even the good ones, were going slower than at the sprint triathlons. I guess everyone was pacing themselves accordingly for the mile so I did the same, although my inclination was to go faster and get the thing over with. I stayed to the side to avoid the faster swimmers but didn't count on the eelgrass that kept getting tangled in my feet. I started to panic but quickly pulled myself out of it, telling myself I was okay. It was such a beautiful day I began singing to myself. As I sang, my strokes got better and I started to relax and enjoy myself. I was even calling out to the volunteers in the water, thanking them for all their help.

"When I got on the bike I was feeling so happy and joyful to just be there. Halfway through the bike course I was on target for a three-hour bike time but on the second loop a strong headwind kicked up. I had to work extra hard to stay on target and knew my legs would suffer for it.

"Back in transition I stretched and took a bathroom break. I don't worry about my transition times. They usually average about five minutes but then again I'm not in a rush to finish. I'll get there when I get there. On my walk-run I couldn't help but notice that I was one of the older and heavier participants. The bright side of that is I get a lot of encouragement from the spectators. So many nice people!

"The miles were going by so slowly and it was getting late and I began to worry I wouldn't finish before the cutoff time. The only participants left on the course were me and what appeared to be an eighty-eight-year old man with broken ribs. With one mile to go the sweeper came by but I begged him to let me finish. He was so sweet and said not to worry, the clock was still ticking. With half a mile to go someone came out on the course and ran with me to the finish. Boy, did I need that boost. When I got to the finish I could tell everyone was just waiting for me to finish so they could go home but they cheered wildly for me and made me feel like a million bucks. It was the third best moment of my life, after marrying Tom and the birth of all my children.

"When I walked to the bike area, mine was the only one left on the field. The volunteers were already disassembling the stanchions. I wish I had a camera to capture the empty field and my lone bike. I broke out with the biggest smile. I was truly beaming. Finishing that half Ironman was one of the most rewarding things I have ever done."

The following month Strahle went back to do the Wyckoff triathlon and in June did a mini sprint with her son, Kevin, an offensive lineman at Fordham University.

"Kevin knows what it's like to train physically hard for a sport. When he decided to do the triathlon with me he knew he had to put in some time on a bike and a pool. Running was already incorporated in his football workouts so he didn't worry about that event. He did some training on a stationary bike but wasn't able to get in any swim practice. He figured, *How hard could that be?*

"Kevin was in the first wave. Standing on the beach, he confided he was a little nervous. I told him to just relax, stay to the side, and swim slowly.

"I was three waves behind him and thought I would catch up to him and we would stay together for moral support but I never found him. When I got back to transition his bike was still there. The mother in me wanted to go find him but the competitor in said to get going. Just then I saw him coming into transition. He had a panic attack in the water and for a split second thought he was going to drown. But he willed himself to relax, and floated on his back till he caught his breath. He told himself that he started this race and he would finish this race, he was not going to be a quitter.

"He did the breaststroke the remainder of the way. Just imagine a 265-pound football-player physique, all muscle, no wet suit, and had never swum in open water before. I was so proud of him.

"He left transition before I did but I passed him on the bike; then he passed me on the run, like everyone does. At the end, I think it finally dawned on him just how hard I have to train for these events. We plan to do it again next year and he promises to put in more training. Oh, and he is going to buy a wet suit!"

In January 2006 Strahle had an operation on her foot to mend a torn tendon. As soon as she is able, she'll start walking, then get back to Spinning class and try to run.

"I know a full Ironman is in my future, I just don't know when. Isn't it ironic that God gave me the passion for sports but not the skills or equipment? Between my bad knees and flat feet I'll never do well time-wise, but I make up for that in tenacity and determination. The triathlon is a great sport and this fat old lady plans to be competing in them for a long time to come. As I said before, all you need is someone to believe in you, and I believe I can achieve all my dreams."

What She Has Learned

"I would recommend that first-timers really train seriously, stretch, strengthen, and listen to your body. Sign up for swim classes, learn the techniques of cycling, work out with a running club. Don't invest in a new bike or other equipment until you know you are hooked. Find good trainers, sports doctors, and massage therapists, preferably recommended by other athletes. You never know when you are going to need one and it is better to know them in advance than need them in an emergency and have no one to call. As fate would have it, two nights before my half Ironman I threw my back out and needed an emergency chiropractic visit. Luckily, I had someone to call."

STACIE SWITZER

DOB: 4-29-70
Residence: Chicago, Illinois
Occupation: Lawyer
First Triathlon: 2000 Mrs. T's Sprint Triathlon, Chicago

Stacie Switzer likes to be challenged. She participated in competitive gymnastics from ages three to seventeen and then switched to running later on. When her only sibling died she increased the miles to help process his death—and the next thing she knew she was running marathons. After a few marathons she needed a new challenge and picked up triathlon. Then she got pregnant and gave birth to a healthy baby girl, Maddie. But then a bigger, life-threatening challenge came her way, one she wasn't prepared for. Weeks after Maddie's birth, Stacie, age thirty-three, was diagnosed with a huge tumor in her spinal cord; and she was unable to move her neck without excruciating pain. Doctors originally thought she would end up a quadriplegic as they ruled out the risky operation. But another doctor determined the tumor was operable and was willing to give it a try. Stacie survived the operation and, after a year and a half in physical therapy, returned to work and resumed taking care of Maddie. Almost two years after her operation she ran a half marathon.

"I'm not sure I would say I was competitive at age three, but I was entering competitions starting at age six. I picked up running in college and increased the distance when I started law school to deal with the pain and confusion over my brother's suicide. It became my coping mechanism, the only time I had to process what was going on in my life. My long runs kept getting longer and I ran my first marathon in 1997, at the age of twenty-seven, while in law school. Since then I've completed six marathons with a best time of 3:37."

After law school, Switzer married Michael, her childhood friend, in a romantic Scottish abbey. They settled in Chicago where she got a job practicing law. She continued her running and added biking to and from work, seven miles one way. Looking for a new challenge, her friends suggested she get into triathlons. Chicago is home to one of the largest triathlon events, Mrs. T's Chicago Triathlon, now reborn as the Accenture Chicago Triathlon. In 2005 the event was filled one month after opening for registration online; it closed at 8,500 entrants. It offers both a sprint and Olympic distance and attracts the pros as well as first-timers.

"I credit my good friends with getting me and Mike into the triathlon. They convinced me I could do it. I didn't have to worry about the run and I was riding my bike to work every day in downtown Chicago, but I wasn't much of a swimmer so that part was a bit daunting. Once I decided to do Mrs. T's, I knew I had to get in some swimming. My office was located right across from the Ohio Street Beach on Lake Michigan. I started swimming during my lunch break, three to four times a week. I wasn't the most graceful swimmer but I learned to get from point A to point B, which is all I wanted. My training was really fly-by-the-seat-of-the-pants, but I did take it seriously as I do all my sports. I bought some training books but had no idea what I was getting myself into. And why I chose Mrs. T's for my first triathlon is incomprehensible. It was insane!"

Switzer didn't invest in a lot of equipment for her first event. She already had a bike, although it was a mountain bike, and opted not to get a wet suit. She wanted to make sure she liked the event before making an investment. With three months of dedicated training behind her, she was ready. The night before the race, she and Mike and their friends went out to dinner.

"The morning of the event we all rode our bikes to the staging area. It was quite beautiful riding along the lakefront at dawn with the sun coming up over the lake, peaceful and quite. But I couldn't help thinking this was the calm before the storm.

"I had practiced setting up my transition area, which my husband laughed at and didn't. I was a nervous wreck as we stood on the beach. It was an in-water start and as I treaded water waiting for the gun I couldn't believe I was doing this. The swim channel seemed so narrow and as I looked around at all these people, I got very intimidated. And the swim was my worst nightmare come true. People were swimming on top of me, underneath me, I was getting kicked, and it was awful. My husband actually panicked and pulled over to the side, but I got angry and started fighting back and that's what got me through it. Lots of powerboats were out on the water and their fumes made me sick to my stomach. By the time I got out of the water I was nauseous and hoped the worst was over."

A true competitor, Switzer didn't waste any time exalting in the fact she'd made it through the swim. She ran to transition, jumped on her mountain bike and went off like the wind.

"I knew how important transitions were and practiced them quite a bit. But my husband laughed at my transition training, until I crossed the finish line first. Then he realized transition training wasn't such a silly idea after all. The twelve-mile bike course was an out and back on Lake Shore Drive, closed off to traffic. There is one very tight turn and I saw lots of cyclists wipe out on that turn. There were so many people on the course that it was quite dangerous. I was actually happy to be on a heavier mountain bike and, quite unexpectedly, my bike time on that heavy clunker was actually faster than some of my friends on road bikes.

"I went all-out on the bike so I was worried I wouldn't have anything left for the 5K run but I was fine, full of energy, and passed a lot of people. The course is lined with hundreds of spectators, which was a great boost, very motivating. Crossing the finish line was a huge thrill. I definitely got caught up in the moment. The energy of the crowd was overwhelming. My dad was there, which made it special. I was definitely hooked!"

After Mrs. T's, Switzer fell in love with triathlon. For her, it was a combination of a new challenge and the diversity of the training as well. A few weeks later she did an all-women triathlon. Her second time she wasn't so nervous and in fact, got a bit cocky.

"I thought I knew what to expect having done one, so I went out harder and faster and my legs were fried by the time I started to run. I realized I had a lot to learn and got more serious. I also bought a new road bike. During the next two years I did about eight triathlons at distances from the sprint to Olympic. In 2002 I started training for a full Ironman when I discovered I was pregnant."

Stacie continued running and cycling (Spinning) throughout her pregnancy. In April 2003, she went into labor on a Spinning bike and gave birth to a baby girl, Maddie. A few weeks after the birth she resumed her training but was hampered with extreme pain in her neck and shoulders. And then one morning she woke up and simply could not move her neck. Tests revealed a large mass growing inside her spinal cord, just below her brain. The tumor within the spinal cord was hemorrhaging. Although not cancerous, the location of the tumor made her condition potentially fatal. It occupied the space of four vertebrae and was slowly cutting off her life. Her doctors were amazed she could even walk at this point. Switzer was faced with the reality that she would never see her daughter grow up. Few neurosurgeons had performed such a risky operation and many shied away from it. But Dr. Edward Mrkdichian, a specialist in spinal tumors at the Chicago Institute of Neurosurgery and Neuroresearch, agreed to perform the very risky surgery. In August 2003, Switzer underwent the operation.

"This type of surgery is extremely invasive and required the removal of pieces of my vertebrae coupled with a rather large incision to open up the spinal cord. I knew enough to know that the spinal cord is not supposed to be cut. I also knew from discussions with many doctors that my marathon/triathlon days were over. Due to the size, location, and type of tumor, I had a very real chance of paralysis. The first thing I did when I woke up was move my toes and fingers. I needed to know I could move. I was thrilled. Unfortunately, I couldn't feel anything from my neck down, couldn't stand on my own without toppling over, and had lost all use of my right arm. The recovery was absolutely brutal. The steroids and drugs I needed to combat pain and inflammation put about twenty-five pounds on my frame. I blew up like a balloon. I also had to relearn daily tasks from scratch, such as using a fork and brushing my teeth."

But Switzer was up for the challenge. Within days of the operation and with the permission of her doctors she forced herself to walk the hospital hallway with the IV hookup in tow and the assistance of the hospital physical therapists. Due to the damage to her central nervous system, she lost all sense of balance. She would have to learn to walk all over again. It took Stacie nearly six weeks before she was able to hold Maddie for the first time and walk short distances without assistance. At three months, Stacie was able to walk one mile in an hour. Finally, at her one-year check-up, Dr. Mrkdichian gave medical clearance for Stacie to attempt running again. That very day, she laced up her shoes and went out for a jog with Maddie in the baby stroller.

"It was a very short, very slow jog. But I didn't care. I was doing something that the doctors told me would not be possible. It just gave me more motivation. The numbness never quite left and for a while I couldn't feel hot or cold or Maddie's soft baby skin. For me, it was never a matter of just getting back to walking, or jogging, or losing the weight. Psychologically, I had to get back to sports to feel whole again."

In December 2004 Switzer did her first comeback race, a five-mile race with her rehab doctor, Christine Villoch, by her side. When she crossed the finish line she decided she was ready to get back to sports and chose a marathon as her goal. She ran a half marathon in the spring of 2005. After the half marathon, Switzer was cleared to train for a triathlon. Just like Mrs. T's, my girlfriends talked me into it. Physically, it was a huge undertaking. Plus I had gone back to work full time and was spending as much time with Maddie as possible. I chose a sprint triathlon in September 2005, in Lake Geneva, Wisconsin. Training was like starting all over again. I knew what to expect, but it was just as hard as my first. The run was hard. All uphill. My dad came, Mike and his family came, and that was special because they recognized how much this meant to me. The biggest difference between this one and my other triathlons was that Maddie was waiting for me at the finish line."

Later that same year, in December, Switzer completed the Las Vegas Marathon in 4:24 and burst out crying as she crossed the finish line. It was a very emotional moment. Just two years prior, she had been learning to walk all over again.

"I was in so much pain after that marathon, but it was a good pain. It meant I was alive."

Switzer is currently training for her first half Ironman in July 2006 in Racine, Wisconsin, with the hope of doing a full Ironman someday. Knowing how much she likes a challenge, don't bet against Stacie Switzer.

"I feel so blessed. I feel like I have this incredible gift of hope that I want to share with others. I never felt sorry for myself, never did the *woe-is-me* stuff. I accepted my tumor and months of painful recovery as another challenge. I still have some tumor remaining and doctors tell me my tumor could come back, but for now I am in a five-year recovery stage. But I am not going to let any of that information interfere with my life with my husband or my child. Life is always full of risks. I cannot stop living my life because of what-ifs. You just have to step up to the challenge."

Her schedule:

Working full time and having a three-year-old, Switzer gets up at 4:30 A.M. She always has a race penciled on the calendar as a goal. She meets her group of women friends and runs up to ten miles two to three times during the week. Two other weekday mornings she attends a Spinning class. Friday mornings are her recovery days and Saturday mornings are for long runs. If she is training for a triathlon she'll get a long bike ride in on Sunday and a long swim on Monday night. During triathlon season, she tries to get in the pool at least two other days during the week.

What She Learned From Her First Triathlon:

"The sport requires preparation, both physically and mentally. You cannot fake it and expect to do well. The mental component is crucial and I like to think that my triathlon training taught me to face my life-threatening condition head-on. It provided me with the mental strength to fight my disease. My first triathlon taught me how to listen to my body in a very different way from the marathon. I cannot kill my legs on the bike. I like to feel as if I could have pushed a little harder in order to have a successful and enjoyable run. I learned that food is fuel. Bad food is bad fuel and makes for a miserable day of training/racing. I learned that some of my most cherished friendships are a direct result of that first triathlon. Most importantly, I learned that the accomplishment of a triathlon is not in finishing in the race, but in the dedication and perseverance needed to properly train for the race. If it were easy, everyone would be doing it!"

SHEILA TAORMINA

DOB: 3-18-69
Residence: Colorado Springs, Colorado
Occupation: Motivational speaker, professional athlete
First Triathlon: 1998 Waterloo (Michigan) Sprint Triathlon

Place your bets on Sheila Taormina. At the 1996 Summer Olympics, Taormina was a member of the gold-medal women's 4x200 freestyle relay team. In 2000, she competed in the inaugural Olympic triathlon in Sydney and made the team again in 2004. Post-Athens, Taormina embarked on a new sport, modern pentathlon, winning the women's senior division of the 2005 Pan American Championships. If successful in qualifying for the 2008 Olympic Games in pentathlon, she'll become the first American to compete in the games in three sports. She has a can-do attitude and self-effacing humor that is contagious and inspiring, two reasons she is a highly sought-after speaker. The youngest of eight kids, Taormina's midwestern upbringing (she was raised in Michigan, where her family still resides) and strong work ethic have taken her on a journey around the world and back to her roots, leaving a positive impression wherever she goes.

"I started swimming competitively with the Clarenceville Swim Club in Livonia, Michigan, from the age of nine all through high school and college. In 1988 I tried out for the Olympic team but didn't make it. In

1992 I tried out again but still didn't make it. I guess three times is the charm because in 1996 I made the Olympic team in Atlanta and won a gold medal in the 4x200 relay team. It was a fabulous moment in my life and a thrill to win a medal at the Olympics. I hung in there longer than I ever thought I would and it paid off. "

After the Atlanta Olympics, Taormina decided to give up swimming. She was tired of waking up at 5 A.M. every morning of her life since she was fifteen, and returned to work. Prior to the Olympics, she received her MBA in 1994 from the University of Georgia and worked in the automotive industry. Her boss gave her time off for the Olympics and afterward welcomed her back. As expected, winning a gold medal was a big deal and it changed her life.

"When I returned home I got calls from local organizations like Rotary Club and Kiwanis and local schools to speak about my Olympic experience. Soon I had more speaking engagements than I could handle. My boss encouraged me to start my own business and become a motivational speaker. He saw that I had an opportunity to impact people's lives so I followed his advice and quit, bought a camper, and started traveling around the country giving lectures."

Taormina became a self-contained, one-woman organization. She booked her own engagements, made her own media contacts, mapped out her route, gave swim clinics, attended sports banquets, and built her client base. In an eight-week period she traveled eight thousand miles. Although she was having a ball, the lifestyle of sitting in a camper all day driving and eating fast food wasn't very healthy.

"By the end of two years on the road I had put on ten pounds and wasn't exercising. Someone mentioned a local triathlon in nearby Waterloo, a sport I knew nothing about. It sounded interesting and certainly would be a challenge. I wasn't even sure I could do one but decided to give it a try. Heck, I knew I could do the swim, and anyone can ride a bike and run. I bought a bike and gave myself four months to train for the event.

"Another reason I wanted to do the triathlon is because I needed a goal to lose the weight and start getting back in shape. I am very disciplined when I have a goal in front of me. And I also wanted to do well. I don't remember my training but I set my own schedule and biked about four times a week. I didn't know what a brick was, never read a book on triathlons, and didn't know anyone who had done one so I really was on my own. Sometimes my brother joined me for a run but that's about it. I didn't know there was such a thing as group rides or runs.

"The day of the event my family came to watch. I was nervous excited. It was not a wet suit swim and I was relieved not to have to deal with that element. The whole thing was such a new scene for me. Standing at the start, I was nervous to do the swim. Here I was an Olympic medalist for swimming and I did not want to get in that water. To this day, I still get nervous at the start of a triathlon.

"I was first out of the water. I don't remember much else about the swim or bike but I do remember coming into transition from the bike and not realizing I had to slow down and dismount before entering the transition area. A very cute guy who was the dismount volunteer was trying to tell me to slow down as I came barreling in and I almost plowed into him.

"The run wasn't too bad and I passed a lot of people. My high school track days came back to me and I felt comfortable. At the end of the race, I had no concept how well I did."

Taormina did very well that day, winning first overall female. A local reporter interviewed her and asked what her plans were for the next competition. She didn't give it much thought, surprised at the attention she received. She'd only done it to lose weight and had no plans to do another one. That was in July, and in October she received a phone call that changed her mind-set about triathlons.

"I didn't do another triathlon, didn't even think of it. In October I got a call from Lew Kidder, the race director of the Waterloo Triathlon, asking if he could coach me. He saw my performance in July and thought I had potential. I was pleasantly surprised but declined. After twenty-one years of intense training for swimming I couldn't imagine picking up a new sport. I tried to tell him I just did it to lose weight but he kept talking to me and asked if I wanted to work out with his team, and that appealed to me. After a few sessions he told me I had the potential to be on the Sydney Olympic team. He even took it one step farther and lined up sponsorship for me and got me a professional triathlon card. Lew really believed in me."

The next step for Taormina was going to a triathlon camp in Curaçao, but money was an issue. She used her business acumen and got the camp director, Doug Stern, to waive her fee in exchange for her services as a swim coach. After the camp, Kidder thought she was ready for her first pro race and signed her up for an all-women Olympic-distance triathlon in South Africa. She had to dip into her savings to go to this one but felt it was worth it.

"In March 1999 I was on my way to South Africa for my second triathlon ever, and as a pro. It was all a bit overwhelming. I was very nervous and decided to strip my bike of everything that weighed it down, including my water bottle cages. Heck, it was only twenty-four miles; I could do that without water.

"I was first out of the water by forty-five seconds and had a nice lead on the bike when the women started passing me. It was over ninety degrees and I tried to push it on the bike but I was hot and thirsty and had no water. By the time I started running I was wiped. I don't know how I did it but I managed to barely cross the finish line and then passed out. While I was sitting in the medical tent with an IV in my arm, I heard them announce I took third place overall."

Things didn't improve much for Taormina in her next three races. Always first out of the water, she would push too hard on the bike, give it her all in the run, and then pass out. But Kidder believed she had the talent to make it to the Olympics; she just needed the experience.

"My next race didn't go any better. My coach put me in a race against the top American women at the St. Anthony's Triathlon in Florida. I had learned my lesson about water so I made sure I had plenty of water but I still hadn't learned about pacing. I was first out of the water again, and this time when the pack caught up to me I didn't surge ahead; I stayed with the pack and learned how to use their power and energy. But I got killed in transition and then sprinted on the run to make up time. As I closed in on the finish at the pier, I could see Karen Smyers in front of me. I was in fourth place and just trying to get to the finish line and realized we had to do a U-turn prior to crossing the finish and circle back. At that moment I knew I wouldn't make it and started to wobble, totally spent. The executive director of USAT, Steve Locke, grabbed my arm and asked if I was all right and I passed out in his arms four hundred meters from the finish. He carried me to the medical tent and I ended up with more IVs. This time Lew was there and I told him I was not cut out for this sport. But he still believed in me and said all I needed was to learn how to pace. Then I threw up."

Unfortunately Taormina contracted a serious muscle disorder, rabomyalsis, a condition where the muscles release toxins into the bloodstream. For three months she couldn't do anything but sleep eighteen hours a day. Once she recuperated, she started training for the World Cup in Switzerland, which turned out to be yet another disappointing race.

"That turned out to be the biggest disaster race I had so far. The good news is that I didn't dehydrate and I paced myself, but when I came out of the water I grabbed the wrong bike in transition. I kept wondering why the helmet wasn't fitting and the bike didn't fit. By the time I realized it wasn't my bike I had to turn around, rack that one exactly where I found it, and go search for my own bike.

"Once on my bike I hammered for all I was worth to make up for lost time and took a corner too fast and crashed into a barricade, flew over the handlebars and landed on my butt. As I sat there watching all my competition fly by I kept saying over and over, 'I hate this sport!'

"I was able to get back on my bike but didn't realize my brakes had locked up and I crashed again. I managed to fix the problem enough to finish the course. The whole day was a miserable experience. That night I called my mom and told her I was thinking of quitting. She told me how proud she was of me and that I had always been a good loser and to hang in there."

That race was a turning point for Taormina. Her string of bad luck seemed to be over and things started to come together for her. Now she was ready to focus on the trials for the inaugural Olympic triathlon. The trials were held in two stages, one in April and one in May. The April trial was held in Sydney on the actual Olympic course, during a World Cup race. Unfortunately, she crashed on the bike at that event. But she came back strong in May and won the trials outright.

"We had a great team for the inaugural triathlon event in Sydney in 2000. I really thought I could medal. My whole family came to Sydney plus many close friends and relatives. The spirit of the games was overwhelming. I was first out of the water by forty seconds but had no one to ride with to pace myself. I was still new to the sport and was up against some great performers who had better biking legs and I lost ground. I finished sixth overall, and felt good about that.

"In 2004 I won the World Championships and made the 2004 Olympic triathlon team in Athens. Again, I thought I could medal. I was first out of the water, was having a great bike experience and going strong, but got a charley horse in my calf. I couldn't shake it and had to stop pedaling. I managed to finish the bike course and was actually in second place during the run but it seized up again and I was forced to walk, finishing in twenty-third place. It was very disappointing."

After the Olympics, Taormina retired from triathlon. At thirty-five, she was tired of training and wanted to experience a life without the stress of competition and all the traveling and demands on her time. She took three months off to do absolutely nothing but visit with her family and then went back to her motivational speaking engagements. She had some thank-you speeches to make to corporations that helped raise thirty thousand dollars to fund her family's trip to Athens. She also spent time trying to find her next passion and started to look around for another sport, one with no transitions. She didn't want to retire on a sour note, feeling she hadn't reached her personal goals. She knew if she did pick up another sport and make it to the Olympics she would be the first American to do so, a pretty impressive goal.

"I thought about picking up cross-country skiing and worked with a coach, Lee Borowski, who thought it was possible to train an athlete in the technique of skiing in a short period of time. For a few months, every two weeks he traveled to the Upper Peninsula of Michigan where I was training. But I didn't like being alone out on mountain trails and couldn't find a group to train with. I started worrying about bears and it was freezing! After a few months of that I quit.

"Then I remembered a conversation I had back in 2003 with Eli Bremmer, a member of the national team for pentathlon. I met him at the Olympic Training Center and he tried to recruit me into pentathlon back then. Told me they like to recruit swimmers and runners and I could be the first American to go to the Olympics in three different sports. My response was, 'What's a pentathlon?' The pentathlon is five sports: shooting air pistols, fencing with an epee style sword, a 200-meter swim, show jumping on horses, and a 3K run. I was intrigued by the idea of doing skilled sports as opposed to endurance sports but decided to stick with triathlon."

In February 2005 Taormina contacted the pentathlon federation and asked how to get into the sport. She flew out to the training center and found herself on a horse, shooting a gun, and loved it. She was ready to train full time right then but she still had a few more professional triathlon commitments to fulfill and hit the road again. Mentally she had already made the switch to pentathlon and wasn't looking forward to going back on the road for triathlon, but it turned out to be a surprisingly good year, finishing fifth in the world. With that, she could finally retire from the sport and turn her attention to the pentathlon.

In June 2006 she moved to Colorado to train full time for the 2008 Olympic pentathlon team going to Beijing.

"You never know what life is going to offer and you just have to be ready to accept it and go with it. I've had some rough times and felt stressed and stretched and isolated from my family. Many times I didn't think I could go on but I always saw the big picture, that sports is my blessing in life, my gift, and although at times it can feel like a curse, I wouldn't change a thing."

SISTER MADONNA BUDER

DOB: 7-24-30
Residence: Spokane, Washington
Occupation: Nun with the order of the Sisters of Christian Community
First Triathlon: 1982 Heels to Wheels Sprint Triathlon, Spokane, Washington

Sister Madonna Buder, a seventy-six-year-old nun from Spokane, Washington, made history with her participation in Ironman competitions worldwide. She set a world record as the first female athlete over seventy-five to complete an Ironman at the 2006 Ford Ironman World Championships in Kona, Hawaii. Earlier in 2005 she won the Ironman Canada in Penticton, British Columbia, for the seventy-five-and-over age group. She doesn't think of herself as a celebrity, just someone with God-given talent. She ran her first marathon at age fifty-two and has gone on to complete more than 250 triathlons, including thirty-three Ironmans. She's been struck by cars at least three times, broken her hip, her arm, and her jaw. But nothing can break Sister Buder's spirit or determination.

"People always ask me how I am able to compete in an Ironman at my age and do so well. I have a very simple answer: I don't know. I think I owe some of it to the strong genes I inherited from my dad. He was a champion oarsman. My mother, who considered herself a champion oarsman widow, finally got to spend time with him when the boathouse burned down. She was very creative and spiritual, which balanced his practicality and physical prowess. Maybe that's what led me to the convent.

"I attended public school until sixth grade. When my mother found out about the kissing games she placed me in Catholic school. I was behind in all the subjects so one of the nuns took me under her wing and tutored me. She was very patient, loving, and nurturing, and was a big influence on my decision to enter the convent, which I did at age twenty-three."

In 1978, while attending a workshop on the coast of Oregon, Buder listened to a priest give a talk on the virtues of running. She was so impressed and moved by what he had to say, she went for a run on the beach.

"I never ran a step before and quite frankly didn't understand the appeal but after that priest spoke I had to give it a try. I ran between the jetties on the beach and truly enjoyed myself. The distance was about half a mile and I did in five minutes. The priest who gave the talk was sitting on the deck when I returned from the beach and he asked me about my run. When I told him my time, he said God had given me a talent and I should keep running. For the remainder of the week I ran the jetties every morning."

When she returned home, she kept running and soon was running one mile every day. A few weeks later she saw an ad for an 8.2-mile race, the Bloomsday Race, in Spokane, and signed up.

"This was a big race with more than five thousand participants. I was forty-nine at the time and the thought of being pushed and crowded in a pack was not terribly appealing but I was determined. After four weeks of training I worked up to four miles but was miserable. Everything hurt. I was coughing, sneezing, having spasms, my knees swelled, my calves tightened, my ankles hurt, and my feet had blisters. My entire body was going through the Stations of the Cross. I didn't know how I would survive the race. I started to cry. When I stopped crying I heard a voice. The Lord was saying to me, 'In my agony in the garden I did not know how many people down through the ages would respond to my act of love either. I also had to step out in faith.' My response to him was, 'Okay, Lord, I can do this if you will be my strength.' Then I dragged myself outside and went for a run.

"After my talk with God I didn't feel any better, but I didn't feel any worse either. How could I? Nothing was left to hurt!"

Part of Buder's problem was that she didn't know how to run. She wore tennis shoes; didn't stretch, drink water, or cool down; and didn't do anything that would have spared her some of her trials and tribulations. Finally a benefactor of the order heard of her training and bought her a pair of running shoes.

"I felt somewhat guilty accepting his offer, especially since I never planned to run again after this race. And still being naive, I bought the shoes within days of the race, didn't break them in properly, and ended up with more blisters. The day of the race was a beautiful, cloudless May morning, just like the morning of the Resurrection. I ran in the back of the pack and quickly discovered that's where all the fun takes place. The camaraderie was wonderful, and to top it all off I placed fourth in my age group. Despite all the hardships and pains I'd endured the last few weeks, I was ready for another race! What the heck, I already had the shoes and it would be a sin to waste them."

After steadily running one race a month for two years, Sister Buder was ready for a marathon. She wasn't content to just finish her first marathon; she set a goal to qualify for the Boston Marathon.

"I thought it would be a good goal to run a marathon at fifty-two and an even better goal to run it in 3:30 or less to qualify for Boston. I don't know how I did it but I ran my first marathon with twelve seconds to spare. I was on my way to Boston!"

Before traveling to Boston, she needed permission from the bishop. To help her case, she decided to raise money for multiple sclerosis.

"After taking pains to explain my situation and stating that it was not my intention to attract unwanted media or create a scandal, he said, 'Sister, I just wish some of my priests would do what you're doing.' I ran the 1981 Boston Marathon wearing a T-shirt the nuns had made with a quote from Saint Paul about racing toward the goal. It was a difficult run and by mile twenty-four my legs had turned to lead. Once again, I felt as if I was walking the Stations of the Cross. Somehow my faith pulled me through. I finished in 3:32 and raised four thousand dollars for MS."

"My next event was a sprint triathlon. At first I rejected the idea as just more foolishness on my part, but the idea would not let go of me. I knew I could do the run, I wasn't afraid of water, and I was pretty sure I could ride a bike. Once again, I did everything wrong but I enjoyed it and two weeks later did a half Ironman, the Troika Triathlon in Spokane.

"For the half, I graduated from a balloon-tire bike to a ten-speed, which was a bit intimidating. Swimming 1.2 miles wasn't so bad, but after the 56-mile bike ride with headwinds, my legs were trashed. I didn't know how I would run 13.1 miles, but I did. It seems I always do things the hard way but I learn from my mistakes. Now I was ready for an Ironman.

"For me, it's always about the challenge. And, of course, my strong faith that I will succeed. I am determined never to give up. I will exert every fiber in my body to finish once I am committed to a race. It is not a fitness thing; it is a spiritual quest. God gave me these talents, and I want to return the glory to him by doing my utmost. The Ironman symbolized my eternal goal. The other reason I enjoy these events is that I love being outdoors. The largeness of the great outdoors has a way of making us realize how small we really are in this pond and that the problems we carry with us are not as overwhelming as we make them. Nothing is too big to handle; everything can be solved. God is everywhere in nature, and observing nature can help us solve our problems."

Sister Buder experienced serious setbacks in her quest to do the 1985 Hawaii Ironman. While riding a borrowed bike with new brakes, and not wearing a helmet, she hit the brakes too fast and went flying over the handlebars right in front of a bus. She had a compound fractured elbow, fractured jaw, dislocated scapula, and multiple abrasions.

"My first question to the doctor was, 'When can I start training again?' He told me to put aside my plans to do the Ironman, that I'd be in the hospital for some time. I wasn't about to let go of my goal just because of a few injuries. I'd slip out of bed at night and run up and down the halls so my legs wouldn't atrophy."

A few weeks later, against doctor's orders, she ran a 10K race with her arm in a sling and a note attached to the sling that read, "Injured runner. No passing on the right, please." She finished fourth in her age division.

"After the accident it was psychologically very difficult to get back on the bike, but I beat down my fears and started riding again. I finished another half Ironman, which helped to lift my spirits."

Another bike accident, this time when a car ran a red light as she was crossing four lanes of traffic, put her back in the hospital.

"Now I was more determined than ever to get to Hawaii and started training again as soon as I could. Maybe the Lord didn't want me doing the Hawaii Ironman because with nine weeks to go while on a training ride in Australia, I was hit by a car. The damage wasn't too bad, a few broken ribs and a chipped heel, so I continued training and flew to Hawaii.

"The night before the event the race director announced that we might be getting a hurricane. Sure enough, the day of my long-awaited Hawaii Ironman, I had to swim in four-foot ocean swells. My ribs hadn't totally healed and I had no strength to pull through the waves. I missed the cut-off time by four minutes and had to DNF.

I decided to bike the course anyway, even though it wouldn't count. God works in strange ways and I think he had a plan for me that day. I met a minister on the bike course who was struggling to finish and in desperate need of some encouragement and friendship. Since I had nothing better to do, I stayed with him and acted as his carrot. With only seconds to spare, he rolled into the bike finish and started his run. I guess it was his day, not mine, and God sent me to get him through."

1986 was finally her year, and after winning her age division at the New Zealand Ironman, she completed the Hawaiian Ironman. She returned to Hawaii in 2000 but that was not a good year for her. Her ninety-two-year-old mother passed away, and Buder lost her desire to compete. She went to Hawaii to try and regain her competitive spirit but strong head winds caused her to crash on her bike and she was carried off the course in an ambulance. In 2004 she broke her arm and couldn't put her helmet on without assistance. 2005 was her breakthrough year, making history by being the first seventy-five-year old woman to woman to enter that division and win it.

"I truly don't understand why I do this, or can do this at my age. I never dreamed I'd be the triathlon nun. It all boils down to an element of faith, belief in yourself and belief in God. My life has been full and varied but not without its trials. My faith always carries my through. Maybe I am destined for a long life to help and inspire others. I've raised money for diabetes, heart disease, MS—you name it, I've run for it. I've advocated for troubled youths. I've written two books and donated the proceeds to charities.

Even though I feel fulfilled by using the talents God gave me, it seems there is always more to do. Life is never at a standstill, and neither am I. This reminds me of the quote from St. Augustine: "We are restless, oh Lord, until we rest in thee."

JULIANA TSAI

DOB: 1-27-75
Residence: San Francisco, California
Occupation: Creative director
First Triathlon: 2002 Harriman (New York) State Park Sprint Triathlon

There is a very large network of people in New York and California that are known as Friends of Julie Tsai. With her engaging personality and passion for the sport, she has turned many people, including nonathletes and "Oh, I could never do that" types, into die-hard fans of triathlon. She rents buses to take groups of friends to events, sends massive numbers of e-mails about upcoming races, and gets everyone to schedule their tri season calendar around social events. Why wouldn't you plan a business trip around a triathlon? Why wouldn't vacations, like a trip to Hawaii, be scheduled around a tri event? A self-described midpacker, she does triathlons for the fun, the challenge, and the chance to convert some unsuspecting spectator into a participant. Since her first triathlon in 2002 she averages six a year.

"I swam competitively when I was a kid. The most important lesson I learned from being on a swim team was to feel strong and comfortable in the water, a lesson that really helped me through my first triathlon. Swimming during a triathlon becomes a contact sport so it is more important to feel comfortable and strong than worry about time.

"As I got older, running replaced swimming as my first love but after three marathons I was ready to cross-train. I wanted to avoid injuries and I was also looking for that first-time high of a new adventure. Triathlons had all the elements I was looking for: a new challenge, new workouts, a new way to keep fit, and developing different muscle groups than I had in running. As a swimmer and runner, I thought all I needed was the bike component and then learn how to put them all together. I was also looking forward to building up muscle mass rather than constantly tearing it down in running. The thought of being more toned overall was definitely an incentive as well.

"I bought the book *Triathlon 101* to learn more about training. I showed up at a family wedding with the book under my arm and was surprised to see my sister with the same book! We now use both copies as a pass-along, circulating them to friends and family planning their first triathlon. We make notes in the book so it has become a personal accounting of first-triathlon highs and lows. They're still in circulation.

"When I made the decision to do my first triathlon, the first thing I did was buy a bike in March 2001. Slowly but surely, a year later I participated in my first race. I didn't want to invest in a bike that would outperform me, rather I settled on a bike that would take me through my first season but not break the bank. I wanted to learn gradually and when I graduated from pedal baskets to clipless, it was a real milestone. Same thing with graduating to the aerobars. I did it slowly and got over the fear issue and learned how to make them work for me. For distances starting with a half Ironman, they really are crucial equipment. The first time I did three loops around Central Park, eighteen miles, I was thrilled.

"I chose Harriman as my first triathlon because it was close to my home and I wouldn't have to travel too far, which adds another layer to the planning that I wanted to avoid. In hindsight, the course was grueling, way too hilly for a first triathlon, but as a novice I didn't think to ask about the course, or check it out on the web, or even drive it, which I could have done. I drove up the night before with a friend and stayed in a local hotel close to the start.

"I was very nervous and went through all the silly questions: *Will I be last? Will I finish?* Everyone looked so pumped and so hard-core, unlike a marathon where you get all sorts of body types. And there were way fewer women than I expected, which kind of freaked me out. I remember thinking, *I must be the only first-timer here,* which of course is silly but that's how I felt.

"When I hit the water I wasn't prepared for the feeding frenzy I found myself in. This certainly wasn't how it felt in the pool doing my laps. I was kicked, swam under, swam over, and almost suffered an anxiety attack, but I pulled myself through it and eventually found my groove. When I got out of the water I looked behind and said, 'Yeah! I'm not last!'

"Running into T1, I was relieved to see that plenty of bikes were left, confirming indeed I was not last! I knew I was here just to finish my first triathlon, but it was added mental boost to know that I wasn't the slowest. With that bit of surge, I got on my bike and set a comfortable pace. Then came the hills. I didn't know what to expect, didn't know what the race protocol was for passing or being passed. I was trying to balance not pushing too hard so there was something left for the run, but I died on the hills. Pulling into T2, I was tired but happy to be finished.

"When I started the run, which I thought would be my easy event, I felt like I wasn't even moving. My legs were wobbly and not doing what I wanted them to do. It was if they had a mind of their own. My natural form and pace never kicked in the entire 3.1 miles.

"Crossing the finish line was exhilarating. I wasn't last, my biggest fear, and I loved it. My first thought was, *I finally did it! My first triathlon.*

That first year Julie went on to do a few more, ending her season with the Santa Cruz Sentinel Triathlon in California that September. It was her first California triathlon and she quickly learned West Coast triathlons are a totally different animal from East Coast triathlons.

"This was my fourth triathlon. It was an odd distance, somewhere between a sprint and an Olympic distance. I still hadn't mastered the swim and here I was about to enter the Pacific Ocean. It was very intimidating, especially when I saw the ten-foot breakers crashing on shore. This was big surf. It was so big that the first wave of swimmers were thrown out of the waves back up on shore. Everyone was fighting to get beyond the breakers so they could start swimming the course. It took so much energy just to get into the water. The big story here for me was the frigid-cold water. The water temperature was fifty-five degrees. I was still wearing a borrowed sleeveless wet suit while everyone else was in full wetsuits, neck to feet, arms covered to wrists with two swim caps. I had no idea just how cold that water was. If only someone had warned me or explained cold-water swimming to me I would have been prepared.

"Jumping into that water was truly a surreal experience. My body went into shock from the cold and froze. I couldn't move. It was overwhelming and I got very frightened. I wanted to quit and tried to swim back to shore but I couldn't. I didn't think I would ever thaw out. All the other swimmers had gone and there I was, treading water and thinking I would die. Twenty yards away to my right was a volunteer on a surfboard and I called out for help but he couldn't hear me. I slowly started making my way over to him and when I reached him I asked if it would ever get better, if I would ever get warm. I think I was also delirious."

As Julie treaded water, her body started to adapt to the cold and she could finally move her limbs. She did a few test strokes and decided to stay in the race and forged ahead.

The swim course at the Sentinel Triathlon is an out and back around a pier. Seals share the water with the swimmers and can be heard barking from the rocks where they perch.

"I could see a few pink caps in the distance so I started swimming. When I got out of the water I never felt so relieved in my life. I also felt very proud for having the guts to stick with it.

"I never truly warmed up and getting back to T1, I was just glad the swim was over. I wore long sleeves and shirts but stayed cold. I felt like I was riding all alone since almost everyone from my wave was already out on the course. I finally warmed up in the run and actually passed people."

Julie learned a lot that day, unfortunately the hard way. If someone had warned her about the cold water and explained how to get through it and that your body does adapt, she would have been fine. Cold, but fine. A masters triathlete died from a heart attack that day in the swim.

The following year she went back to California for the famed Escape from Alcatraz. She was now prepared for the cold water but not for fighting the strong currents and tides of San Francisco Bay.

"Riding the boat out to Alcatraz was very intimidating. The water was choppy and the coastline seemed to get smaller and smaller. When the boat stopped, I jumped feetfirst into the bay, almost like jumping out of a plane. Bodies quickly scattered as they got pulled in all directions from the tide. It was a long swim and I was exhausted from fighting the tides. At one point I felt as if I wasn't even moving, in fact going backward. It was frightening being alone in the choppy water, exhausted, losing sight of my focal point on land. The nearest rescue person was so far away, I knew I would never reach them. My only option was to just swim and try to swim straight to shore. It took me fifty-nine minutes to complete the swim and when I reached shore I burst with relief, tired and grateful."

But there wasn't time to rest. The bike and run awaited, and Julie describes it as the hardest bike and run she ever did. Why does she do it?

"What makes triathletes so crazy that we keep signing up for more events even though we have such painful stories? It's for the feeling afterward. It is pure bliss when I cross the finish line, and I want to capture that feeling over and over. I need the bliss-blast. There's nothing as personally satisfying as knowing you've pushed yourself mentally and physically to your max. Regardless of the performance, it's that sheer high and grand sense of accomplishment that no one can question—simply because you did it! You finished it!

"There's no arguing that going to the start line of a triathlon is a self-imposed jail sentence. I think part of the reason we feel such personal satisfaction in doing triathlons is because it is one of the few sports that is individually performed. And you can bask in that sensation . . . and bask as long as you like . . . or as I like to think, as long as you need. It's a great drug.

"Of course, staying in shape (or as I often think of it, breaking even on the scale), having fun while training with friends, meeting new people and exploring new grounds, new towns, afoot or on bike, or even discovering new pools are all fringe benefits too. Seeing personal performance improve is always fun as well, especially for the average midpacker like myself who isn't necessarily out there for the podium.

"Because the race *is* the culmination of all the training (workout schedules, ups, downs, soreness, happiness, endless decisions, crazy choices, camaraderie, exhaustion, fatigue, ailments, successes, highs, lows, trials, and stewing over race prep, logistics, gear, gear, gear, et cetera), afterward you feel all that satisfaction boiled up into one giant smile. That smile, for me, usually stretches from my head down to my toes, both inside and out. No earthquake can shake that smile. And that is why I do 'em!"

What She Learned

"I think the lesson about acclimation to cold water deserves attention. If someone had just told me how cold it was going to be, I wouldn't have been in such shock. If someone had just told me to feel the water temperature ten minutes before the race, I might have been better off. If someone had told me I'd feel like I was having a seizure, but that it would soon pass and I'd be fine, I would have been in a much better place in those first five minutes of the race.

"I did Alcatraz a year later and the water temperature was also fifty-five degrees. But I swam in the bay the day before to prepare and got the freezer-burn-cold sensation out of my system. And then I knew what to expect. Sure enough, on race day I jumped in and was okay. My body felt the same as it did that Sentinel morning, but at least I knew the sensation of my frozen head was only temporary and would soon pass and that all my parts would be working shortly."

Other tips for first-timers are:

"Learn race protocol. In the run, don't throw your water cup unless you know you're clear of another racer. Keep alert and aware of what the other racers are doing. If you are not sure of race etiquette, ask the race director or race volunteers.

"Shave as much time as you can during transitions. Visualizing your T1 while getting out of the water can make for an efficient transition. Likewise, visualizing T2 in the last mile of your bike leg can also help shave off lots of minutes to your overall time.

"Practice your weakest link and spend more time training for it.

"Brick workouts are crucial. During the winter I do an hour Spinning class at the gym and then jump on the treadmill for a few miles. Once the weather gets warm, I do the same drill outdoors.

"You can't always pee in a wet suit, especially if the water is cold. Physically impossible. Make sure to hit the port-a-johns before the swim."

ROB UDEWITZ

DOB: 9-9-66
Residence: Manhattan, New York
Occupation: Psychologist
First Triathlon: 2003 Central Park (New York) Sprint Triathlon

Rob's first-triathlon story is a classic. He is a great runner, a lousy biker, and afraid of the water. Nothing in his past suggested he would want to do a triathlon. Running his first marathon at age seventeen, with a PR of 2:56, he knew what he was good at and probably should have stuck with that. But love makes people do silly things, including a triathlon.

"I'm a lousy swimmer. At summer camp when I was a kid I never made it out of Minnows. To be a Shark you had to swim the length of the lake and I wanted to be a Shark worse than anything. But on the day of the Shark test I got scared and sank to the bottom. That was the end of my swimming career. I wasn't any better on the bike. I grew up in Brooklyn. What did I need a bike for? I loved tennis, football, and basketball. Not the formal games, but pickup games in the streets and alleys. Like most New York City kids who grew up watching baseball, I dreamed of being a professional baseball player. My favorite television show was ABC's *Wide World of Sports* with Jim McKay. I had a respect for all sports and loved the drama that television packaged so well. Heck, I'd watch barrel jumping if it was on. When *Wide World of Sports* covered Julie Moss crawling across the finish line of the 1982 Hawaii Ironman, desperately trying to get to the finish line, looking like a punch-drunk boxer as she staggered, then fell, then got up and staggered some more, then fell, then got up, then fell, and eventually began to crawl toward the line, I was totally captured. It was one of the most amazing events to this day I have ever watched on television."

When he saw the New York City Marathon on television, he knew he had to run it. During his college years, Udewitz ran in Division III track at Binghamton University in upstate New York. Although he prefers the mile or 5K, he has run eight marathons.

"The media made the marathon bigger, better, and more interesting than a 10K. If you think about it, the decisions we make are heavily influenced by the media. If the sport of curling got national coverage and had funny beer commercials and hip athletes, we'd all be curling. After getting caught up with the media hype that the networks did on Grete Waitz and Bill Rodgers, I had to do it. And it turns out I was good at the marathon, so I stuck with it. That's the type of advice I give my clients. If you are good at something, stick with it. Too bad I didn't follow my own advice.

"Okay, I'll admit it. My girlfriend and I were drifting apart and I wanted to impress her so I told her I would do a triathlon. What was I thinking? I really didn't want to do it."

The first thing Udewitz had to do was face his fear of swimming. That was probably the only benefit of the entire experience.

"Fear is a learned behavior. My mother passed on her fear of swimming to me. I look forward to having kids someday and I don't want to pass my fear on to them. So it wasn't such a bad thing that I had to force myself to take swimming lessons. I quickly learned that just because I was a good runner with strong leg muscles didn't necessarily translate into being a good swimmer or that it would come naturally. I was still that little Minnow at camp. After a few lessons I got comfortable being in the water but never really took to it. I knew I wasn't going to drown, but I just couldn't settle and get the breathing thing down. I don't float well either. I had to borrow a bike, which was old and I didn't try out prior to the event. I really don't bike much."

The Central Park Triathlon begins with a quarter-mile swim in Lasker Pool, at the north end of the park, utilizing the lap lanes. The pool is only four feet deep so Udewitz didn't have to worry about drowning, although the water was cold and he did not wear a wet suit. The bike course is two loops around Central Park, twelve miles, and the run is five miles.

"I made it through the swim, barely. By the time I got out of the pool I'm sure there was only three feet of water left as I drank a few gallons attempting to swim. I wore tri shorts so I didn't have to do much in transition except get on the bike. The thing that bothers me about the bike event is the amount of money people spend to get a faster bike. That doesn't seem fair. I could be in better shape but if the guy next to me has a more efficient bike, he'll beat me. That's why I love running. It's pure. Not even an expensive pair of sneakers will make you run faster if you haven't put in the time and training. I'm a runner at heart so the bike wasn't terribly comfortable. I don't know how hard to push. I have no gauge like I do in running. I think like a runner, not a biker. *Do I brake on the hills? Do I coast?* If I ever take up this sport seriously, I'll have to put a lot more time learning about cycling.

"Finally, I got to run, the one event I knew I could do well in and was waiting for all morning. *Why didn't I just go for a run this morning? Why did I have to swim and bike before I got down to doing my favorite thing?*

"In the end, I have to say it was hard to relate to the sport. For me, raising the bar means doing something better, not necessarily doing multiple things really average. Okay, I did one. I still didn't get back with my girlfriend, so the experience has become somewhat tainted in my memory.

"I don't want to sound negative about the sport. I know I didn't train properly and my heart wasn't really into it. I would like to do another one and start over and do it right. Only then will I develop an appreciation for the sport and what it takes to compete at the top, like I do with my marathons. I will take swimming lessons and do the drills, join a masters team. I'll invest in a good bike. I'll put everything into it that I do with my running. On a mental level, I also lacked the confidence. I know I can build more confidence in my swimming and biking through practice but the biggest challenge for me would be to start thinking like a triathlete and not a runner. I really don't know if I will ever be able to do that."

What He Learned, Mistakes He Made

I did everything wrong and learned that I have to want to do one for myself in order to do one right. Having said that, the truth is I would do it all over again for exactly the same reason as the first."

REBECCAH WASSNER

Photo by Laurel Wassner

DOB: 9-1-75
Residence: Manhattan, New York
Occupation: Professional triathlete
First Triathlon: 1997 Danskin Women's Sprint Triathlon, Baltimore, Maryland

Rebeccah (Bec) Wassner started swimming on a year-round YMCA swim team at age eight. In junior high, she and her twin sister joined the cross country team. Their talent became immediately apparent, and running soon became just as important. By the time she was in college running had eclipsed swimming as her main event.

"I always thought about doing a triathlon. My high school swim coach was the first person to suggest I do one and then a teammate on my college track team, a pro triathlete from Australia, talked about triathlons and it sounded so interesting. With those words of encouragement and the fact that I was already a competitive swimmer and runner, it seemed like the natural thing to do.

"I had just graduated college and was living at home with my family in Maryland when I heard about the Danskin Women's Triathlon in Baltimore. The timing was ideal. I also liked the fact that it was a rather small field, just a few hundred women, and a sprint distance, which would be comfortable for a first-timer.

"I have to admit I really didn't train for it. I was still running road races, swimming occasionally, and I had a hybrid bike I used to get around campus but I didn't train on it. On the day of the race, my sister showed up with her road bike thinking it would be better than my hybrid, but it was a real clunker, old and rusty. Still, it was better than my hybrid, so I took a few spins around the parking lot right before the race and decided to use it."

Through her background in sports, Wassner is naturally competitive and thought she had a chance to place, even with the lack of training and preparation. But when she got to the staging area she was a bit overwhelmed by the professional-looking women, their expensive bikes and other equipment, and their definite demeanor of having done this before.

"I was a bit taken back at all the equipment being laid out. All I came with was an old bike and a pair of running shoes. I come from a sport where all you need is a pair of sneakers and you're off. But I didn't let it get to me and the flip side of being a first-timer is not knowing how under-prepared I was. All the expensive bikes and gear and wetsuits were lost on me. I hadn't a clue what I was looking at. Ignorance truly was bliss that morning."

Wassner did what every first timer does in the staging area: she looked around and copied everyone else. But all she had to lay out on her towel was her running shoes.

"Standing at the edge of the water waiting for the start, I thought I would be confident but as I looked around at the other women, some of them looked like they were pretty decent swimmers as well. And the swim was in a river, a triangular course, not the pools I was used to. I was thinking how different this was from my normal competitive swimming, when I had a lane all to myself. Instead, I was looking at cold, dirty water and I started to get nervous.

"I hit the water and swam as fast as I could but got lost in the shuffle. I gradually caught up and came out of the water in the top ten.

"Running back to transition, I forgot where I put my bike and kept circling the staging area until I finally found it. Out on the course, people were passing me like I was standing still. Young and old, all sizes, it didn't matter. I was not getting anywhere fast. This was a new experience for me. As a runner, I'm used to people passing me and then at some point I pass them and we play this competitive game to wear each other down. That's the strategy in road racing, but in this case, there was no way I could stay with anyone passing me. Although this was new to me, the fact that I couldn't figure out the right strategy bothered me the entire twelve miles."

Getting off the bike, Wassner was still fresh because she hadn't pushed herself. That wasn't a conscious ploy; she just didn't know how much to push. In retrospect she could have gone a lot faster but was using her background as a runner, not a biker, to guide her.

"Finally I got to run and started passing people right and left. I was running hard and the spectators kept yelling at me to slow down. But to me a 5K is nothing and since I didn't hammer on the bike I had plenty of energy left and ran the 5K around 18:00 flat."

She placed in her age group and came home with an award. She decided to give the sport a chance and bought a triathlon bike. However, just a few weeks later, she was invited to participate in a highly selective marathon training camp. Wassner decided not to pass up on this opportunity, and shifted focus back to running. She joined the training camp with the hope of making the Olympic marathon trials. Over the course of the next two years she ran three marathons with a PR of 2:55.

"When I didn't make the trials, I decided to go back to the triathlon. Marathons are just too tough on the body. And besides that, it takes months of training and all that preparation can be blown in one day by something as elusive as the weather. I felt I had a better chance with triathlons."

At age twenty-seven, Wassner joined a masters swim team, dusted off the new bike she had yet to ride, and concentrated solely on triathlon training. She was working full time as a CPA and after doing a few more sprint distances and one Olympic, she set her sights on qualifying for the Triathlon World Championships. To qualify she had to be ranked in the top sixteen of her age group by USA Triathlon, the governing body of the sport. If she made it to the worlds she decided she would go professional.

"I met experienced age-group triathletes who took me under their wing and taught me about cycling. I also swam regularly at Chelsea Piers and continued to run with my competitive running club, Moving Comfort. The running coach, Gordon Bakoulis, was a world-class marathoner so I knew I was getting great training. I kept racing and every time I did a tri

I learned something new and improved my splits. For me, the bike was the biggest area of improvement, and it took about a year before everything just clicked and I felt comfortable competing on the bike. I also worked out with a coach who gave me a plan to follow, which really helped. I needed the structure of following a routine and positioning the workouts for the best overall results.

"In 2003, the World Champs were held in New Zealand. I had always wanted to go there and I knew that the Southern Hemisphere is where the toughest competition is, so I set my sites on qualifying. It was an expensive trip, but worth it. The course, in Queenstown, was very hilly and challenging and I was happy to take sixth place in my age group.

"That was a real turning point for me and at the age of twenty-eight, I made the decision to go pro. A professional development team was forming in Florida so I joined them. They paid for coaching, travel expenses, and race entry fees. I was on my own for rent and food. In my first year, I won enough to live on but not much extra so I worked full-time in the off-season. I also started looking for a sponsor to offset my expenses and in 2005 decided to live part of the year at the Olympic Training Center. I also became a member of Team Lipton, the professional cycling and multisport team. That's been a tremendous help in gaining national exposure and also getting outfitted with top-of-the-line gear."

After a promising 2004 season, in which she was named USA Triathlon's Elite Rookie of the Year, Wassner suffered a pelvic stress fracture in early 2005. The fracture took eight months to heal, so she spent the entire triathlon season on the sidelines—rehabbing and recovering. "The injury was devastating because I was in great shape and I had finally figured out what it takes to be a professional. I was looking forward competing in World Cup races and climbing up the world rankings."

As a professional, her life has been reduced to training and traveling to events but she loves it. Her current goal is to make the US triathlon team for the 2008 Olympics in Beijing.

"Most of what I do revolves around training and racing. As for a social life, I usually allow myself a few nights a month to have fun and blow off steam. When I'm living at a training camp, with a team, we are all doing the same thing. Everyone gets up early and goes to bed early. When I'm back home in New York City, it is a bit harder—it is hard to explain that I need to be in bed by 8 P.M.! But I'm focused on my goals and do what it takes to make the most of my workouts. My friends and family are used to it by now and it doesn't feel different. It's what I've been doing for a few years now and I love it. I've learned that you have to have balance; it can't just be triathlon all the time."

Wassner explains that a typical day's training starts around 5 A.M. and finishes up in the afternoon. A hard day of training usually starts with an hour-and-a-half swim, followed by an hour of Pilates or weights. A few hours' break for eating, stretching, and recovery, then back out for a midday bike ride, lasting from one to three hours, and finally, an afternoon run—either a track workout or a distance run.

"Not every day is that intense; on some days, all I do is a long run. These are the days when I actually get to fit in something different, like rock climbing or kayaking. Even though I am no longer working full time, it still seems like there are not enough hours in the week to fit everything in."

Wassner is also looking down the road at her future. If she makes her goal of competing on the Olympic team, she can retire and feel fulfilled. If she doesn't, she still has lots of options and the realization that she lived out her dream of being a professional triathlete.

Wassner made a list of essential equipment and things to do the morning of the event:

Essential Equipment (should be a checklist kept by the duffel bag)

bike

helmet

swimsuit

wet suit

running shoes

goggles

towel to lay on the ground to mark your transition area (a bright one that it is easy to spot)

elastic shoelaces

spare tubes

CO_2 cartridges

water bottles (one filled with water, one with sports drink)

GU/PowerGel (this can be taped to the bike)

sunglasses

Triathlon Racing Kit (to keep in the race bag)

Sportslick—for blister prevention.

sunscreen

medical tape (helpful in taping things to the bike)

GU

race belt

Nonessentials (but nice to have)

floor bike pump

running hat

extra clothes to change into after the race

Things to Do Race Morning

"Get to the race early so that you can get a good transition spot.

"Make a mental note of where your transition area is—maybe by counting how many rows you are from the end.

"Set up transition area: lay out everything you need.

"Put Sportslick in your running shoes (don't skimp!).

"Ride your bike around to make sure it is working properly, if something doesn't seem right, visit the bike mechanic on-site.

"Make sure your tires are pumped up.

"Rack your bike after making sure you've left it in the right gear.

"Familiarize yourself with the course, especially the entrances and exits of the transition area.

"Figure out exactly what time your wave goes off, so that you can time your warm up and when you need to eat.

"Eat something about an hour before the race (I usually eat honey on a bagel and drink coffee) and make sure you are well hydrated."

DAVID WEINGARD

DOB: 9-26-63
Residence: Manhattan, New York
Occupation: Microsoft sales
First Triathlon: 1991 Westchester Sprint Triathlon, Rye, New York

David Weingard has a passion for running and doing triathlons. He ran the 1980 New York City Marathon when he was just seventeen years old and did his first triathlon in 1991 when the sport was still being discovered on the East Coast. His athletic life took a sudden crash in the summer of 2000 while he was training for an eight-stage survival triathlon. Overly fatigued, he went to the doctor and was diagnosed with type 1 diabetes. Never the quitter, he learned how to live life as a diabetic and went on to run the New York City Marathon ten weeks after the devastating news, finishing the race one minute off his 3:43 PR. In 2003 he completed the Lake Placid Ironman and two years later did the 2005 Ironman Coeur d'Alene in Idaho, raising more than twenty-four thousand dollars for the Juvenile Diabetes Research Foundation. "I'm trying to spread the message that we can get through rough patches one step at a time," says Weingard. Up until his diagnosis, his life was a pretty smooth ride.

"I started running at fifteen and ran on my high school cross-country team. As I became a better runner, I gravitated to long distance and loved it. I did my first marathon at age seventeen in 4:07.

"When I heard about this new sport that involved swimming, biking, and running I was interested and then got really excited when I saw the Hawaii Ironman on television. It looked like an amazing challenge and I thought the cross-training would be good for my running."

Although Weingard was very impressed with the Hawaii Ironman, he never entertained the thought of doing one. He thought it would be just as cool and satisfying to do the shorter distances. Plus he looked forward to the challenge of learning to swim and bike effectively.

"I started to read triathlon magazines, searched for information on how to train, and joined a pool to become a better swimmer. Married with my first child on the way, I thought the focus of training would relieve some of the stress I was feeling. I wasn't looking to win, just wanted to finish.

"I broke out my old college clunker and did some fifteen-mile rides and that was it for the bike training. I didn't do any brick training and as a runner, didn't bother with any special running drills. It actually never dawned on me to link the three sports together. I viewed them as three separate events, not three consecutive events linked with no rest in between. I didn't even bother with a wet suit because I didn't know if I would like the sport enough to incur costs. My attitude was to just wing it and have fun.

"The day of the event, the field of seven hundred mostly first-timers at the Westchester Triathlon didn't really know how to pull this together or what to expect. I clearly remember when people came out of the water they literally took off all their clothes, dried off, and changed into their bike clothes. Men and woman, standing naked in front of each other and not caring. That's how new the sport was. We didn't have the benefit of all the instructional books and magazines that are available today.

"After getting on the bike, I realized I should have done some more bike training. I was tired from the swim and my old college bike, hefty to begin with, felt like it weighed five hundred pounds. That was definitely the low point of the three events.

"Finally, I got to run, the event I had been waiting for all morning. At that time, the run finished on a high school track and I felt like a million bucks crossing the finish line. It was an amazing day and I held on to that T-shirt for fifteen years. Although the marathon was a bigger event, I felt extreme pride in finishing a triathlon."

Back in 1991, to finish a triathlon was a huge deal even at the sprint distance. Weingard did two more sprint triathlons that season and continued to do them for the next seven years, juggling his training while attending to his family of three sons (Steven, Daniel and Jacob) and more job responsibility. In 1998 he stepped up to the half Ironman Triathlon in Rhode Island and finally got hooked.

"After the half, I knew I had to do a full Ironman. I was now committed to investing in a new bike, wet suit, the whole nine yards. There was no going back."

He worked with Long Island Team in Training (TNT) and pioneered their efforts with triathlon. He chose TNT for the its support for finding a cure for cancer and related diseases. His mother died of breast cancer at the age of forty so he wanted to raise money for the Leukemia Society in her honor. For six months he juggled family life, a full-time job, the training, and fund-raising for TNT in order to get ready for the Roth Ironman in Germany, in June 1999. At the time, there weren't many Ironman events in the United States, which is why he made the decision to go to Germany. While training, Weingard made the psychological switch from marathoner to triathlete, incorporating all three sports into his weekly training.

Back from Germany, he kept up his weekly training and the next year began training for an eight-stage survival triathlon in the Shawangunk Mountains in New Paltz, New York, called SOS. Feeling abnormally fatigued and experiencing rapid weight loss, he went to the doctor for some blood work and was given the news that would change his life forever. He was diagnosed with type 1 diabetes, formerly referred to as juvenile diabetes, characterized by high blood glucose levels. The disease occurs when the body's immune system attacks and destroys the insulin-producing cells in the pancreas, which stops producing insulin.

"My first thought after hearing the news was, *Will I die?* Then I heard all the potential complications like heart problems, loss of vision, amputation. I couldn't believe it. I didn't even know what type 1 diabetes was and I had it. I went home with a blood test kit, an insulin pump, and a needle.

"The only thing I knew for certain was that I would give 100 percent of my energy to fight this the best way I could and vowed not to let the disease change my life. Trying to keep that vow has been a humbling journey."

With a lot of conviction and personal faith, ten weeks later he ran the 2000 New York City Marathon, finishing one minute off his personal best time. He checked his blood levels every three miles during the marathon with a testing kit he carries in his shorts pocket. He also carries glucose tablets and an insulin pump clipped to his shorts. But Weingard doesn't let the extra baggage of having type 1 diabetes interfere with his running or his life. In June 2001 he ventured back into triathlons, a very risky undertaking.

"The risk of doing a triathlon of any length as a diabetic is that I have to disconnect from my insulin pump during the swim. For anywhere from half an hour up to two hours, my body is exercising at a high level but not getting the insulin it needs. I could become groggy, disoriented, I could pass out; and I could even die.

"I selected a sprint distance for my first reentry into the sport and was very scared. I was literally starting out all over again, being very cautious and conscientious. I had to prove to myself I could do it. My doctors weren't comfortable with it, just told me to be careful. The irony of diabetes is that the one thing you can do for maintenance prevention is exercise, stay in shape, and follow healthy nutrition. But doing exercise, especially extreme exercise, and keeping on top of my blood sugar levels is very complex. To prepare for the triathlon I did simulations of what I would do on the day of the race: got up at the same hour, ate the same foods at the same time. The swim is the most difficult phase of the triathlon for me because during the swim I can't monitor myself."

He pulled off the sprint distance early in the summer 2001 season and then took a chance and competed in the Escape from Alcatraz Triathlon in San Francisco, a major comeback for Weingard for many reasons.

"I was very, very nervous doing Alcatraz. For the first time since being diagnosed I would be without my insulin pump for almost two hours. I left the pump inside my bike helmet at transition and walked away thinking I could die out there in the chilly waters of San Francisco Bay. Boarding the boat to Alcatraz, I kept looking at the shore hoping I would make it back. The mile-and-a-half swim seemed to take forever. Halfway there, I looked up to see San Francisco in front of me and Alcatraz behind me. I had been gone for over an hour. I knew I had to focus and not panic if I wanted to reach shore and see my kids again. I put my head back in the water and didn't stop till I reached shore. Finishing that triathlon was a turning point for me. I knew I could go farther.

In 2002 he completed the Eagleman Half Ironman in Maryland, his first major distance triathlon as a diabetic. He practiced for months, monitoring his blood sugar levels, insulin regulation, and diet. He taped a testing kit to his bike aerobars and tested his blood sugar seventeen times during the six hours and twenty minutes it took him to complete the course.

"I cried when I crossed the finish line at Eagleman. I felt in some way I had beat diabetes. And I knew I could go on and do a full Ironman as a diabetic."

He immediately started training for the 2003 Lake Placid Ironman, and raised eleven thousand dollars for the Juvenile Diabetes Research Foundation (JDRF). He completed the event, becoming one of a handful of type 1 diabetics in the world to ever complete an Ironman race. After Lake Placid, David continued marathon and triathlon racing, and in June 2005 he completed Ironman Coeur d'Alene in Idaho. He clocked his fastest swim time despite breaking a bone in his hand four weeks prior to the race. In November 2005, he ran his twenty-fifth New York City Marathon in 4:37, just thirty minutes over his time as a seventeen-year-old. Every day, every event, is a test for Weingard. At Lake Placid it rained and his testing kit stopped working. Now he travels with a backup kit. "My testing kit looks like a cell phone propped up on my bars and I get a look of crazy looks. Someone asked me if I was sending e-mails during the race.

"We all have tough moments in life and need to know we'll get though them. Living with diabetes and continuing my life as a triathlete has taught me anything is possible. My triathlon life came full circle in 2005 when I returned to the Westchester Triathlon. When I did my first one in 1991 I was a young, healthy twenty-seven-year-old kid. Fifteen years later I returned a dad of three boys and with diabetes."

Weingard has raised close to fifty thousand dollars for JDRF and the

Leukemia Society. He is a sought-after speaker and inspires everyone who meets him with his courage, discipline, and accomplishments. He doesn't let diabetes get in the way of meeting his goals. He receives e-mails and letters from people around the world asking for advice and thanking him for his positive energy.

Weingard is currently looking for a way to combine his professional background with his passion for helping people with diabetes by launching an online service, www.fitness4diabetics.com, that will provide integrated fitness and nutritional services to people with diabetes.

"The Ironman motto is 'Anything is Possible.' I've taken that motto as my own. In believing that anything truly is possible, my accomplishments have allowed me to make a difference in the world by giving people the confidence that they too can live with, and overcome, their own obstacles."

What He's Learned

"I can sum this up in two thoughts: Always be prepared for anything, and always have a positive attitude no matter what obstacles come your way. Being prepared means having backup gear. Flat tires happen. Make sure you have a spare and know how to put it on. Warm days turn cold and vice versa. Make sure you have extra clothes for any weather condition. As a diabetic, my backup gear also includes extra insulin pumps, testing kits, and other medical supplies. If any of my medical supplies fail me, it can be a lot worse than a flat tire; it could be more like a flatliner.

"And if that flat tire happens, approach it with a positive attitude. Don't waste energy brewing and stewing over what went wrong. Fix it and get on with the race. You never know who else may have had a flat tire, or a bad swim, or developed a sore blister. Stay focused on your own race and in the end, be proud of your accomplishments."

SCOTT WILLETT

DOB: 12-20-61
Residence: New Paltz, New York
Occupation: N.Y. University triathlon coach, Team in Training N.Y. City chapter coach
First Triathlon: 1980 Carleton College Sprint Triathlon, Northfield, Minnesota

The first thing you notice about Scott Willett is his English accent. The second is that he is darn funny. He's the type of coach who keeps you laughing all the time even though you're in pain from the drills. His coaching mantra is: If you're not having a fun time, you won't have a good time. He doesn't keep records or logs, preferring to view every race—and he has done over 250—as his first one. He's proud of his midpack finishing times, although he has won a few triathlons along the way to becoming a full-time coach. He has a true passion for the sport, which he feels he grew up with, and wants everyone else to love it as much as he does. But Willett is the first to admit he hasn't grown up yet and loves being a kid and surrounded by kids, especially his own. The last thing he tells his athletes before a race is to enjoy the process. "Your split times will fade, but the memory will stay forever."

"I spent my formative years in England, in a countryside commuter town south of London. My athletic experience was limited to riding to the store for bits of sweets. Maybe I took too many rides to the candy store, as I was a bit chubby. I only ran when other kids chased me and my swimming event was the plunge, an event that consists of diving off the side of the pool and gliding at the bottom to the other side. The winner is the one who can glide the farthest. There's no real swimming involved. I also played soccer and rugby, poorly.

"In 1979 I transferred to a small liberal arts college in Minnesota, my first time in America. I was shy but having an accent made me a bit of an anomaly, so I had to make friends. I fancied the female lifeguard at the pool so I started swimming laps. One of the other lifeguards mentioned a triathlon at a local school, Carleton College, an event that combined swimming, biking, and running. None of us had ever heard of a triathlon since the sport was in its infancy stages, but it sounded interesting so I entered the event. I didn't do any training, just showed up on race day with a borrowed bike.

"It was a pool swim and since I had been doing laps that wasn't too bad. Then we biked the country roads. I was enjoying myself until I fell off my bike. My shoelace had wrapped around the pedal crank and I wasn't paying attention because at that moment a dog was chasing me and I was pedaling furiously to get away from the dog and suddenly I was yanked off the bike. Freaked out, flipped over, and landed on the ground. I got back up, dusted myself off, and kept going. It was a long, windy twenty-mile ride and it wasn't fun.

"When I finished the bike and dismounted to go back to T2, I saw a chap sitting on a folding chair cheering me on. I'd seen him at the beginning of the race so I knew he was a competitor and thought to myself *What a loser; he must have quit to be sitting there so calmly.* Turns out he had finished way before me and was resting. That's how far behind I was.

"I can still visualize the run. I say I was running but I really wasn't. My legs had locked so badly from the bike, I couldn't get them to move. Usually my legs are like strong saplings but that day they turned into oak trees and wouldn't perform at all. I resembled Forrest Gump, pushing myself to Run, Scott, Run. I finished the event in a tortured state. It was a horrendous experience.

"The next year I transferred to New York University. Some of the athletes were talking about starting a triathlon club and since I had done one I thought it would be an excellent opportunity to torture others the same way I have been tortured by my friends who got me into this sport. With funding from the university, we started out with sixteen members and today have more than one hundred. I guess you could say we grew with the sport. It's a very vibrant group of like-minded people. We started out doing sprint-distance triathlons and moved up to the Ironman. In 1998, WNBC Sports did a documentary on me and some members of the NYU club training for the Florida Ironman.

"Anyone who gets into this sport has to realize they come to it from their own choosing. They are the ones pushing the 'on' button and at any time they have the power and freedom to push the 'off' button. As a coach, I don't necessarily torture people as much as they are torturing themselves. As to why I coach triathlon, I'd need years of deep analysis to figure that one out but I have always fancied an adventure. I swam around Manhattan, I've attempted a triple Ironman (7.2-mile swim, 212-mile bike and 52.4-mile run) and other ultra-events. For me, there is something about the repetitive motion of endurance sports that I find pleasantly lulling."

Willett didn't do another triathlon after Carleton College until four years later. He was busy hitchhiking across the country and doing his own Zen style of maintenance.

"In 1983 I did my next triathlon, a sprint distance, in Annandale, New Jersey. I really didn't consider the Carleton College Triathlon a proper event so I needed to do one where I got the full impact. I bought my first Trek bike for the outrageous price of four hundred dollars. I've always bought into the mantra that if you believe you can do it, you can. I still didn't know how to train but for some reason I came out of the water first (it was a mass start for all participants—in those days there were no 'wave starts') and was on a huge high as I ran into T1. I never practiced transition areas and didn't have all my gear neatly lined up so I just grabbed the first thing I saw, which was my bike helmet, a big round Bell V1 Pro, which looked and fit like a hat umbrella. The next thing I grabbed was my bike shirt, which I tried to pull over the helmet. The shirt got stuck on the helmet and I stood there for what seemed an eternity trying to pull it down, which only made matters worse. My girlfriend was screaming from the sideline to take off the helmet, which made perfect sense but I had no sense at the time. Finally, I took off the shirt, removed the helmet, and did it in the proper order. I learned two things that day: Women are usually right, and practice transitions.

"By now, I blew my big lead from the water and was passed by at least fifty people. On the run I was passed by another fifty and ended up at the back of the pack. It was a real challenge and I truly enjoyed it."

Six weeks later Willett did his first half Ironman at Tupper Lake, and a month later he did an Ironman on Cape Cod. He was hooked.

"My goal has always been to avoid getting better so I don't have to compete against myself and I don't ever have to take myself seriously. It gives me the perfect excuse for being slow. Nowadays my goal has become to just cover the distance and finish. I'm not talented but I am willing to work hard. That and sheer luck gets me through my triathlons. I still remember the first one I won. I was dumbstruck with awe. I thought there must have been a huge mistake, a quirk in the universe that day."

These days Willett is busy with his NYU Triathlon Club as well as being the Team in Training triathlon coach for the New York City region since 2002. He is also co-founder of a group called TriLife Coaching. He still competes 'with dignity.' His life is also filled with a wonderful wife, Julie Denney, an accomplished triathlete, and two kids, Wells and Lake, so he has learned the importance of balance.

His Advice for First-Timers

"I always tell my students to keep in touch with their motivation, and always keep foremost in their head the reason they are doing the triathlon event in the first place. We all have an inner athlete inside us and I tell my students to start the practice session by greeting their inner athlete. How you define yourself as an athlete is how you will face challenges.

"Don't do what I did, which is to go into the event blind. I spent years making mistakes and getting injuries. With the knowledge and training advice offered today there is no reason for injuries if you practice caution and patience.

"Focus on the things that need attention. What is your weakest link? Most first-timers, and some experienced athletes as well, view their weak link like the white elephant in the room: Everyone sees it but them.

"Know what your body feels like when it is pushed or called upon to do more. High-intensity training is important so that on race day you know when to push and how much to push before you spend it all. Don't let the song, 'Eye of the Tiger' fuel you with false intensity. You want to finish the race strong. Train hard during practice so you can finish hard at the event.

"On event day, race your own race, not someone else's. It is very risky to go out too fast just to keep up with others. You want to finish and make it a memorable day, not DNF. Start to sprint and try to beat someone else when you can hear the finish-line music, not before.

"Be flexible with your training plan. If you scheduled a Spinning class and the weather allows for outdoor biking, then go outside. Spinning classes do not make up for road biking. They are a great adjunct but cannot replace getting out on the road.

"Strengthen the quads and lungs with squats and lunges. You'll need the strength in your legs for the bike and run.

"The most important word of advice I can give to all levels of triathletes is to be patient.

"Finally, always remember that life is full of challenges. What defines you as an athlete is how you respond to those challenges. If you train and race properly, you'll be rewarded with challenges for a lifetime."

JAYNE WILLIAMS

DOB: 8-1-63
Residence: Mountain View, California
Occupation: Grant writer, author
First Triathlon: 2002 Wildflower Mountain Bike Sprint Triathlon, San Antonio, California

It takes a lot of chutzpah in our weight-obsessed culture to write a book about yourself called Slow Fat Triathlete, *but that is what Jayne Williams did. She ventured into the sport and found she belonged. After years of poor eating habits and steady increments of weight gain, she chowed her way up to 269 pounds before deciding she'd have enough of being the fat girl and found the stamina and discipline to do something about it. She started walking around the block and slowly added more distance, then jogged, then more jogs and kept walking and jogging all the way to her first triathlon. Nothing about Jayne is traditional or standard. She has a BA in Russian from Harvard, an MA from UC Berkeley in Slavic literature, has organized whitewater-rafting expeditions in Siberia and camped on the banks of the Zambezi River in Africa. She feels that all these experiences prepared her in some strange way to take on triathlons. In her book she combines two f-words,* fat *and* fun, *and invites the reader into her world which turns out to be more about the fun and less about the fat.*

"I decided to write my book for people like me, who have struggled their whole lives with a few extra pounds and always talked about doing something about it but never did. It's certainly not a diet book and it certainly isn't a training book for serious triathletes. You won't get faster but you may lose a few pounds.

"When I was growing up I was a mixture of the tomboy, active kid, and bookworm. If I didn't have my nose pressed to a book, I was outside running around climbing trees, riding my bike, playing basketball and softball but I never made it onto a high school sports team. During my senior year at Harvard I took up rugby and loved it. After college I attended UC Berkeley. I had great plans to be a teacher but the administrative end didn't appeal to me so I turned to research. I stayed active riding my bike and swimming but never ran. Berkeley has a lot of hills and I got some great riding in before my bike my stolen."

Despite being active, Jayne steadily gained weight and at 220 pounds on her five-foot-nine-inch frame, she was overweight. Her biggest downfall was poor eating habits, which contributed to a greater risk of injury.

"When I got injured I'd stop exercising but still indulge in the junk food and put on the weight again. Then I'd start exercising, get down to 170, and get injured again and soon I'd be right back where I started. I was definitely on the yo-yo plan."

A desk job didn't help matters. She sat in a cubicle all day working on a keyboard. That lead to tendinitis in the shoulder and she stopped exercising. Her weight ballooned to 269 pounds.

Jayne was determined to lose the weight. She started walking and stuck with it. She also restricted her calorie intake and between the two disciplines the weight came off. For the first time in her life, at age thirty-six, she started to feel healthy.

"The walking turned into jogging. A year after I started my exercise program I ran my first 5K, then did a 10K. Around this time, in 2001, a friend of mine did his first sprint triathlon and I went to cheer for him. I didn't realize there were triathlon distances less than the Ironman, which I had seen on television. Everyone seemed to be having so much fun, like being a kid again. You spend some time in the water splashing around, get out, ride your bike for a while, and then go for a run. Heck, I did that all day long as a kid. I also remember seeing all the different body types and being surprised that not everyone was a zero-fat hard lean athlete. I walked away from that event thinking I could actually do one. The biggest draw for me was the fun part. This was a very friendly low-key triathlon. Among the five-thousand-dollar bikes were old-time Schwinns with straw baskets on the handle bars and some with streamers blowing in the breeze.

"The more I thought about doing a triathlon, the more appealing the thought became. I knew I could swim and ride a bike and could get through a run even if I had to walk it. I hadn't ridden a bike since mine was stolen at Berkeley so I bought a recumbent bike, which is kind of like a luge with a backrest on wheels, but then I found out they are illegal for triathlon events so I bought a bike on eBay for $375."

Jayne also joined the Silicon Valley Triathlon Club in the fall of 2001, realizing she needed a support group and professional advice on how to tackle her first triathlon. The club was welcoming, friendly, and everything she needed. She worked out with them doing weekend rides and runs, lap swimming, and track meets. They practiced transitions and did a series of bricks. She also put her nose back in books and studied triathlon like a history geek.

"I gave myself a long lead time before settling on a triathlon. My research skills came in handy as I searched for the ideal event. I wanted to do one the next spring and signed up for Wildflower Sprint Mountain Bike as it was the earliest spring event; my club sends about a hundred members to the event, and it becomes like a huge party. I also chose the mountain bike event because a mountain bike was easier for me to ride than a road bike with all my tendencies to get tendinitis. I was putting in an average of one hour a day, six days a week. I already knew I was going to do more than one and trained hard."

The Wildflower Triathlon weekend is nothing short of a blast. Thousands of triathletes of all levels camp out in a beautiful valley. The air is filled with excitement and an intense level of energy. You can't help but be swooned by its song. The weekend events include a mountain bike sprint distance, a half Ironman, and a full Ironman. It's the Woodstock of Triathlon.

"Going into the event, I had no fear, just pure elation. I knew I was ready and would finish. In fact my tri club had a workout on the exact course a month before so that was an added bonus going into the race. My only concern was not injuring myself. That, and getting in and out of my wet suit."

In her book, Jayne devotes two pages to her purchase and use of a wet suit. She bought her first one on eBay three weeks before the event and was thrilled when it arrived, but the thrill quickly turned to torture when she tried it on. In her attempt to yank and pull up the "constrictive monster" she poked a hole in it with her fingernail, not an uncommon occurrence for first-time wet suit wearers. As she stood in her living room wrestling with the monster, her husband got concerned she would actually injure herself just getting into the darn thing, never mind doing a triathlon.

"Let me add that although I didn't have any fear I was full of anxiety and the wet suit had a lot to do with that. Would I get it on? Get it off? Would I bonk on the bike? Crash on the run? Also, it was my first open water swim and I worried about staying on course. At Wildflower you enter the water from a boat ramp. Being large and very comfortable in the water, I decided to just get right in the flow and use my size and my rugby skills from college to plow right up the middle of the pack. The swim was great, very peaceful once I found my spot. The morning sun was coming up over the hill and it was just so beautiful. I was loving it.

"Running back to transition I was able to work on peeling off the wet suit and managed to get it off rather quickly and get on the bike. Since I had already done the course there were no surprises. I actually passed people on the bike, which was awesome. The last mile of the bike course is all downhill. I entered transition all pumped and rarin' to start the run.

"I knew the run wouldn't be my best event, even though it's only two miles. My legs were like rubber when I tried to get going and I realized I'd probably gone too hard on the bike. I was barely managing eleven-minute miles. But it's a pretty run, rolling hills along the lake with lots of vistas and scenery. The last half mile I was grimacing and gasping and pumping my legs to try and get up a hill that my grandma wouldn't notice on a bad day. When I saw Tim standing at the finish cheering for me, I actually picked up the pace and went from a grimace to a huge grim. It's a beautiful finish line and when I cross it I am ecstatic. Volunteers surround me draping a medal around my neck, clipping off my chip from my shoe, handing me a towel, T-shirt, water, and fruit. Such luxurious treatment! I couldn't believe it. I was so proud of myself. After months of training and reading and dreaming, it finally happened. I did a triathlon and couldn't wait to do the next one."

Two weeks later Jayne did another longer sprint distance but had to DNF due to a flat tire. Being a true competitor, she did the run anyway even though she was disqualified. In her first triathlon season Jayne did four triathlons, two at the sprint distance and two at the Olympic distance. So far she has done twenty, averaging about six a season, and worked her way up to a half Ironman in 2003 and 2004.

"I am a triathlete. It's so cool to be able to say that and really believe it. I like all the triathlons I've done and they have taken me to great spots like Fairbanks, Alaska, and Las Vegas. My weight continues to be an issue and I don't lose weight just doing triathlons. When I want to lose weight I rely on Weight Watchers. They actually have a Weight Watchers online triathlon club and I've met some of the gals at events.

"I know I will do a full Ironman some day but will have to lose weight first. I can't think of doing one carrying all that extra weight around with me. Not a good idea. I've picked out Ironman Canada later in 2006 so if I can lose the weight in time, I'll go for it. I plan to live out all my athletic dreams and I am not going to let my slow, fat body stop me."

What She Learned

"The most important lesson for first time triathletes is to just have fun. Don't worry about a time or transitions or how many people are passing you. Unless you plan on standing on the podium, relax and enjoy yourself.

"Never buy a wet suit without trying it on first. And don't pull on it with your fingernails in your attempts to get it on.

"Always have a checklist of your essentials before going to the event.

"Don't be intimidated by all the speedy bikes. Just because the bike looks fast doesn't mean the owner is.

"Don't invest a lot of money in equipment before you know you like triathlon and plan to do more.

"Make up a positive mantra and repeat it to yourself throughout the event.

"Try to cover the bike and run course before the event if possible. If not, at least try to see the last few miles of the course."

TEAM EXCEL

In 1990, physical therapists Matthew Gibble and Gary Flink, who compete at triathlon distances ranging from the sprint to the Ironman, started Excel Orthopedic Rehabilitation in Fort Lee, New Jersey. Matthew Gibble has completed Ironman USA three times. Gary Flink is a four-time Ironman finisher, having completed Ironman Canada two times, Ironman USA, and the Ironman Triathlon World Championships held in Kona, Hawaii. Their practice soon attracted the top professional athletes in the tristate area who required physical rehabilitation such as Jason Kidd of the New Jersey Nets and Patrick Ewing.

Hoping to promote good health and physical fitness through proper exercise and good nutrition, Gibble and Flink started Team Excel in 1999. According to Flink, "Joining a team is the best way to train for a triathlon. It gives a sense of camaraderie, support, an in-depth knowledge base about the sport from other members, and, most importantly, group training. It's hard enough to put in the training to compete in a multi-sport event but to do it alone makes it more difficult. Knowing your buddies are waiting for you at six o'clock on a Saturday morning for a group run makes it easier to get out of bed."

Team Excel is geared to all levels of triathletes, from beginners to Ironman competitors, and they have seen a rise in membership in the last few years as the sport has caught on. "Everyone has different goals and we accommodate that," says Flink, who has seen many members start out content with just the sprint distance and before long begin training for an Ironman. "This sport is contagious. Members are always reevaluating their goals as they get stronger and more experienced."

Here are some Team Excel members:

BILL EICKELBERG

DOB: 5-21-53
Residence: Leonia, New Jersey
Occupation: Health and physical education teacher, Leonia High School
First Triathlon: 1998 Oyster Bay (New York) Sprint Triathlon

Bill grew up in Amityville, New York. He was swimming at age six and surfing by age ten. In high school he took up soccer and continued at Adelphi University with the dream of being a professional. Reality set in and he returned to competitive swimming by joining the college swim team.

"Even though I took many lessons and I was a competitive swimmer as a kid, when I started swimming again in college the lessons and techniques I learned from my coach, Bill Irwin, were light-years ahead of what most other coaches knew. He brought in ballet dancers to teach us the details in movements, how the angle of a hand can change a stroke. In graduate school at Penn State, I was a graduate assistant for the men's swim team. During the summers I coached swimming at country clubs." After graduate school, he became a physical education teacher in Leonia.

Eickelberg's good friend Dave Thompson, also an Irwin swimmer, was the head coach at Hamilton College. Together they started their own swim camp in 1989 at Hamilton in upstate New York. They wanted to focus on technique for competitive swimmers ages ten to seventeen. The camp is successful to this day.

"I started running when I played soccer. I liked it and did a few races, mostly 5Ks. In 1994 I joined a running club, North Jersey Masters, on the recommendation of my friend Pete Shanno, the track coach at Leonia High School. I wanted to become a better and faster runner, and the club was great. I injured my hamstring and had to go to physical therapy. I went to Excel Rehabilitation and met one of the owners, Matt Gibble, who was an Ironman triathlete. I couldn't run for a while but I could bike so I went home and dug out my thirty-year-old Schwinn ten-speed and had a ball as I remembered how much fun biking was."

During his rehabilitation, Gibble told Eickelberg that he was a natural for the triathlon and suggested he sign up.

"Matt and Gary were great coaches, gave me lots of tips and advice, and I headed off to my first triathlon. I didn't officially join the team as yet, I just wanted to try it out for size and see if it was something I'd be interested in doing. When I got to the event site and saw the hundreds of people I realized for the first time I had no clue what I was getting myself into.

"I got mauled in the swim, my supposedly best event. On the bike, everyone passed me like I was standing still. I'm sure they were all laughing at my antique bike. It was totally demoralizing. The run wasn't any better. I thought I knew how to run until my legs didn't work when I got off the bike. The whole experience was horrible but something about it appealed to me. As I drove home and distanced myself from the event, I started thinking I liked it. Actually, I started to realize there was plenty of room for improvement so I made a decision to join Team Excel and learn the sport.

"What I enjoy most about being part of the team is the camaraderie and group training. All anyone on the team has to do is go to the website and find out where the next group ride, run, or swim is taking place and they are ready to go. There isn't a feeling of intimidation if I can't keep up. There are people of all levels. I also get discounts at sports stores and quick turnaround on service at participating bike and running shops."

Eickelberg is happy doing five or six events a season and has stayed at the sprint level, although he is interested in doing an Olympic distance soon.

"I would definitely recommend joining a team for any level of triathlete. This has been a great experience for me. Everywhere I go I find an Excel person."

GERRY CLARK

DOB: 11-29-65
Residence: Ridgewood, New Jersey
Occupation: Financial adviser
First Triathlon: 2001 Wyckoff (New Jersey) Sprint Triathlon

Gerry Clark was a professional golfer for six years. Sounds exciting and athletic, but Clark says just the opposite. "It's a terrible business. Lots of eating, smoking, and drinking, and little in the form of exercise." He put on the pounds, eventually quit golf, and became a financial planner. His neighbor in Ridgewood, Matt Gibble, offered to do a health evaluation—and the results were pretty dismal.

"I had to face the facts. After being athletic most of my life, I had become a smoking, overweight, sedentary middle-aged guy. With two young daughters who deserved good examples of a healthy lifestyle in their lives and a wife who was already a Weight Watchers success story, my reputation was on the line. I stopped smoking in 1998 but was still stuck behind a desk or going out to dinner with clients. Something had to change and the catalyst to the change was my neighbor, Matt Gibble. When he offered to do a health evaluation I jumped at the chance.

"I wasn't surprised by the results of the test. He told me I was a physical

226

mess. I couldn't even run a mile and weighed 205. But little by little Gibble worked with me and I slowly started to see some progress. I also had four knee surgeries in my former sports life when I golfed, did lots of trail biking, and ran cross-country so I wasn't looking to run marathons."

Gibble thought triathlon would be a good sport for Clark because it wasn't all running; it combined other sports. Clark was up for the challenge. It was just what he was looking for to get his physical life back on track.

"I'm the type of guy who buys lots of health and exercise magazines with the best intentions of working out but never do. The magazines get recycled and I go back to the couch. But now I had someone who was willing to help me, coach me, and hold my hand through my first race. I couldn't say no. Matt even found a bike for me, an old clunker from someone on the team that probably weighed two hundred pounds and was a potpourri of borrowed parts. To me, it was perfect."

Clark marked the date of the triathlon on the calendar, mentally committed to it, talked it up with his family and friends, and settled down to a training regime.

"The first time I went to the pool to swim, I thought they would have to pull me out with a meat hook. I couldn't swim a lap. But slowly and with lots of encouragement from Matt and the team, I kept at it, and when I swam my first half mile they all celebrated with me. Everyone on the team was so helpful and encouraging even though they were all so much better and faster than me. I know I asked lots of stupid questions but they never made me feel that way.

"The morning of the triathlon, Matt picked me up and we drove together listening to heavy metal blaring on the radio. He had given me a checklist of things to bring and one item was a tub to clean my feet. I didn't know what size or anything so I grabbed a huge washbasin. I thought Matt was going to lose it when he saw that.

"He gave me a wet suit and told me to put Pam on my wrists and ankles so it would be easy to take it off but I decided to use a little extra and basically basted myself in Pam. I put on so much of the stuff that my race numbers, which were just marked on my body, started to drip down my arm and leg. I felt like a Thanksgiving turkey ready to go into the oven.

I was a wreck. I was so nervous that when I started pumping my tire, it burst. At that point, Matt took over and tried to calm me down.

"Heading down to the beach didn't make me feel any better. I was petrified and my heart was pounding through my chest. To me, it looked like legions of people all waiting to get in the water. I waited till the first row went in and then jumped into the fray, getting kicked, pounded and smashed to pieces. I floated on my back for a while wondering what in the hell I got myself into. I had no business being here. But pretty soon I passed the first buoy and that made me feel better."

When Clark got out of the water he was absolutely exhausted and didn't think he could make it back to transition. But there in front of him were his wife and daughters holding a big sign saying GERRY'S GIRLS! That inspired him to pick up the pace and get back to transition.

"Now I had to get off the damn wet suit and man, did I smell! I spent about twelve minutes going through my checklist, putting baby powder on my feet, and all the while Matt is screaming at me to get on the bike and get outta there. By the time I got on the bike course, there wasn't anyone around. I was all by myself and actually made a wrong turn.

"By the time I got on the run, I was shot. I really didn't know if I could finish but I saw my in-laws and got some high-fives from my kids and buckled down and dug deep. Real deep.

"When I finally crossed the finish line I was an emotional wreck. I was crying, my girls were hugging me; it was a huge highlight in my life. For the first time in a long time, I really felt good about myself."

It was also a huge turning point in Clark's life. He made a vow that day never to go back to his sedentary lifestyle. He gained confidence that transferred into his business, and his sales revenues went up.

He does five or six triathlons a season and in 2004 he did his first half Ironman. In 2005 he hired a coach, Don Fink, to prepare him for his first Ironman, Lake Placid in July 2006.

"Sometimes I pinch myself because I can't believe this is me. I've gone through such a total lifestyle change. It's been great for me, my business, and my family. My daughters are starting to get into the sport and participating in youth-level triathlons. I actually can't wait to go to my high school reunion because I know I am in the best shape of my life."

ARLENE FLINK

DOB: 8-21-65
Residence: Franklin Lakes, New Jersey
Occupation: Nurse, Hackensack Hospital
First Triathlon: 1999 Wyckoff (New Jersey) Sprint Triathlon

For those who say they don't have time to train meet Arlene Flink, a mother of four, a part-time nurse up until 2004, and triathlete who always finds the time to train. She completed her first triathlon eight weeks after the birth of her third child. She got in her training by being flexible and creative: She did it at her local YMCA where the kids were in nursery school or Tot Drop day care; she did it on a treadmill when the babies were napping; she did it before and after her husband came from work; and she saved the weekends for her long rides and runs. "Training for triathlons is a great way to stay in shape and it gets me out of the house," says Flink.

"I've always been active but not in an organized way. I didn't do team sports as a kid, just a little of everything. I got interested in triathlons when I watched my husband do his first. As I saw the people cross the finish line I noticed the women, who came in all different sizes and shapes. They didn't look like pros, more like the women I pass on the sidewalk in town. I thought anyone who did triathlons had to look and act like a pro but after seeing this woman I thought I could do this. I was pregnant at the time and it seemed like a great way to get back in shape."

Six months after her second child was born Flink decided to do a duathlon instead of a triathlon because she didn't know how to swim. She won her age division. After that, she was determined to learn how to swim and do a triathlon. But she got pregnant again and had to postpone it.

"To train for the duathlon, I put my older child in nursery day care and the baby would nap at my side while I rode the CompuTrainer, an indoor bike, at home. Whenever my husband was around I went for a run outside. I still had to learn how to swim and decided I could do that while pregnant. My ever-expanding body felt very comfortable in the water and I started to do water aerobics. Gary then taught me how to swim.

"Eight weeks after giving birth I did my first triathlon. I wanted to prove to myself I could do the whole thing after training for it. The day of the event I was very excited. I wasn't really nervous, just wanted to enjoy myself, take my time and get through it. I actually felt more comfortable with all the other women swimming around me. At least I wasn't alone and knew I wouldn't drown. As I came out of the swim, my mother was there holding the baby and the other kids. They all high-fived me and it was so great to see them. I was in no rush and took my time through the transition.

"For the bike leg I had a decent bike that I'd used in the duathlon so I felt comfortable using it. The run was tough but I managed to run the whole five miles. I think all the 5K races I did in the last few years helped me get through it. I always find it is easier to just put on my shoes and go out for a run if I don't have time to do anything else."

Flink was thrilled to finish and immediately started planning how she could better her time. But she got pregnant again and now had to train with four kids all under the age of six. With four kids, timing and training is everything.

"Most of 2000 was spent pregnant with number four so my goal was do the 2001 Wyckoff Triathlon and better my time. I took six months to train. I would drop the kids off at Tot Drop at the YMCA and take a Spinning class and do my swimming. When Gary got home I'd go for a run. That year I placed fourth overall female and won my age division."

When it comes to races, Flink is very competitive. She can hang in there and dog down the next female in front of her. In 2002 she did a half Ironman in St. Croix, a very hilly course.

"I really didn't know what I was in for at the half. I did six long bike rides, which wasn't enough, but I was in good running shape, which helped to pull me through. I didn't place but I was glad I did it. In 2003 I ran the New York City Marathon in 3:32, qualifying for the Boston Marathon, which I ran the following spring in 2004. In 2005 I did another half Ironman at Eagleman in Maryland. In 2006, I took up tennis."

Flink still does the Wyckoff Sprint Triathlon. In 2006 the kids were finally old enough to stay at home alone with the oldest babysitting. Flink won second in her age group but didn't stay for the awards ceremony as she was anxious to get back and see how the kids were coping.

"I admit I have good strong running genes, which certainly helps me. I don't train hard or a lot. For the marathon I trained three days a week. That's it. For my half Ironmans I get up at 5:30 A.M. and bike one sixty-miler and a few fifties. I am a minimalist when it comes to training. I don't believe in overtraining. It works for me and my family lifestyle."

Flink has no desire to do an Ironman. "I'll leave that to my husband," she says. "I see no point in it. My training keeps me in shape and my sprint-distance and half Ironman triathlons and marathons are very achievable goals. I love getting outside to run as it helps me plan my day and I get to spend quiet time with myself away from the kids. I don't need any more than that."

Flink still goes on training rides with her Team Excel partners and encourages them in their events. She gives full credit to Team Excel for helping her reach her triathlon goals.

"Being on Team Excel means new friends to hang with, train with, challenge your endurance and speed. I trained with the nicest guys for the marathon. They pushed me to a limit that I didn't know I had. Being on the team got me motivated those days that I truly did not want to get up and out of bed. I would definitely recommend a team to someone just getting started. You can always find someone at your level—or, even better, someone above your level—to push you to your limits. Initially it can be overwhelming because you are unsure of where you stand physically. I remember the first time I went to the masters swim at the YMCA, I was so overwhelmed and I was unsure of what to do, but there is always someone there patient enough to explain things to you."

THE POWER OF THREE: FIRST-EVER ALL-AMPUTEE TRIATHLON TEAM

Sabrina Wisniewski, Denny Chipollini, and Christie Adams are the Power of Three, the first all-amputee relay team to compete on the East Coast, at the Philadelphia Triathlon in June 2006.

Wisniewski, thirty-five, of Flemington New Jersey, the swimmer, had her left leg amputated below the knee at fifteen as a result of a childhood form of arthritis, which also caused stunted growth in her left arm. She gets all her power for the swim from her right arm and right leg.

Chipollini, fifty-three, of Skippack, Pennsylvania, the biker, lost both of his legs in a car accident in 1989 but doctors were able to reattach one. He has completed over three marathons in his prosthetic left leg.

Adams, thirty-two, of Bridgeport, Pennsylvania, the runner, was born missing a fibula in her right leg, which was amputated when she was seven.

The three athletes, all personal trainers for abled and disabled athletes, met through their prosthetics maker, who suggested they form a team. "All abilities, become disabilities, if we don't use them," says Chipollini. At the triathlon they raised funds for a nonprofit group started by Chipollini in 2001 called Generation Hope, which spreads the message that amputees are just like anyone else and that inspires able and differently able people to live life with No Excuses . . . No Limits! (www.genhopeusa.org). "If we can do it, anyone can," says Chipollini. "Life is about sharing and helping each other."

Unfortunately for Sabrina the swim portion of the triathlon was canceled due to flooding on the Schuylkill River. The event director decided to add a 5K leg on the 10K race, which meant that Christie had to run 9.3 miles instead of 6.2.

DENNY CHIPOLLINI

DOB: 5-26-53
Residence: Skippack, Pennsylvania
Occupation: Motivational speaker, personal trainer
First Triathlon: 2005 Philadelphia Olympic Distance Triathlon

"I was a fat kid. In seventh grade I was already over two hundred pounds. I have no excuse for being overweight. I ate too much and didn't exercise. It's as simple as that. I come from an Italian family and there was always a big bowl of pasta in front of me.

"After high school I took up running and started to get in shape. I liked the new me and the way it made me feel. So did my girlfriend, who became my wife. Life was looking better and better every day."

All that changed for Chipollini one rainy morning in September of 1989. While driving his car on the Pennsylvania Turnpike he hit a slick patch of road. The car skidded out of control and hit the guardrail. The impact of the crash forced the guardrail through the car and sliced through his legs, severing them from his body.

"When the car stopped spinning and I could assess the damage, I saw my left leg on the dashboard and right foot on the passenger seat. The pain was intense and I started to panic. I forced myself to stay calm, which helped to slow the loss of blood. Minutes later police and EMS were at the accident, cutting me out of the car and transporting me by helicopter to the nearest trauma hospital."

He spent a total of three and a half months in and out of the hospital and underwent fifteen operations to try to save his legs. To complicate matters, his wife was pregnant and about to give birth.

"The doctors managed to connect my right leg but the left leg had to be amputated. During the operation, my wife went into labor. When I opened my eyes, the first face I saw was my newborn son. The doctors made a decision that since I couldn't be at the birth of my child, they would bring him to me."

Complications and infections continued for the next few years until the technology advanced and the doctors could finally get the right leg perfectly connected. Chipollini worked hard in physical rehabilitation to make the struggling steps from a wheelchair to crutches to a cane to finally walking with a prosthetic leg. During the next few years he fought bouts of depression and got fired from his job.

To help get his life back on track Chipollini decided to run a 5K race in his hometown. He missed running and knew he had to get it back to feel whole again.

"Three years from the date of the amputation I ran a 5K wearing my prosthesis. My wife ran as well pushing our son Nicholas in a baby jogger. I finished last but it didn't matter. I was back! The whole town showed up for the race and there was an outpouring of emotion, tears, and good wishes.

"That day was a turning point for me. As I was leaving the race, a little boy came over to me and said I was his hero. That brought tears to my eyes. It also made me realize how important it was for this young child to see me as normal, not a man with disabilities. That incident sowed the seeds for my motivational talks and the formation of Generation Hope, the nonprofit organization I created to inspire and educate adults and children to overcome adversity and accept diversity in others."

Five years later he and his wife received the devastating news that their eight-year-old son had an incurable genetic disorder, neurofibromatosis (NF), which causes tumors to grow on the nerve endings of the body internally and externally. NF also carries along with it learning disabilities, ADHD, and Tourette's syndrome.

"My wife and I got through the hard times only because of the love and support from our friends and family. My mother came to our house five days a week to watch our son when my wife went back to work. Neighbors raised thirty thousand dollars to help offset our medical expenses. The spiritual and physical healing was finally taking place."

Chipollini started giving talks at Nicholas's school to help his classmates understand his disorder. He challenged them to ask themselves if they would pick on someone who, for example, has a prosthetic or some other difference, or if they would instead befriend and help that person.

"My talks in the classroom definitely had an impact on kids and it made a difference. It motivated me to continue sharing the message with others so they can find ways to connect with the compassionate and inspired side of life instead of focusing on a person's disability and making them feel different."

In 1999 he ran a ten-mile race in Philadelphia. A year later he ran his first marathon in under six hours. He went on to run two more marathons before switching to triathlons.

"In 2002 I biked across Pennsylvania to draw attention to Generation Hope. I stopped at schools and community groups and talked about my message."

But another curveball hit Chipollini. He contracted hepatitis C due to a blood transfusion received after the car accident. He started drug therapy, which continued for more than a year.

"By 2005 I was back on my feet again and needed a new challenge. I read about the inaugural Philadelphia Triathlon and decided that would be my goal. First, I had to learn to swim.

"For the first time since I lost my leg, I got into a pool. I did one lap and thought I'd die. There was no way I thought I could do this. I couldn't breathe. I was gasping, kicking my one leg, and not going anywhere. A group of masters swimmers who witnessed my miserable attempts took me under their wing and taught me to swim. I worked my way up to swimming three times a week. I already had a bike from my cycle across Pennsylvania, a nice Trek, donated to me by the company. It was a hybrid but I didn't care. Halfway through the swim, after panicking with every stroke, I calmed down and made it through. Once I got to shore I was helped up to my crutches and got to transition, took off the wet suit, and put on the bike prosthesis. It seemed to take forever and in fact took over six minutes. When I returned from the bike I took that leg off and put on my running leg, which is decorated with simulated snakeskin, for the run. It was an amazing day, absolutely incredible and I accomplished a new goal in life."

As much as it was a major thrill for him, it was also a day he realized how much admiration the crowd had for him and what he had achieved. Something clicked inside him and he realized he had to get more amputees into the sport. To Chipollini, this was the perfect venue to show that amputees are no different from people who wear prescription eyeglasses; they are both disabilities.

"I asked my prosthesis maker if he knew other amputees who might be interested in doing a triathlon and he hooked me up with Christie Adams and Sabrina Wisniewski. When we met, we clicked right away and became the Power of Three."

Over the next few months they did most of their training separately, but met occasionally to discuss race-day details and transition-area logistics, and to give each other support. Chipolloni was the only one out of the three who had done a triathlon.

"On the day of the event the swim was canceled due to flooding in the river. The directors decided to add a 5K run before the bike, followed by the 10K run. We were all disappointed that Sabrina would not get to participate. Since Christie had to do double runs and would be tired at the start of her second run, I felt pressure to push hard on the bike to try and make up time. I did the best I could. It was an amazing day.

"Life throws us things sometimes and it's up to us to use them in a positive manner. If we are fortunate enough, with the help of God's love, to recognize them as gifts then we can use these gifts to help others and in turn we will be using our lives to the fullest."

Chipollini received the United Parcel Service's Community Service Award in 2000; Ford Motor Company's National Blue Oval "Commitment to Kids" Award in 2001; is featured in Montel Williams's book, *A Dozen Ways to Sunday;* ran with the Olympic Torch in Philadelphia; and carried the 2002 Paralympic Torch in Utah.

CHRISTIE ADAMS

DOB: 11-29-73
Residence: Bridgeport, Pennsylvania
Occupation: Exercise physiologist
First Triathlon: 2006 Olympic Distance Philadelphia Triathlon

Christie is a right congenital below-the-knee amputee, the result of a missing fibula at birth. She has been active her entire life because her parents didn't have a problem letting her be involved in sports such as track, swimming, and soft-ball. She began working out more regularly in a gym with her sister after she graduated from high school and became committed to kickboxing group exercise classes and weight lifting. She received a bachelor of science degree in exercise sport studies and has been working in corporate fitness in Philadelphia.

"From the time I was born until I learned to walk I was in a cast. I never knew any other way of life so it really wasn't a traumatic experience when my leg was amputated at the age of five. My parents made sure I did everything able-bodied kids did. I swam, was a cheerleader, did gymnastics, and participated in high school track.

"I ran with a prosthetic but fifteen years ago the technology wasn't that great. The prosthetic never fit correctly. Every minor change, like a shift in the weather, affected the fit and caused blisters and sores. And most prosthetics makers worked with older people, not kids, so I was like an ex-

237

periment to them. They weren't used to active people who constantly needed adjustments. Another problem was the cost, extremely prohibitive at that time. I could have bought a car instead of a state-of-the-art prosthetic. "

Adams attended college in North Carolina and kept running but still had issues with her prosthetic. It wasn't worth it to run more than three miles as she would get blisters. She concentrated on her studies and got in great shape by exercising at the gym. Finally, in 2005 she turned to the biomechanics company Ossar and got a new leg which enabled her to run without pain or discomfort. Ultrathin, ultrastrong and ultratough, the philosophy behind the new generation of prosthetics is to create an artificial limb that is an extension of the human body, not just a strap-on device. For athletes like Adams, Chipollini, and Wisniewski, the technology enhances their quality of life.

"When I got my new leg it felt great to run. I was running three times a week and getting in some good distance. My prosthetics maker told me about Denny and doing the Philadelphia Triathlon and I was definitely interested. I called Denny, we met, and I agreed to do the run."

Adams wasn't fazed in the least that they would be the first-ever amputee team. She doesn't think of herself as an amputee. To her it was an opportunity to be on a relay team and do a triathlon.

"I feel like any other person. I'm not special just because I don't have a leg. Most of the time I don't even notice I'm missing a leg. It's just how I have always been. I'm like any other person."

The biggest challenge for Adams was running outside. All her running to date had been on a treadmill inside.

"Running outside was so different. I had to learn to pace myself and deal with the weather and other elements of being outside. I had seven months to make the transition so I wasn't worried. Dealing with the heat was the biggest problem. I knew I had to get in more distance and signed up for a ten-mile race. I thought a race atmosphere would be good for me. I needed to get used to running in a pack."

Adams was happy with her performance in the ten-miler. It gave her confidence to do the 10K leg of the triathlon. The three members continued to train on their own but met for press conferences and public relations appearances. A lot of media hype was being generated over the team's appearance at the triathlon.

"The morning of the event things started to go wrong from the start. We didn't have time to eat as it was so hectic dealing with the traffic, the media, the cameras, and just the general confusion of a triathlon event. When we arrived at the start we found out the swim was canceled due to flooding in the river. When I got the news that I had to do double runs I was concerned. I knew I could do it but I wasn't mentally prepared to run more distance. I also do better when I don't have to stop and start up again and now I had to run a 5K, stop for about an hour and run a 10K.

"I was also very upset for Sabrina. She put in all that training and now couldn't participate on the team. She's not a runner so we couldn't ask her to do the 5K. When the decision was made that I would run the 5K, I turned to Sabrina and said, 'I am doing this one for you. You are a part of this team no matter what.'"

Adams held a nine-minute pace for the 5K and felt good but was worried about starting up again when Denny returned from the twenty-four-mile bike leg. The heat was also a factor. Nothing was going right for Adams.

"When I started out on the 10K I was nervous. I didn't feel as strong as I'd like. The last two miles of the 10K my calf started cramping, something I never experienced before. There was nothing I could do to make it stop. If I slowed down it was still there. It really hurt and threw off my time. By the time I finished the run it looked like a softball was lodged in my calf and I had to go to medical tent for icing and a massage afterward."

For Adams, it was a thrill to be on the Power of Three team and compete in a triathlon, but not because she considers herself disabled.

"Anytime I run I feel it is a huge accomplishment and not because I am an amputee. Anyone who gets out and runs is accomplishing something. It's not about my prosthesis, it's about me. Of course it's hard work for me but it's hard work for anyone. I feel the same as any runner does when I finish. What a relief!"

SABRINA WISNIEWSKI

DOB: 6-25-70
Residence: Flemington, New Jersey
Occupation: Personal trainer
First Triathlon: 2006 Olympic Distance Philadelphia Triathlon

Diagnosed at age two with a childhood form of arthritis called scleroderma, Wisniewski had her left leg amputated above the knee at age fifteen. The disease also caused stunted growth in her left arm. When she was diagnosed, doctors advised her parents to keep her active so her joints would stay mobile. They immersed her in sports programs. She was a very active kid and didn't miss a beat, keeping up with the neighborhood kids. In high school she was on the tennis team and took up running in her twenties. She met her husband, a prosthetic practitioner, who suggested she join the triathlon team.

"It's true that you adapt to what you have and what you are given in life. When I was diagnosed at age two with scleroderma, a rare form of arthritis that arrests one's growth by causing scarring and tightening of the skin, the doctors told my parents to keep me as active as possible to keep my joints mobile so they wouldn't fuse together. I've been into sports all my life. I thank my mom for making me do all the things normal kids did and never treating me any differently.

"I participated on the town softball team, swam, and played tennis.

By age six, all the damage from the disease had been done but the doctors wanted to hold off on the amputation until I finished growing, which is why they delayed it till I was fifteen.

"Although I swam a lot when I was young, tennis became my sport of choice in high school. I was lucky to have a decent-fitting prosthetic, because my condition makes it difficult to fit. I have no fat on my leg, the skin is scarred, and I have limited mobility in my hip and scoliosis in my back. During college I didn't swim or play tennis. I concentrated on weight training. At twenty I picked up running for a while but it was really hard on my sound leg. I kept getting stress fractures and had to walk around with my one foot in a stability boot and a prosthetic on the other. Not a great way to get around."

Wisniewski also had four operations performed on her hand, which had become very arthritic and had limited mobility, to increase her range of motion. In her late twenties she started going to a new prosthetist, Kevin Towers, CP, of POSI (Prosthetic Orthotic Solutions International) where she met her future husband. Because of her condition, Wisniewski needs to protect her skin when she wears her prosthesis and starts with a gel sock. Over that she wears a thermoplastic inner liner, like a sleeve, before donning the artificial leg. There's also a microprocessor in her prosthetic knee, which she has to charge every night.

"Once I started going to POSI, I felt the difference right away. It was like going from wearing a standard model to the new top-of-the-line model. As a personal trainer, I'm on my feet all day and this made my life so much easier."

Denny, Christie, and Sabrina all went to POSI but had never met. It was her husband who talked with Denny about the triathlon team. Denny was looking for a swimmer, and he volunteered Sabrina.

"I was thrilled when I found out about the team. I had always wanted to do a triathlon and this was the perfect format. We had about six months to train and since I hadn't been swimming in years, I immediately joined a masters swim club and got back in the pool."

Wisniewski is being a bit modest about her swimming background. In 1996 she tried out for the Paralympics swim team. She didn't make it but had the guts and determination to try. It didn't surprise anyone who knew her that she was going to do a triathlon.

"The masters swim coach was a great find. He didn't treat me differently. I did the same drills as the rest of the team. He had never worked with a challenged athlete so he had no preconceptions and pushed me to keep up with the workouts the other triathletes were doing."

Workouts consisted of two-mile swims plus drills three days a week. On the other days she did weight training. She felt prepared and ready by the time of the event. Unfortunately things didn't go her way.

"The night before the race Denny called and warned me the swim might be canceled. Due to all the heavy rain the Schuylkill River was flooded and they didn't think it would be safe for the swimmers. He was very upset and said the team would wait for another one if I couldn't participate. I told him that wasn't necessary; we were still a team and should go through with it regardless.

"On the morning of the race—my birthday, by the way—everything that could go wrong did. We got caught in traffic, couldn't get close to the media site where we were supposed to be located, and in the middle of all the frenzy I got a call from my husband that the swim was canceled.

"I was devastated. It was a huge disappointment and I started crying. My first thought was that there wouldn't be any payoff for all the hard training and on top of that I couldn't even take over the added run for Christie as I hadn't run for years."

Although she was very emotional, Wisniewski held it together for the team and all the media that surrounded them. She kept telling herself things happen for a reason and let it go at that. As she worried and fretted over Christie having to do double runs, Denny and Christie were as sympathetic to her disappointment.

"What came out of this was a stronger bond for the team than we ever imagined. After that weekend we tried to find another triathlon so I could finally do my swim but logistics keep getting in the way and we still need to plan one. I can always use this experience as a lesson when I give talks to teens about self-esteem and having a positive attitude. Life presents many opportunities and we have to look at them all."

TEAM WAESCHE

One of the pleasures of being an athlete is introducing a sport to others. It's even better when they are family members. My nephew Jacob did his first triathlon with me last summer. I use the term with me loosely, as he is six foot four and 185 pounds of solid muscle and is on the crew team at Brown University. He cycles thirty-five miles a day for cross-training. This summer we did the triathlon again and he took second in his testosterone-infused age division, twenty to twenty-four years old. He could be the family's first Ironman.

I introduced my three nieces to road racing a few years ago at the Cherry Blossom ten-miler in Washington, DC, on a cold sleeting day. Other family members cheered from the sidelines, umbrellas in hand as they raced around the looped course to catch us from start to finish. It was a day filled with laughter, fun, and family togetherness. All three nieces have gone on to run half marathons. Last summer we all did a triathlon together. That day will stay with them forever as a testimony to their devotion to one anther, a summer memory that started in the waters of Long Island Sound and ended in the sand beneath the finish line.

WENDY WAESCHE LAVALLE

DOB: 4-3-75
Residence: Norwalk, Connecticut
Occupation: Marketing
First Triathlon: 2005 Sprint Niantic Bay Triathlon, Niantic, Connecticut

The oldest of the three sisters, Wendy was always a good role model for her younger siblings. Athletic as a kid, she was captain of her high school swim team in Westport, Connecticut. She would like to get more involved with athletics but with a new marriage and a demanding job and just completing a master's degree at the Stern School of NYU, there's little time for anything else. Training for a marathon, which is on her list of things to do someday, will have to wait. A sprint triathlon was the perfect respite from the routine of work and study, and training with her sisters made it even more appealing. Incredibly close, the sisters at one time or another have shared apartments, see one another on the weekends, and are one another's best friends.

"I always considered myself somewhat athletic, but not competitive. For me, it's never been about placing or winning. I'd rather enjoy a nice relaxing run than compete in a race. When I played on the youth soccer team in town I found it very intimidating. I was always comparing myself with the other girls, who were much more aggressive, and it made me nervous. I shied away from them and never pushed myself. I didn't really enjoy it.

"Swimming, on the other hand, was always fun. I was good at it and found it comfortable. The swim team at Staples High School had a reputation for having a nice group of girls and I found my niche. However, there was still a level of intimidation when it came time to compete. Every time I stood on the block, I got nervous and lost my self-confidence.

"At Connecticut College I joined the sailing team, which was really hard-core. We had Olympians on the team and sometimes I would return from practice covered in bruises but I loved it. I still have wonderful memories of great sails on the Thames River."

Wendy didn't pick up running until her junior year at college. She went out for an occasional jog but then someone told her she wasn't built for running and would never make a good runner. Instead of feeling defeated, she got angry and made it her business to become a runner.

"I started to take running more seriously and loved the rush I felt afterward. In 1998, I was working at Greenwich Associates and did a corporate 5K just for fun and was shocked how much fun I had. Later that year I did a ten-miler with one of my sisters and was hooked. I realized this was a sport I wanted to do for the rest of my life."

Wendy got married in 2002. Adjusting to married life, working long hours, and commuting every weekend into New York City for her master's program, she was stressed and found it difficult to even fit in a relaxing run. She relied on her sisters for closeness and understanding as time became her worst enemy.

"The summer of 2005 was very special for all of us. Our family still managed to carve out two weeks of family vacation in our family house in New London, Connecticut, where we've summered since we were babies. My sister Dana had moved to California and we were all eager to have her back in the fold. This was our time to unite again as a family, sleep on the porch, have long talks into the night, and build campfires on the beach. I was really stressed out over finals for the MBA program and needed the family ties to pull me through.

"Someone, I think it was Dana, mentioned doing a triathlon. She had done the Niantic triathlon last year and Erin had just done her first a few weeks ago so I was the only one who hadn't done one. If I was ever going to do one, this was it. I couldn't have asked for a better set of coaches."

Wendy was nervous, as she didn't think she was in good shape. With the triathlon just a week away, the sisters started swimming every morning, followed by a run. The bike leg would be an issue as she had a heavy hybrid, but nothing was going to stress her out. This was all about fun and being with her sisters.

"I wasn't intimidated at all. The swim would be easy; the only thing I wasn't sure about was putting it all together. Even if I was the last person, I didn't care. I wasn't in running shape and that bothered me. I worried about not having any energy left after the bike and not being able to finish."

The day before, they picked up the race packets and checked out the swim and run course. That night they all had a big, boisterous dinner and tried to get to bed early. The next day they drove to the beach, excited with anticipation of the day's event.

"I remember standing on the beach waiting to start the swim and Dana came over to me and said, 'Don't worry about anything. I'll stick with you the whole time.' It was such a sweet, soothing thing to say and I thought how grateful I was to have such a caring, sensitive sister."

Wendy did well on the swim, feeling natural and comfortable. In the frenzy of the swim start she lost track of her sisters but when she turned her head to breathe, there was Dana right next to her.

"With every breath, I saw Dana. It just felt so natural like we were just doing our regular morning swim. Then I saw Erin on the other side and I couldn't believe how lucky I was.

"We all got to transition about the same time, and just laughed and enjoyed ourselves while everyone else around us was rushing off. We didn't have a care in the world. Heck, I wasn't worried about shaving off seconds!

"On the bike I got passed by a lot of people but I didn't care. Erin took off ahead of us but Dana stayed right next to me. My hybrid wasn't the best choice of bikes but I managed a steady pace, until my chain fell off."

She told Dana to go ahead, not wanting to hold her back. As she struggled to get it back on, a man stopped and took the time to help her. Thankful, she got back on the bike and tried to make up for lost time. She was worried about having to do the run alone and finishing last.

"When I got back to transition, there was Dana, waiting for me. The love I had for my sister at that moment was absolutely immeasurable. She is such a good athlete and gave up a good time and a decent finish for me. That's a gift.

"Starting the run, I had a crazy feeling as if I was having an out-of-body experience. My legs wouldn't work; I didn't feel connected to my body. It took about a mile before I settled down and fell into a rhythm. As I started to sprint to the finish I saw Erin, and David, my husband, who ran the last few yards with me, and my aunts and parents all waiting for me and it was so beautiful and I finished strong and happy with a huge smile on my face.

"It was definitely the best way to end our family week. I will definitely do another. My dad calls us his 'jock' daughters. What I've realized is that I want to be fit forever and always be in shape to do athletic events like triathlons, runs, hiking and swimming. Someday I'll have kids and I want to play with them and take them on hikes and teach them to swim and sail. My parents taught me two important lessons in life: Always put family first and practice a healthy lifestyle. I'll definitely pass those on to my kids."

DANA WAESCHE

DOB: 10-18-77
Residence: San Francisco, California
Occupation: International market research
First Triathlon: 2004 Sprint Niantic Bay Triathlon, Niantic, Connecticut

Dana is the middle sister. Growing up, she fought with her siblings as sibs often do, but soon they became one another's confidants. Whereas Wendy and Erin went to Connecticut College and moved back home afterward, Dana carved a different path to William and Mary; after graduation she worked for AmeriCares, flying into disaster areas around the world. She was at Ground Zero three hours after the Trade Towers were attacked. She was in Iran one day after the Bam earthquake, and she frequently traveled to Africa to address health issues, such as malnutrition . The job was exciting and rewarding but took an emotional toll. When she made the decision to move to California, it wasn't without a sense of loss and longing for her sisters. But she kept in daily contact, keeping up with the family news and staying involved from the other coast, and is everyone's trusted confidante. Dana knew before anyone in the family that Erin's boyfriend was going to propose. No matter how far she is from her sisters, Dana will always be connected.

"I always enjoyed sports. From age five through fifteen, I played on the youth soccer team and loved it. Unlike my sisters I loved the competition. I played all the positions from striker to goalie. In high school I branched out into lacrosse and running, a little bit of everything. I tried track but kept getting shin splits that turned into stress fractures so I had to lay off the running for a while.

"I didn't go the swim route like my sisters because I have certain fears of the water. I enjoy swimming, but have a fear of what lies beneath the water and a fear of being in the water too far from shore. Both my sisters were lifeguards and couldn't understand why I didn't want that job. How could I be responsible for someone's life if I didn't like getting in the water!

"In college I tried to get back to running and took it easy so I wouldn't aggravate my old injuries. After college I joined a gym to keep in shape and tried to keep running after work."

Dana did a few local road races with her sisters and was planning on joining them at the Cherry Blossom ten-miler but her leg issues came back so she had to miss it.

"The summer before I moved to California I was very nervous about my decision. I was having some anxiety about leaving my family and starting my life over in a new place. I knew it was the right decision but I was scared of the unknown. I needed something to challenge me and get my mind off it so I decided to do a triathlon. Looking back, that triathlon was a metaphor for my life at the time. I needed something I could accomplish that would give me the self-confidence for the move. If I could finish a triathlon, I could move to California."

Dana gave herself a few months to train. She talked to people who had done them but basically went into it blind. She trained for each leg but often did them in a different order since it was easiest to bike to the beach, then swim, then bike or run back.

"I never did a brick. I felt if I could do the legs separately I'd be fine on race day. But the swim scared me. I never conquered my fears and had to force myself to swim. Part of me loved it but I became anxious when I put my face in the water. The fear would surface and I would lose my focus. The goggles made me claustrophobic, my ears hurt, and I would panic. One day I had a meltdown in the water and started crying. I tried to push through it and kept swimming but every time I put my head in the water I felt blind and deaf. The only way I could swim was to do it with my head out of the water."

Besides the fear of swimming, another disadvantage for Dana was her bike, an old clunker hybrid she borrowed from her sister. She didn't tell anyone she was doing the triathlon and when the family found out they questioned why she was doing it.

"At the race packet pickup the day before, I was getting very excited. I checked out the swim course and talked to some people about what to expect. That night my family had our normal big, boisterous dinner and I was getting very psyched."

The next morning Dana realized what a rookie she was when she saw the gear and all the high-tech bikes in transition. She showed up in tennis shoes, a borrowed swimsuit, her bike, and a towel.

"I copied everyone and did whatever they did. I didn't even know how to rack my bike; some guy showed me how. Another guy told me to get my body marked and I didn't know what he was talking about! I was so clueless.

"It was a cold morning and most of the swimmers wore wet suits. I didn't even realize I needed the swim cap that was in my race bag. I thought it was just a nice freebie. With minutes to spare a kind woman told me I needed my cap and I had to race back to transition to retrieve it. Another woman, sensing my anxiety, advised me to stay back and swim to the side. When I first got in, the rush of the cold water startled me. Then I started getting kicked and couldn't breathe. But I fought through it and found my space and settled in. I finished somewhere in the middle of the pack, which made me feel confident.

"By the time I left T1, some of the people I beat in the swim passed me on the bike. I chalked it up to being on a hybrid as they passed me on their road bikes. I actually received a lot of encouraging comments about my hybrid as people passed by. I took it all in good humor since I wasn't trying to prove anything.

"When I started to run, my legs wouldn't work. An older woman and her daughter were running by me and we all encouraged each other and made it through. Running down the beach on the final stretch I saw my family, which made me run even harder. Actually, I could hear my family screaming for me before I saw them!

"I'm sure that day I planted the seeds for my sisters to do one."

Fast-forward one year. Those seeds took hold, and Dana's two sisters joined her at the Niantic Triathlon.

"Erin was first to join in the plans. I could sense that Wendy was holding back. She didn't think she could do it. I didn't want her to be left out and I knew she could do it if she took it easy so I made a pact with her and said, 'Wendy, I need you to get me through the swim and I'll get you through the run.' That seemed to give her the confidence and she agreed to be a part of the team.

"Doing the triathlon with my sisters was all about being together. I didn't care how long it took or what happened along the way. My goal was to make it a positive experience for all of us. Being away from my family is difficult for me so the times we have together are precious. The triathlon made it even more so. It's a memory we will always have, something we laugh over, recall fondly, and probably even embellish a little. The photographs of that day bring it all back and help to keep my sisters in my life when I am away from them."

Dana has adjusted very well to her new life in San Francisco. She's running half marathons and has gotten into the habit of laying low on Saturday nights so she can get up early on Sunday morning and go for a long run through the marina or up the cliffs to the Golden Gate Bridge and across to the Marin side.

"It is such a rush to run through San Francisco. I forward to those long runs all week. What's also really fun is having a bunch of friends who are also new to tri. We've all gotten together and are doing a series of triathlons this summer. The triathlon community has been a great find for me. I now have lots of swimming coaches so I'm sure I'll be able to conquer those fears for good."

ERIN WAESCHE

DOB: 6-16-80
Residence: Bridgeport, Connecticut
Occupation: Finance
First Triathlon: 2005 SoBe Mossman Sprint Triathlon, Norwalk, Connecticut

The fact that Erin, the youngest sister, could do a triathlon at all is a tribute to her gutsy, steadfast belief that she can do anything. Diagnosed with Lyme disease at age four, some mornings she has to fight her way out of bed. Every bone and muscle aches. Her legs won't work. The pain flares up and it hurts just to walk. She's been on antibiotics for more than ten years and even though she is finally off medication, there is no guarantee she will ever be free of this illness. But Erin is a determined fighter and as a kid danced her way around the pain and then in college ran her way through it. Nowadays what keeps her dancing and running, and now doing triathlons, is focusing on the good days when the pain is at bay. That, and her engagement to George.

"Like my older sisters, I played youth soccer but I didn't like it. The girls were too aggressive for me. Dancing was my sport. I loved to dance and took lessons three times a week through high school. And like Wendy, I was captain of the swim team. I wasn't the fastest but I had a lot of spirit and loved the girls.

"In college, I didn't participate in any sports. I started running to stay grounded and found I really enjoyed it. I always felt refreshed after a run and looked forward to the next one. But some days the Lyme was so bad I couldn't do it."

After college Erin kept running on the good days. Her very first race was the ten-miler in Washington, DC, with her sister Wendy, while Dana cheered on the sidelines. In 2004 she ran a half marathon.

"I watched Wendy and her husband, David, run a half marathon and thought I could do that. Then Dana did a triathlon and I thought I could do that too. It's very empowering to watch someone do a half marathon or a triathlon, something that seems so difficult, and then thinking maybe, just maybe, I could do that."

Erin was living in Bridgeport at the time and riding her bike to work. She also started swimming again. The idea of a triathlon appealed to her at the same time she was getting a little bored with just running. Watching Dana do her first triathlon was the final kicker.

"When I saw Dana cross the finish line and seeing how excited she was, I knew I had to do one. I decided to do the Norwalk sprint triathlon the following July. My training started in the spring with a ten-mile bike ride to work. It was a beautiful ride through Fairfield County along the beaches of Westport, Southport, and Fairfield. After a hard day at work, when the last thing I felt like doing was riding the ten miles home, the views and the water always refreshed me. When the water was warm enough for swimming, I went out early, around 6 A.M. The only one around was an old fisherman. I loved my morning swims. One morning, a week before the event, I went for my swim and hit a huge jellyfish. It stung me all over and I panicked. It definitely left me with a fear of going back in the water."

By race day, Erin was confident and excited. Her goal was just to finish, have fun, and never look at a watch. Unfortunately she had another jellyfish attack during the swim.

"As much as I was warned about the swim, I got kicked in the face and pushed and then got stung again. It wasn't a great experience and I couldn't wait to get out of the water. In transition I couldn't find my helmet. Someone had kicked it and I finally found it in another spot. Since I had already ridden the course, there were no surprises except for all the people that passed me. I didn't care, I sang and smiled and had a ball. It was actually interesting to see all the neat bikes. I actually started doing some bike shopping, picking out which one I might want to buy.

"When I started the run my legs wouldn't move. They felt like the jellyfish I just swam through. My whole family was watching me and I couldn't move. I tried talking to them but they weren't hearing me. A man passed me, heard me complaining and said, 'Welcome to triathlons, honey!' "

At the finish, Erin sprinted for all she was worth. Three weeks later she did the Niantic Triathlon with her sisters. As much as she wanted to stay with her sisters, she was still pumped from her first one and wanted to beat her time.

"It was so much fun standing on the beach with my sisters. We all started the swim together and I felt like I was in this school of Waesche fish. Dana was on one side, Wendy on the other. We all came out of the water just about the same time. We hung out in transition for a while but I headed out before Wendy and Dana.

"I worried about them and part of me wanted to be with them but I knew Dana would stay with Wendy. The run went better for me this time but again, I missed my sisters. The run is a loop and on my second loop I was hoping to see my sisters. Finally I saw their blond ponytails bobbing along the course and I started to scream and calling their names and making a complete spectacle of myself. We hugged and high-fived and then I kept going. It was the best part of the event."

WHAT NOT TO DO AT YOUR FIRST TRIATHLON

The following article is reprinted with permission from slowtwitch.com. Its author, Dan Empfield, is an entrepreneur in the world of multisport, inventor of the speed wet suit—Quintana Roo in 1987—and the tri-specific racing bike in 1989. Today Empfield is the editor and publisher of the popular on-line triathlon news and commentary website slowtwitch.com.

This article captures many of the mistakes made by first-time triathetes. Dan was gracious and generous with his time and told me the real story of how he came to name his company Quintana Roo.

In the mid-1980s Dan did quite a bit of traveling in Mexico and always brought his bike with him. One of the places he visited and rode in was Quintana Roo, a state in the Yucatán Peninsula. When he developed the first triathlon-specific wet suit and went into business, he looked for a name for his fledgling company that would bring attention as well as sound somewhat mysterious. Quintana Roo was the perfect fit.

Mrs. T's Chicago Triathlon: The World Championship of "Whim Racing"

Dan Empfield

slowtwitch.com   August 27, 2001

Kona's "sweet spot" is between twelve and fourteen hours. People who finish faster than that have expectations (usually unmet).

Those who finish in the sweet spot have no expectations, just hopes and dreams. They are the athletes who've trained hard enough to finish in a respectable time while remaining utterly unpretentious. If you want to watch a race, watch the pros. If you want to watch a finish, go eat dinner at the Chart House and return around the twelve-hour mark. That's when Kona gets interesting.

Quite the opposite at Mrs. T's in Chicago. The pros leave last, and all the good stuff happens first thing in the morning. The "good stuff" here, though, is a little on the lighter side. Nobody does Kona on a whim. Kona is serious business. Mrs. T's is the world championship of whim racing.

You see it all at this race. Like the guy who has his wet suit on inside-out. Zipper in the front. Size tag protruding from his chest. Do you tell him? He may not be able to get the suit off and back on again before his wave goes off. (Sometimes it's better not to know.)

We take our seats on the curb right outside the bike corral, at the bike mount-up point. Every imaginable species of rider comes out of the corral, pushing every imaginable species of bike. They mount up in front of where we're sitting.

A fellow appears who carries no fewer than 350 pounds on a five-foot-ten-inch frame, wearing a De Soto skinsuit. De Soto is an advocate of Lycra power and now so am I. It's unimaginable how that suit stays together.

A lady exits T1 wearing her helmet backward. She's not alone. Perhaps every five minutes an athlete exits transition sporting a helmet back-end-first. One guy gets ready to mount his three-speed commuter bike in his tennies but is informed by an official that a helmet is mandatory. He's shocked . . . shocked that there exists such a rule. A spectator loans him a helmet. He puts it on—backward—and rides off.

Another lady rolls her bike out of transition and we notice her chain has derailled. We try to warn her. We're all there: Rich and Chris, managers of Mission Bay Multisport's two Chicagoland shops; Steve Hed, John Cobb, and Mark Vandermolen, marketing manager for Profile Design. It's an entire row of people who make their living trying to help people enjoy their riding experience, yelling in unison: "No! Stop! Don't pedal! Lady, your chain! Don't do it!" She doesn't hear. She's in the heat of battle. The fog of war. Our screams and pleas are without purchase, just din and clamor. White noise. Background music.

She mounts the bike. "No! Don't! Your chain, lady, it's your chain!"

Nothing we do or say will stop her. She tries to put one foot in the pedal and can't get it in. We still have time to grab her attention, but we may as well have been screaming in Arabic. Click, she gets the shoe to lock in. Pushes off with the other foot. It's too late. Nothing to do but watch.

Now she's got both feet clicked in, and surprise? She's spinning her cranks at 120 revolutions per minute, and going nowhere. Now she understands but, sorry for her, too late. Like the *Titanic* she starts to list.

She's like a Douglas fir after the lumberman makes his final chainsaw crosscut. She's gaining speed, but on the wrong axis. The bike is pointing north. She's traveling west. Splat.

Chicagoans are fearless. This is why I admire them. They think nothing of doing this race on no training whatsoever. Many of this race's entrants fit that model. You can tell this with precision just by looking at their bikes.

You will see equipment here you haven't seen in eight, twelve, fifteen years. Entire bikes that come from a distinct technological age. A Centurion Ironman with original Scott DH bars, original foam armrests still in mint condition. Aerospokes, Gripshifts (the oldest ones), and handlebar tape that hasn't been manufactured since the late 1980s. This bike has been ridden, it is obvious, a dozen times since 1989, once each year on a particular day in August.

Same guy has a late 1980s vintage foam Giro helmet that comes with the Lycra cover. Except no Lycra cover. And, of course, it's on backward.

IS IT ABOUT THE BIKE?

Entire books are dedicated to the task of buying bikes. Andrew McKinnon, owner of Ridgewood Cycle, Ridgewood, New Jersey, and an Ironman, has been around bikes most his life and offers some basic guidelines for purchasing a bike for first-time triathletes. His father owned the store before him and McKinnon grew up putting together the bikes displayed in the store. According to McKinnon, Lance Armstrong brought biking into American homes. "Before Lance, only geeks and freaks were serious cyclists. In the last decade, there has been a 400 percent growth in the sport with women making up almost half that figure." Women's sizes and frames didn't even exist until a few years ago when manufacturers started realizing women were the buying force behind the increased sales in bikes. Now companies like Giant and Trek market their bikes with female-specific properties.

For many first time triathletes, investing in a new bike is intimidating and confusing. It's also an expensive purchase so you have to be sure you like the sport and will amortize the cost of the bike over time. That's why many first timers drag out the old college clunker or borrow a bike. And unless you've spent years in the saddle developing biker legs, endurance and speed, and embrace the thought of hill workouts, you're not going to make up any significant time on the bike leg of the event.

Types of Bikes

Most adults who own a bike usually have a hybrid or a mountain bike. They offer a more comfortable ride and are more durable for family rides and weekend trips. But they are also heavy and not aerodynamically designed for speed or lightness. McKinnon suggests first-time buyers looking to get into the sport buy a road bike, not a triathlon-specific bike. Here's the difference: A tri bike has a steeper seat post angle that moves the rider more forward into a position that simulates running. They come with aerobars with shifters at the end. It's effective for triathlons but not very comfortable for just touring around. "Unless you are a serious triathlete it doesn't make sense to invest in a tri bike right out of the gate," says McKinnon.

The Price Factor

There's a huge price range in bikes depending on the manufacturer, materials, and components such as wheels, brakes, gears, and do on, that go into the bike. The four big manufacturers are Trek, Specialized, Giant and Cannondale, not necessarily in that order. Lance happens to ride a Trek Madone but not many people have his income or need for speed. "A good entry-level road bike has a range of six hundred to a thousand dollars," says McKinnon. A lot of buyers come into his store and their first question is usually about price. *What can I get for (fill in the blank)?* If you aren't familiar with all the differences and nuances in bikes and aren't an experienced enough rider to appreciate them, an entry-level bike should be fine. For McKinnon, an entry-level bike will come with an integrated shift/brake levers, usually Shimano or Campagnolo, and clipless pedals. "Clipless pedals are definitely the way to go," says McKinnon. "Some practice is required but it is worth it for the comfort and efficiency they bring to the ride."

The intermediate buyer looking to trade up can expect to pay from a thousand to twenty-five hundred dollars. For that they will get higher-end parts, a higher grade of steel and aluminum, usually a carbon-fiber frame. Frame material makes up a big piece of the price. Frame material impacts how a bike feels as well as speed and lightness. In choosing a frame, consider its stiffness and lightness. A stiff bike that doesn't "give" over bumps may not be good for someone with lower back issues.

Aluminum frames are a popular choice. It's affordable, but in comparison with better materials, can be a rough ride.

Titanium frames have the capability to be light and stiff but also compliant and comfortable. They have a high life expectancy and a high price tag. A titanium frame will add about five hundred dollars to the price tag.

Carbon-fiber frames are light and forgiving over bumps. Over time they have become more durable as more manufacturers have experimented with the material and perfected it along the way.

An advanced rider with many years in the saddle and miles on the odometer can expect to pay from twenty-five hundred dollars to "the sky's the limit," says McKinnon. Another option if you don't want to purchase a new bike is to bring the clunker in for a refurbish. For approximately sixty-five dollars and up you can get new brake pads (old ones dry out and get brittle, explains McKinnon), tires, and a tune-up. "I encourage people who aren't sure if they want to continue with the sport to refurbish their old bike," McKinnon says. "That way, I know they will be riding a safe bike and if they do like the sport they will be inspired to trade up to a new one."

If possible, test ride a few bikes before you buy one. Consider the feel of the bike on the road, on hills, and on flats. Does it feel stiff? Does it "give"? Most riders claim they know in a minute when they find the right bike. It's like being one with the road. After all the research and testing and kvetching, sometimes it just comes down to a good feeling.

ADVICE FROM THE PROS

In this section well-recognized coaches from each discipline will give a blueprint for training for first-timers and explain the best way to survive and enjoy your first triathlon. Then Dave Scott, "The Man" himself, will describe how to pull it all together.

The advice is geared to first-timers but can be reviewed by all levels of triathletes as a refresher course. It's kept simple and basic, enough to get you started. Books and websites are provided for digging deeper into drills and other training modes.

The first thing anyone interested in doing a triathlon, or any sporting event for that matter, should consider is why they are doing it. I believe all athletes should start out defining goals and then develop a program to reach them. Maybe your goal is to just finish your first triathlon, or do better at your second, or if you are feeling brave and competent increase the distance to an Olympic or even a half Ironman. Whatever your goals are, they need to be defined. Chris Carmichael, who contributes the cycling section in this chapter, defines goals by their level of reachability and describes three levels:

Dream goals: These are at the top of the chart, the ultimate goals that will push you to the limits of possibility. You may not even admit to or talk about your dream goals but they are there in your mind to inspire you and drive you to succeed and exceed your limits. Set your dream goals high. A dream goal could be to do an Ironman one day.

Confidence-building goals: These goals are realistic to achieve with the proper training. They can actually be a series of goals, such a starting out with a sprint distance in the beginning of the season and building up the confidence to tackle an Olympic distance or half Ironman by the end of the season.

Action goals: The details of your daily or weekly training are your action goals, providing a link to accomplishing the confidence-building goals. Daily goal setting is an integral part of training and the one most sidetracked. If you don't stay true to your daily goals, you might as well forget the others.

Once you have defined your goals, select an event to match. Then fill in the registration form, lay down the money, and write it on a calendar to make it real. When you commit to something with time and money, it is easier to train for than an abstract time or event. Some people keep their goals quiet and personal, choosing not to share with others. Then there are those who shout them from the rooftop and make it part of every conversation. Don't be afraid to share your goals and dreams with the people closest to you. You'll need their support and understanding as you go through the process, and you'll certainly want them at the finish line to share your accomplishments and take the photos.

THE SWIM

I was thrilled when Terry Laughlin agreed to participate in the coaching section of this book. I searched for the right swim coach for first-time triathletes and Terry came highly recommended by just about every professional I spoke with. After speaking with him, I knew he was perfect—especially when he told me he was cut from the first swim team he ever tried out for, a CYO team. "It doesn't get worse than that," says Laughlin of his poor swim start in life. He stars off his conversation explaining that he was the slowest member of any swim team he was on and no matter how hard he worked to catch up, all he did was expend energy and still finish last. He was never able to rise above an average level of performance, despite a willingness to sacrifice and work extremely hard, and never understood why some swimmers were much faster than him, despite always making it look easy. It took years for Terry to figure it out but once he did, the blinders came off. His approach can be taught to anyone who wants to learn to swim, or thinks they know how. His many books on swimming for nonswimmers are best sellers because his main point is not to make his students the first out of the water or the fastest; he wants them to become optimistic and aspirational swimmers who enjoy the sport and feel comfortable in the water.

Terry Laughlin is a world-renowned swim instructor, writer, founder and owner of Total Immersion. At twenty-one, he became the youngest head coach in the NCAA, at Kings Point Academy in New York. Over sixteen years, his athletes won fourteen individual and relay titles at NCAA Division III, National YMCA, and US Junior National Championships. His students also qualified for Olympic Trials in 1980, 1984, and 1988 and produced a number of world-ranked swimmers.

Following the Olympic Trials in 1988, Laughlin stopped coaching age group swimming, partly from swim-parent fatigue and partly to find out what else he could do well. For the next four years he earned a living primarily as a writer but missed teaching. So he started a new camp for masters swimmers at Colgate University in Hamilton, New York, adopting the name Total Immersion from some popular foreign-language courses of the time, thinking it ideally suited to swimming. Since 1989, TI has taught tens of thousands of swimmers; the vast majority are not only swimming better, but love swimming and expect to continue improving and learning for life.

How Swimming Is Different from Running

The path to swimming improvement is not to make more energy available through training; it's to waste less energy by improving your stroke. Increasing your energy efficiency even modestly—from, say, 3 percent to 4 percent—can translate into a 33 percent improvement in your swimming. Many of my students are runners who want to learn to swim but always seem to hit a wall, like Joe.

Joe, a longtime runner for whom a five-miler is barely a warm-up, decides to try a pool workout one day. Within a few minutes, he's panting for breath and wondering: "How will I ever get in a decent workout if I can't even make a hundred yards without dying?" Experiences like that probably convince many adult athletes that swimming is only for those who swam millions of yards as kids, and wondering if the time and effort required to master will even be worth it.

But mastering the "art of ease" in swimming is decidedly worthwhile. Not only will a good stroke allow you to enjoy and thrive in triathlon, but it provides a fitness-building *and restorative* workout that can give new life to your legs. The good news is that I've yet to meet a runner who could not learn to swim well enough to gain these benefits. All they have to do is discard everything running has taught them, as soon as they enter the pool.

Anyone from occasional joggers to dedicated marathoners knows this fundamental truth: Increase your mileage or intensity and your running improves. But when they apply the same logic to swimming, most novices quickly achieve what one of my former students christened "terminal mediocrity"—after a few months, no amount of effort produces any further progress.

Here's why: The world records for the mile run and the 400-meter swim are virtually identical. If you were to run once around the track with Alan Webb, America's best miler, he'd beat you easily, but—even if you're purely a recreational jogger—by running easily and efficiently, you could nearly match the *number of strides* he took to cover 400 meters. If, on the other hand, you tried to swim 100 meters with Klete Keller, who broke the American 400-meter-freestyle record in Athens, not only would he beat you easily but—assuming you *could* complete 100 meters—the difference between his stroke count and yours would be staggering. Keller and other elite freestylers can easily swim twenty-five yards in seven or eight strokes (counting each hand entry as one stroke), while beginner triathletes typically average twenty to twenty-five strokes for the same distance.

And that threefold difference in stroke efficiency is only half the story. A world-class runner is about 90 percent mechanically efficient, meaning that ninety of every hundred calories expended produce forward motion, while approximately ten are lost to muscle heat, ground friction, wind resistance, etc. Because water is almost 900 times thicker than air and highly unstable as a medium for applying power, a world-class swimmer is only 9 percent mechanically efficient—which means the typical beginner triathlete probably has energy efficiency of about 3 percent. Thus, the path to swimming improvement is not to make more energy available through training, it's to waste *less* energy by improving your stroke. If you can increase your mechanical efficiency even modestly—from, say, 3 percent to 4 percent—that will translate into a 33 percent improvement in your swimming capacity. No workout program can produce those kinds of results, but I've routinely seen swimmers in Total Immersion workshops achieve that sort in a single weekend.

Running Is a Sport; Swimming is an *Art*

What makes swimming different? Simply put, running is a natural activity, while swimming is a "natural struggle." The world's best swimmers move through the water with grace, economy and flow, while novices are awkward, clumsy and inefficient. You needn't lose any sleep if this describes you; my extensive teaching experience suggests that very few people have the innate ability to swim fluently. But I've also learned that the rest of us *can* learn to swim well if we take the time to master swimming as an *art* before tackling it as a *sport*. When you focus on swimming more and more yards, you just imprint what I call "struggling skills." Instead focus on swimming short distances slowly without fighting the water or yourself, then patiently develop your ability to do that for progressively greater distances or at marginally faster speeds. Here's a quick plan for learning to *move like water* in the pool:

1. **Swim slowly.** Racing the clock—or other swimmers—will only cause you to thrash and splash. Swimming slowly is the best way to begin developing habits of efficiency and economy. And while swimming slowly, practice the following:

2. **Count your strokes.** Your best measure of efficiency is how many strokes you take getting across the pool. Set an initial target 10 percent lower than your norm. If you usually take twenty-two strokes per length (spl), make twenty your goal—using ease, not strain, to make it. After any length that exceeds your target, rest longer—try five or more deep, slow breaths as a recovery interval—before starting again. Allow at least two to three hours of cumulative practice, over several thirty-minute sessions, to adapt before reducing your spl further.

3. **Look Down.** Forget the old rule about looking forward; a high head position is bad for your neck and spine and creates extra drag. Look directly at the bottom and focus on a long "head-spine line." Ask a friend to check that no more than a sliver of the back of your head is visible above the surface.

4. **Swim silently.** Noise and splash are the clearest evidence of wasted energy. Anything you do that results in a quieter stroke will also increase your efficiency, lower your spl, and reduce fatigue.

5. **Swim less, drill more.** If you find yourself unable to reduce your spl to a consistent twenty or fewer strokes per twenty-five yards, your stroke inefficiencies are so stubborn that every lap you do simply makes them more permanent. The quickest way to build new "fishlike" movement patterns is to practice skill drills rather than conventional swimming. Try doing up to 80 percent of your laps in stroke drills for the next month or two and see how your stroke reacts.

Happy laps!

BASIC SWIMMING MADE EASY

Why a novice swimmer should practice "martial arts" to transform frustration into flow. I get many letters and inquiries from athletes who want to take up triathlons but can't swim. Or worse, they think they can swim but when they get into a pool they can't swim a lap without losing their breath. It's very frustrating for them. Trying harder works with most other sports, but in swimming it only gets aggravating and most give up. The harder they try without the proper instruction, the slower and more tired they get.

You *can* figure out the swimming-improvement puzzle *and* have fun doing so! You have difficulty with swimming—and not with other sports—for this reason: You have human DNA. The other sports come more easily to you because they don't happen in the water. Your coach's frustration is likely because he's guided by traditional "Human Swimming" principles that haven't changed much in fifty or sixty years. The old way of thinking goes like this:

1. Swimming is an ordeal; if you get tired, then you need to train more and harder to survive it.

2. Technique—if you get around to working on it—mainly means "how you use your hands to push water toward your feet."

Total Immersion has succeeded with novices because we understand that training to "get in shape" mainly ensures that your "struggling skills" get more permanent. We also emphasize that avoiding drag is far more important than how you push the water back.

Swimming as a martial art. Next time you visit the pool, spend ten minutes watching other swimmers. You'll see that every stroke looks exactly the same. Your stroke is a habit pattern, deeply imprinted in your nervous system. The phrase "practice makes perfect" gets it only partly right. "Practice makes permanent . . . whatever you happen to practice" is far truer.

When trying to improve your efficiency, your success depends on practicing only the movements you'd like in your "muscle memory" and on scrupulously avoiding whatever you don't want imprinted there. Normal swim repeats will limit your progress because the imprint of millions of previous strokes is so resistant to change.

Each year we teach about fifteen hundred students in TI weekend workshops. Their average stroke count at the beginning is twenty-one to twenty-two for twenty-five yards. One day later that average has improved to seventeen strokes, or an overnight efficiency gain of 20 percent. The two primary reasons for such progress are "muscle amnesia" and "martial-arts swimming."

Avoiding struggle. After we videotape our students doing a length of freestyle on Saturday morning, they don't swim another length of whole-stroke until Sunday afternoon—by which time they've spent six hours practicing efficient swimming movements without a single "old" freestyle stroke. By teaching with movements their nervous systems don't recognize as swimming, we've given them "muscle amnesia," a blank slate for learning new skills and bypassing old habits.

The second key to success is the "martial-arts swimming" part. Formal swimming instruction has existed for a few dozen years, while martial arts have been taught for thousands of years, giving martial-arts masters considerable opportunity to refine the best way to teach movement skills. Their non-negotiable rule is: "Never practice movements you cannot perform correctly." So they start with movements that seem ridiculously simple and progress by small steps. The more patiently they practice basics, the more fluent and effortless they'll be at advanced skills. TI employs the same kind of progression.

Four essentials for achieving a "swimmer's high." Because of your human DNA, the skills that make you more economical won't come naturally. You'll need to make a mindful, organized, patient effort to make them as instinctive as the inefficient habits they'll replace. Here are the guidelines for success at swimming:

1. Saving energy is more important than getting in better shape. If you're fit enough to run a mile, you're fit enough to swim a quarter mile nonstop; if you can't it's because you spend too much energy making waves and creating turbulence, and too little moving you forward. The typical novice swimmer wastes as many as ninety-seven of every hundred calories. If you can increase your energy efficiency by just a little bit, you could swim lap after lap with little fatigue.

2. Get rid of "that sinking feeling." When we videotape novice swimmers at TI workshops, nearly all have poor balance. Hips and legs sink, meaning much more surface area is creating drag. And because they feel themselves sinking, most of the energy they put into stroking is actually devote to "not sinking" rather than to moving forward. Working on your pull is fruitless until you learn to achieve an *effortlessly horizontal* position. Balance drills are the fastest way to begin saving energy.

3. Pierce the water. Because water is 887 times denser than air, drag is the main reason you can't swim as far or fast as you'd like. By learning to slip through a smaller "hole" in the water, you'll immediately go farther, faster, with less effort. Two things that will make a big difference: (1) Keep your head in line with your spine, and (2) use your hand to lengthen your body line—and let "pushing water back" take care of itself, while you focus on extending the *other* hand.

4. No more bubbles, noise, or splash. Water is a *fluid;* thus any rough or rushed movement is hugely penalized, while smooth movement is hugely rewarded. Listen for noise or splash and watch for bubbles in your stroke. Do whatever it takes to eliminate them. You'll immediately feel a *lot* better.

Your goal with every length, should be to not only move through the water better but also enjoy it more. In fact, make it a primary goal to feel good every time you swim. This can help create and sustain what we call a flow state, an almost euphoric condition, similar to the "runner's high," in which you virtually lose yourself in the satisfaction of the activity. Start with simple movements and drills and with just a few movement cycles. Progress gradually and patiently to longer distances and more advanced movements.

Eventually your nervous system will have taken so many "snapshots" of smooth swimming movements that it becomes easy for you to assemble them into a complete "movie." And because humans' natural efficiency in water is so limited to start with, there's virtually no "improvement ceiling" when it comes to good technique. Whether you're a beginner learning basics or swam competitively in your youth, if you practice mindfully, there will always be some new breakthrough in store. After thirty-six years of swimming and thirty of coaching, I still make exciting discoveries that make me feel better than ever in the water.

This article is excerpted from the book Triathlon Swimming Made Easy. *For information call 800-609-7946 or visit www.totalimmersion.net. Questions on swimming? Send them to Terry Laughlin at totalswimm@aol.com.*

A Few Words About:

Pool toys, such as kick boards, zoomers, hand paddles, and fins: Laughlin isn't a big fan of these, referring to them as old-school techniques. They are used to strengthen individual body parts, but Laughlin's swim approach is built on integration, not separate pieces. "No real learning happens if you are relying on toys to teach you balance or form," says Laughlin. "Skilled movement is the best teacher." He cites the example of swimmers who use zoomers, short fins, in the pool to build speed. "The zoomers make them go fast but you can't use them in competition so what's the point? To impress your friends at the pool? And if they think they are building leg muscle, then think again. It's the worst thing to do. You want your legs to barely be working in the swim as you will need them more the bike and run."

Variety of strokes: Although most triathletes stick with freestyle, Laughlin, who competes on a high-ranking masters team, likes to incorporate different strokes in his own workouts. He believes you learn something about yourself and your body with each different stroke. "I wouldn't use the butterfly stroke in a triathlon but when I use it in the pool I learn something. Swimming all strokes in training teaches you how your body interacts with the water."

Injuries: According to Laughlin, the most common swim injuries are shoulder tendinitis and torn rotator cuff. These injuries can be avoided by learning to swim properly with the right stroke techniques. "It all goes back to balance," he says. "Injuries are caused by swimmers constantly slamming their arms into the water at the wrong angle, pressing down at full extension. It's an accident waiting to happen and over time an injury will most likely occur."

Wet Suits: Although Laughlin isn't a personal fan of wet suits, he realizes that first time triathletes wouldn't think of "going into battle without their armor." He prefers the feeling of moving through the water on his skin rather than neoprene. He also wants to dispel the myth that wet suits keep you buoyant. They do, but so will learning to swim correctly with the right balance and movement.

More information on wet suits can be found later in this chapter.

THE BIKE

If Chris Carmichael can coach Lance Armstrong to seven consecutive Tour de France titles, imagine what he can do for your cycling leg at your first triathlon. Carmichael is the founder, CEO, and president of Carmichael Training Systems (CTS), and longtime friend and coach to Lance Armstrong. He was also the cycling coach for the 1992 and 1996 Olympics and has been honored as the US Olympic Committee's Coach of the Year and as well as being inducted into the USA Bicycling Hall of Fame in 2003.

Before becoming a coach, best-selling author of books about cycling and fitness, and peak-performance expert, Carmichael was first and foremost a cyclist. He was a member of the first American team to ride in the Tour de France (7-Eleven, in 1986) and was a member of the 1984 Olympic cycling team. He's been competing since he was a ten-year-old kid in South Miami, Florida. Carmichael is the only person to coach both a Tour de France winner, Lance Armstrong, and an Ironman winner, Peter Reid, in the same year.

The advice he gives here can be found in his 2004 book, The Ultimate Ride: Get Fit, Get Fast and Start Winning with the World's Top Cycling Coach.

Welcome to my world of cycling: Whether you are digging out that old clunker from the back of the garage or riding a ten-thousand-dollar custom bike won't make much of a difference if you don't know how to ride properly. Let's start with the basics. Regardless of the bike used for your event, a proper fit to the bike is essential. Changing your position even slightly can have a significant effect on overall comfort, performance and efficiency. Cycling during a triathlon, even if you are not competing for time, is different than cruising downtown on a Sunday afternoon. It's more strenuous, you can't control the route (i.e., avoid hills) and there will be lots of other riders all around you. A proper fit to the bike will help reduce the risk of injuries, especially to the knees and lower back. Think of your bike as an extension of your body. Reputable bike stores can do a fitting, although they may charge for the procedure.

Now that you have the proper fit, start your ride with a good warm-up. Just as you would do in any sport, give the muscles a chance to warm up and get flexible and supple before you start to make them work hard.

Get comfortable on the bike: The most important point in cycling for a first-time triathlete is to just get comfortable riding. Become familiar with your bike, how the gears work, how it rides, how it handles on hills and over bumps. The more time you put in on the bike, the more comfortable and adept you will become by race day. This is going to be different than riding your bike around town when you were a kid. You'll have a set course that will probably entail hills. You'll be in close proximity to other cyclists who will be going much faster and some much slower than you.

You should also practice using a water bottle while cycling. If you don't have a water bottle bracket, it would be wise to get one. Even if you are not riding at top speed, you'll be working hard and using up energy, which will need to be replaced with fluids, especially if it is a hot day.

Build aerobic capacity: In the beginning, you will need to build aerobic capacity. The first few weeks on the bike should be all about strength training and focusing on pedal mechanics. The most important work a first-time triathlete can do, more important than sprinting or high-intensity intervals, is to increase the power of your aerobic engine. Generally, sixteen weeks is sufficient to build aerobic capacity and strength but if you don't have that much time, try to fit in as much as you can prior to the event so you will feel competent in completing the course. Try to get out for a ride two to three times a week, for anywhere from ten to twenty miles. Don't worry about time. Concentrate on volume.

Build pedal cadence: Cadence refers to the revolutions per minute of the pedal stroke. It is a cycling skill in itself and how many cyclists define themselves. The ability to pedal at different cadences is important for your development as a cyclist. The cadence you use during cycling can affect how fatigue impacts your riding. When you pedal slowly, you're pushing against more resistance with each pedal stroke, which means you have to recruit a lot of muscle fibers in your legs to generate enough power to keep going. The trouble is, many of those fibers fatigue quickly, no matter how fit you are. Pedaling faster reduces the resistance you're pushing against with each stroke, which shifts a good portion of the stress of pedaling from your leg muscles to your heart and lungs. Since your heart and lungs don't fatigue the same way skeletal muscles do, this shift allows you to keep riding longer before your legs get tired.

Drills: As your leg muscles develop your training should include longer intervals of riding. I suggest you integrate the following three drills into your weekly workouts:

Tempo workout: This drill develops the upper-end aerobic system. Tempo workouts should be performed without disruption, i.e., traffic signals, intersections, stop signs, etc. The goal is to complete an uninterrupted, continuous ride at medium speed, low pedal cadence, for at least forty-five minutes. Try to stay in the seat when climbing hills for as long as you can.

Steady state interval: These are like tempo workouts, but faster. On flat to rolling terrain, pedal fast for eight to twenty minutes, two to four times. The concentration in this workout is on intensity, not cadence.

Fast pedal: The fast pedal drill helps increase pedal efficiency and allows you to develop a smooth pedal stroke. On a relatively flat surface, with low pedal resistance, start out with a cadence of between ninety and ninety-six rpm, or fifteen to sixteen pedal revolutions per ten-second count. After two minutes, slowly increase your speed to eighteen to twenty-two pedal revolutions per ten-second count, or between 108 and 130 rpm. Keep your hips steady with no rocking. Concentrate on pulling through the bottom of the pedal stroke and over the top. Sustain this cadence through the remainder of the drill, five to twelve minutes, one to five times.

Tapering: For most people, this is the favorite time when all the months of training kick in and you are performing at your best. Weekly volume is reduced, intensity is at its highest and training is specifically focused on the event. As much as this is an exciting time, it is also a fragile one as you don't want to get injured or fatigued after months of training. Keep the workouts short and sweet. During this period, use all your previous training skills to perfect your ability to move quickly and confidently on your bike at high speeds and pedal cadences. But don't get too tired. Ideally, you should taper one week before your triathlon.

The event: You are ready! Here's what to do the night before:

Make a list of all your gear and check it twice before you go to bed the night before the event. Pump the tires as well so that task is one less worry on race day. In the event something happens to your tires or bike, don't fret as most USAT sanctioned events have bike mechanics and bike work stations set up to aid the athletes.

Helmets are required at all sanctioned triathlons so don't leave home without it.

Setting up transition: Try to situate yourself closest to the bike exit of the transition zone. This will decrease the time you have to run with the bike.

Rack your bike by the handlebars.

Organize your gear in a way that makes it easy to grab and is in the order you will be using it. Start by laying your towel out in front of your bike.

Have your shoes loosened and lubricated with Vaseline if not wearing socks.

Next to your shoes, have your gels or bars opened and ready.

Place your bib-belt or running shirt with the bib already pinned on it, hydration belt, and running hat last in the line of gear.

Preparing to get off the bike: In the last two miles of the bike course try to keep a high cadence with your pedal strokes. This will take the stress off the muscles in your upper legs for the transition to running. The goal is to get off the bike with enough energy and fresh enough to complete the run. Our experience has shown that conserving a little energy on the bike leads to a much faster run, but a very fast cycling leg can wreck your running performance. You can crank out a huge bike lead and gain several minutes on your bike time only to lose more time in your run due to fatigue.

Transition two: Rack your bike by the handlebars (no matter how tired you are or how rushed you feel, don't ever throw your bike down on the grass and leave it for someone else to rack or, worse, step on).

Grab some fluids or energy bar.

Get ready and run!

A Few Words About:

Indoor trainers and Spinning classes: A stationary trainer is essential equipment for anyone who takes their cycle training seriously, especially if you live in climates with extreme weather changes like snow, ice, or intense heat. With a trainer, there is no excuse to put off a workout or distance ride. If you don't want to invest in a stationary trainer, spinning classes are a good alternative and should be available at a local health club or fitness center. Make sure to take an introductory class before joining in with more seasoned spinners.

Weight resistance training: I am a firm believer in resistance training to gain strength, not bulk. Athletes need a strong, solid core and this is especially true for cyclists and runners who need to call upon upper body and lower back muscles.

Group rides: One of the best tools for everything from motivation to training is the group ride. They should be regarded as supplements to your personal training program and opportunities to add variety, racelike conditions, and tactical practice to your overall preparation. Besides, if you know your pal and training partner is waiting for you at six on a Saturday morning, you're more likely get you out of bed and resist the temptation to roll over and shut off the alarm.

Stretching: Flexibility in the hamstrings, lower back and quadriceps is important for optimal performance. Stretching after your workout, when your muscles are warm, is the best time for improving flexibility and preventing injury. When stretching at the beginning of a workout, it's best to ride easy for ten to fifteen minutes to warm up your muscles, then stop and stretch.

Sports drinks: Drink fluids containing sodium, potassium, and magnesium during and following the race are essential for recovery. They are also an important source of carbohydrate energy. Water alone won't replenish the minerals or energy lost in the overall effort.

The seventh day: I believe all athletes should incorporate a *complete* day of rest once every seven to ten days. The positive impact of one full day of rest outweighs the potential benefit you would see from adding one or two more workouts to that seven-to-ten day period. You'll come back feeling stronger, having better workouts, and enjoying training much more.

Heart rate and heart rate monitors: I think they are a great tool for determining the intensity of your training. I prefer using average heart rates (instead of maximum) as they yield better responses from athletes at all ability levels and minimize the risk of overtraining.

Clipless pedals: This is a more functional pedal system than standard pedals and were designed for more aerodynamic pedaling. They provide solid foot-to-pedal contact and work the leg and pedal more efficiently. The pedal cleat and shoe system cost more than standard pedals and take some time to get used to but if you are going to become a serious triathlete these are the way to go.

Aerobars: Considered part of "fast" equipment for serious riders, these specialty bars fit over the handlebars angled upwards. They are designed for the more advanced rider who is looking for a more aerodynamic ride where every second counts.

THE RUN

I knew just who to turn to for the best advice on running: the ambassador and guru of the running community, Bart Yasso. He has been running for more than twenty-five years, completing more than 150 marathons in places like Antarctica, Mount Kilimanjaro, and on every continent. He has completed the Badwater ultramarathon—146 miles through Death Valley, considered the world's toughest endurance race—and when not out running on assignment for Runner's World *magazine, where he holds the title of race and event promotion director, he is cycling. He was the United States Biathlon Federation long-course national champion in 1987, an event that earned him a feature in* Sports Illustrated. *What motivates a guy to run 150-plus marathons? "I ran the first seventy-five or so for time," he says. "But lately they've been either work-related—I've helped lead a lot of* Runner's World *pace teams over the years—or just for fun." He knows everyone in the running community who looks to him for advice, and as a friend. His sense of humor is evident in the lectures and clinics he gives around the world for* Runner's World. *He is self-effacing, hysterically funny, and a bit nuts. Or maybe it's his wife, Laura, an ultra-marathoner, who's nuts. "Laura says we need to run every marathon in Italy," says Yasso. "We got married there and ran the Rome Marathon the very next day. It was awesome and I am very proud to say it was one of my slowest marathons. The thing is, there are fifty marathons in Italy, and we've only done four of them. We need to get busy. I can't wait."*

Yasso's knowledge and years of experience running and biking are invaluable for successfully completing the run component of a triathlon.

Before I start, I am going to assume you know how to run and can run three miles. Don't worry about speed for now. If you don't know how to run or haven't started jogging at least a mile then look to my buddy and *Runner's World* colleague Amby Burfoot, winner of the 1968 Boston Marathon, who has written a few books on the subject of how to run.

Physically, the run is the most demanding of the three sports in a triathlon. You can float in the swim, coast on the bike, but in the run there is no escape. You have to haul around your total body weight for the long haul. And you start the run already fatigued, sweaty, hungry, and thinking, *Will someone please remind me why I signed up for this in the first place?*

There's only two things you have to know to successfully complete the run in a triathlon: Pacing is everything and yes, your legs will feel like jelly when you first get off the bike, but with the right training and workouts you can overcome that and run like the pros.

I've trained a lot of people to run marathons and races at other distances and the one thing that I find essential is a plan. You need to work out a training plan and tack it up somewhere you'll see it—and follow it—every day. For a first-time triathlete doing a sprint distance, a twelve-week training plan is a good place to start. When I am training marathoners, I have them running six out of seven days, with a gradual buildup of distance. But for triathlon training, you have to squeeze in swimming and biking workouts as well so I'd cut down on the numbers of days you run. But that means no junk days. Every day you run, whether it's three or four days a week, make it count.

One of those days should be a long run, 100 percent longer than your race-day distance. If you're racing a 5K, train up to a 10K. If you're racing five miles, train up to ten. Building the endurance and distance will help you significantly on race day. However, keep the "double your long run" rule only for sprint and Olympic distances.

As I mentioned, pacing is everything. If you look at the elite marathoners, they can hold their race pace almost to the second for 26.2 miles. It's the smart way to run. It's the way Deena Kastor won her bronze medal in Athens in 2004. As you train, wear a watch and learn how to mentally run at the pace you want to set race day. If you're running a 5K and want to finish in twenty-five minutes, that's an eight-minute-per-mile pace. If you're running a five-miler and want to finish in forty-five minutes, that's a nine-minute per mile pace. Pace charts are very helpful. You can find one on the *Runner's World* website, www.runnersworld.com. Even if your goal is just to finish and you don't care what your time is, proper pacing helps you expend energy more efficiently. It's easier and more efficient to run at a steady pace than go through spurts of fast to slow. That kind of running, especially in a triathlon when you are already tired from swimming and biking, usually results in a dead stop.

I'm a big believer in negative splits and think they are especially important in the triathlon because the fatigue from the swim and bike ease into the run. Run the first mile at a pace fifteen to twenty seconds per mile slower than race pace. Then gradually pick it up until you feel comfortable with the pace. Hold that comfort zone and then try to go a little faster the last few miles to achieve the negative split.

Speaking of running efficiently, this goes along with learning to pace correctly. Learning to run efficiently means running with the least amount of swing and movement to your form, which conserves energy. The form of an elite runner is beauty in motion: arms at the hips, hands relaxed not clenched, arms pumping in a backward motion in rhythm to the foot strike, body bent slightly forward, back straight, and head square on the shoulders, not drooping down. Even a tired runner can have good form. Don't flail your arms around wildly like a crazy person. Keep your arms at your sides pumping in tune to your feet. Relax your whole body, starting with the facial muscles, all through your shoulders, back, arms, hips, legs and feet. The more you relax, the faster you will run. You'll also look a heck of a lot better in the race photos and the sag wagon won't be following your every move.

When you encounter hills, shorten your stride on the uphill and pump your arms more. On the downhill, relax your arms and keep your body lean even with the hill. I call it the "nose over toes" look.

Now, about those jelly legs. What causes your legs to feel like large oak trees when you first get off the bike and start the run is the body's challenge of switching gears from using biking muscles to using running muscles. Your body has to reroute the blood supply away from the biking muscle and to the running muscles. The more you practice this transition, the faster your body will become at adapting to the switch. The first time you do this you'll feel like you've forgotten how to run. Your legs won't cooperate and you can't rely on your mind because that's spent as well. The only thing that really helps is brick workouts. Set up a transition area on your lawn or at the gym by spinning and then hitting the treadmill. Even if you run for just ten minutes it will help the body adapt. Brick workouts should be done once or twice a week, fifteen to twenty minutes of running right off the bike.

On race day, remember to keep focused on your pace, form, and run transition. If you are the competitive type that notches up the testosterone when someone passes you, learn to rein it in. That sort of macho attitude will get you nowhere. The smarter runner who is pacing well will most likely pass a lot of fatigued participants who haven't learned the secret of pacing and staying steady to the drumbeat of a real runner.

Specifics

Check your shoes for wear and tear once a month. Never run more than four hundred miles on a pair of shoes. The midsole wears out first and isn't visible to the eye, like the outer wear and tear you can see around the heel and toe of the shoe. A good tip is to write the date of purchase on the shoe box so you can see how long the shoes lasted.

Practice grabbing a cup of water on the run and try to get more inside you than on you.

Recovery

Rest and recovery is part of training. A rest day is as important as a speed workout. One thing I learned from my trips to Africa is that the Kenyans run very easy on their easy days and very fast on their quality days. You must recover so you can increase the quality of your workouts. Here is a sample run week schedule:

Monday, rest day; Tuesday, three- to six-mile tempo run; Wednesday, rest day; Thursday, speed workout or hills; Friday, brick workout; Saturday, easy five-mile run; Sunday, six to twelve miles starting out ninety seconds per mile slower than 10K race pace, middle miles sixty seconds per mile slower than 10K race pace, last few miles thirty seconds per mile slower than 10K race pace.

A Few Words About:

Sun protection. Always lather up before the run. Sunglasses and a visor or cap will also help keep the sun off your face.

Running shoes with lace locks or elastic laces will get you moving faster. If you prefer not to wear socks, bring some foot powder to keep your feet dry and Vaseline/BodyGlide to help get your feet into your shoes quickly.

If you don't have a bib-belt, make sure to bring an extra running shirt with your bib number already pinned to it.

It's always a good idea to bring multiweather clothing just in case it rains or turns cool.

PUTTING IT ALL TOGETHER: DAVE SCOTT

The most recognized athlete and coach in the sport, Dave Scott is a six-time winner at the Hawaii Ironman and the first inductee in to the Ironman Hall of Fame. At his first win in 1980 at the age of twenty-six, he wore high-top white tube socks and had his parents follow him along the course in their car just in case he needed something. He won in 9:24:33 and went back to win in 1982, 1983, 1984, 1986, and 1987, earning him the nickname "The Man." Dan Empfield refers to Scott as the God of Triathlon. In 1994, at age forty, he came back to competition after a five-year hiatus and came in second. In 1996, at age forty-two, he finished the bike sixteen minutes behind the lead pack and went on to run a 2:45 marathon, finishing fifth overall.

In 1989, his most dramatic Hawaii finish, Scott had a memorable show-down with Mark Allen, battling side by side for eight hours. Allen narrowly edged Scott out to win by seconds. Their marathon splits were 2:38 and 2:39, respectively.

He is highly respected by his peers and is considered the last word on training and drills. He now coaches full time at his establishment in Boulder, Colorado, and still competes. In this section, Scott will discuss training for a developing triathlete (he doesn't use the word beginner*) gearing up for a first sprint-distance triathlon.*

Setting Goals

The first thing I ask my clients is to define their goal for the event. Do they want to win outright? Win the age division? Just have fun? It's important to know what your goal is before the event. Most developing triathletes say their goal is just to finish but they want to finish in the best possible way for them. I call this being internally competitive and I think it is a good thing. It's what motivates us. In your first event you want to do the best you can and then if you go on to do more, it's logical to want improve on your time.

After you have defined your goal, pick the event and start a log. Working backward from the date of the triathlon, designate a sixteen-week training period.

Integrating Three Sports

If you are already doing one or more of the three events, it is natural to want to gravitate to that sport—it's comfortable. If you're a runner, you'll want to run more than bike or swim. If you're not a runner you'll most likely put it off as long as possible, as it is the most difficult of the sport to integrate into your training because it takes a toll on the body and is aerobically the most difficult. If you are not a swimmer you'll have to force yourself to get in the pool and learn to swim and breathe correctly. It is the most technical of the three sports, and it takes time to learn to swim efficiently and fast. And even though most of us rode bikes as kids, riding in a triathlon is not the same as cruising through town on your banana-seat bike with no gears. Try to get out on a road bike and learn to use a few gears and feel comfortable in the saddle for ten to fifteen miles. Hybrids and mountain bikes are fine if that's all you have but they will slow you down. If you are going to borrow a bike, at least give it a few spins around the block before the event and try to remember what it looks like when you get to transition when it will be racked with hundreds of other bikes that will all look alike that morning.

Short- and Long-Term Goals of Training

Throughout the sixteen-week training period, keep going back to your goal. A developing triathlete doesn't need to master each sport but just feel comfortable doing them for the duration of the event. The overall long-term goal of the training period is to build confidence in mastering your first triathlon. The specific short-term goals are to slowly build the distance and intensity of each sport and then start to combine them, adding one then two and incorporating some brick workouts.

Training Cycle

During the first six weeks you should be slowly increasing distance, 7 to 10 percent per week for all three disciplines, three sessions per week per discipline. Saturdays should be reserved for long days and the other two days are short workouts.

At beginning of the seventh week start doing multiple sessions, combining workouts. A twenty-minute swim followed by a twenty-minute bike, or a twenty-minute bike followed by a twenty-minute run. Your sessions should gradually be getting longer in distance and intensity, following the 10 percent rule, and at the same time shortening the gap between the multiple sessions. If you are swimming twenty minutes in the morning and running twenty minutes in the afternoon, try to bring them closer together each week, hitting your peak with two weeks before the event. The maximum sustained effort and maximum time for each level triathlon before tapering is:

Sprint: 6-10 sessions
Bike: 2 hours
Run: 75 minutes
Swim: 1200 meters
Olympic: 6-10 sessions
Bike: 2 hours and 30 minutes
Run: 90 minutes
Swim: 2000 meters
Half Iron: 6-10 sessions
Bike: 3 hours and 30 minutes
Run: 1 hour 40 minutes to 2 hours
Swim: 2800 meters
Iron Distance: 8-10 sessions
Bike: 4.5 to 6 hours
Run: 1 hour 50 minutes to 2 hours and 30 minutes
Swim: 3600 meters

Incorporating Brick Workouts

Incorporating a brick workout is fine provided you don't compromise the overall length of your training sessions. Total time per week is the number one priority in training. You need time on the bike and in your running shoes as well as hill workouts on the bike (nine to eighteen minutes of climbing) and the run (six to twelve minutes) before you consider a brick workout. Ideally, brick workouts should come after twelve weeks of base training.

Tapering

You should hit your peak training period two weeks out from the event. This doesn't mean you can take off the last two weeks; it just means reducing the intensity of the workouts. If you back off too much and sit around doing nothing with two weeks to go, your fitness levels could fall off. You need those endorphin cues to stay sharp in your brain. One week prior to the event is plenty for a developing athlete to ease off the training but you should still be keeping your muscles tuned up and toned. Go for an easy run or bike ride just to keep the legs moving.

Overreaching

If you are feeling stale and a general malaise begins to take over your workouts, you may be over-training. Take two days completely off and come back slowly.

Tips for Swimming

Definitely take a few strokes in the water before the race starts. This isn't just for the elites or pros to get a good warm-up. Getting familiar with the water can be calming and reassuring. First-time triathletes who've never swum in open water before tend to panic when they put their face in cloudy lake water with eelgrass, and start to panic, which causes short, shallow breathing—which can bring on a panic attack. Instead of going into full panic mode, relax in the water and do slow deliberate inhales and exhales.

Think about your breathing. For the first fifty yards, exaggerate your inhale time, allow your hips to rotate, and look up at the sky. This can be calming. Relax your recovery arm and rotate it with a high swing back into the water. This helps to open the shoulder blade. Don't push hard until you feel comfortable and are ready to surge ahead.

Wiggle your fingers on the recovery arm. It helps to relax your arms.

Wiggle your toes while swimming, which mimics the foot movement of biking and running and helps to keep the blood flowing to the legs. Try to avoid keeping your feet in a planed position, which can cause cramping in the calf.

A great universal drill I give to my developing triathletes is to swim while holding tennis balls, one in each hand. It forces you to feel the pressure in your forearm. The most common fault of all swimmers is the tendency to hold their head too high, drop their hips low, and drop the elbow on the catch. None of this is efficient use of the body's form. When you swim with the tennis balls you'll feel how important it is to stay streamlined while swimming.

Tips for Biking

Periodically stand up in the saddle to stretch out the lower back and hip flexors. This position also simulates running and changes the muscles in the legs, which will help if overused muscles get tired.

When in the standing position, push your hips toward the stem for a better stretch and pedal in an upright posture.

Stand up early, which helps to smooth the transition to running.

Tips for Running

Do walk if you feel like it, especially in the first mile or so when your legs feel heavy and worthless.

Don't force long strides until your legs are ready to adapt.

Swing your arms to get the entire body moving along with the legs.

Try to avoid hunching over and bunching your shoulders. This will cause your shoulder and abdominal muscles to tighten, which will in turn cause short, shallow breaths—not an efficient way to run. To alleviate this, run with the palm of your hand open upward and your thumb pointing out to the side, like you're carrying a tray. This motion will open your shoulders and help your posture.

About Transitions

For developing athletes, the transition area is the best place to shave off some time. You can eat up minutes by not having your gear laid out properly or fussing with clothing or equipment. I highly recommend setting up a practice transition area and practicing T1 and T2.

Swim-to-bike: This is the easier of the two transitions because your legs are still fresh and the swim is the shortest of the three disciplines. If you are wearing a wet suit, start to peel it off down to the waist as soon as you come out of the water. At transition, quickly take it off (refer to Chris Gebhardt's section on wet suits) and get on your biking shoes or sneakers. Socks are optional, but only if you have practiced biking and running without them. The most important thing to remember in T1 is to grab your bike helmet and your fluids or gels if you are using them. In USAT-sanctioned events you must walk your bike out of T1. Don't run with the bike. For sprint distances, most athletes stay in their swimsuit or throw a pair of running shorts over the suit. The bike distance is not long enough to feel any discomfort if you choose to stay in your suit.

Bike-to-run: This transition is harder due to the leg factor, but can also be the quickest as all you have to do is doff the helmet and rack the bike (only if you are not wearing clip shoes). If you are wearing bike shoes, try to loosen them before you dismount so you can kick them off in transition and slip into running shoes. Lace locks allow you to just pull the laces of the running shoes and tighten them, avoiding the extra seconds of tying and double-tying laces.

Over-reaching, Going (Too) Big: Avoiding, and Recovering from Over-Reaching and Over-Training *Reprinted by permission from* Triathlete Magazine *and Dave Scott*

At some point during your athletic career you will experience fatigue—either for a few days or, possibly, for several months. Fatigue in otherwise healthy triathletes is typically the result of emotional, psychological or physical overload—or a combination of all three, and, ultimately, it takes a toll on your ability to perform. Endurance athletes are particularly vulnerable to physical overload. Too much progressive training combined with incomplete recovery can create an over-reached athlete and an over-trained body.

The term *over-reaching* was adopted by exercise scientists to describe the short-term overload that can be managed within a few days. However, over-reaching can develop into over-training (from which it can be more difficult to recover) if the athlete does not mitigate the factors that caused the over-reaching or fails to allocate proper recovery time.

First, it's important to recognize that an athlete who repeatedly overloads his or her body without allowing adequate recovery time will eventually reach a state that requires rest. The length of the required rest period is one difference between over-reaching and over-training. Secondly, over-reaching symptoms can sometimes be masked by an overzealous, type-A athlete. An athlete and/or a coach must objectively recognize the patterns and fluctuations in a training year to prevent the compromised results that accompany chronic over-training.

To begin, let's take a look at the characteristics that produce over-reaching. It is important to remember that individuals may demonstrate a broad range of causes. However, over-reaching is most commonly caused by:

1. Too much too soon, such as a 10 to 20 percent increase in training volume over a three- to four-week period.

2. Frequently combining two harder variables in one training session (e.g. combining a long run with challenging hills or a tempo session with speed work).

3. Two or three high-intensity (i.e., near or above lactic threshold) workouts in one week on either the bike or run.

4. Not allowing two days of easier sessions between the challenging workouts described in 2 and 3 above.

5. Overload in psychological or emotional stress in other facets of your life.

6. Lack of sleep.

7. Poor nutritional habits before, during or immediately after workouts.

8. Loading up your racing season with too many events.

If only one of these statements matched your training style, then you might be able to get through the year. However, if you nodded your head to two or more then you are likely destined to experience over-reaching and possibly slide into over-training.

Walking a Fine Line

The three training parameters that dictate success for an endurance athlete are progression, overload and recovery. Without repeated days, weeks and months of workloads that break down and rebuild you, physiological progress would come to a standstill. And, indeed, there are times throughout the year during which you need to train in a fatigued state. Your muscles may, at times, feel sore and heavy, but there is a fine line between preserving your body's ability to repair and rebound and pushing yourself into a spiral. In fact, *rebound* is the key word that differentiates a tired athlete from one who has gone too far and has crossed the line separating over-reaching from over-training.

As with the above causes of over-reaching, the symptoms of the condition demonstrated by each athlete may vary. Still, many commonalities exist:

1. Physiologists, coaches and athletes have looked at morning pulse rate as an indicator of over-reaching, and studies have confirmed that a pulse rate of four to six beats above your baseline normal can be an initial indication that you are fatigued but not necessarily over-reached. An easy

day or a day off will usually bring your resting pulse back to normal. A more accurate indication of over-reaching is an inability to elevate your pulse rate and sustain it at a sub-threshold level. The body seemingly has a set governor that acts as a protective mechanism. When you are over-reached your muscles cannot and will not allow you to drive up the workload.

2. This inability to increase the pulse goes hand in hand with a muscular heaviness or overloaded feeling. Quite often there is a simultaneous tightness and stiffness in the joints. Regardless of the length of your warm-up, the muscles remain lethargic and heavy.

3. After a hard session the muscles can experience millions of micro-tears that can cause tenderness and soreness. The delayed onset of muscle soreness is a common symptom post-exercise (twenty-four to sixty hours). However, if the muscles are sore for an extended period, even with light exercise, this can be a sign of over-reaching. In an effort to repair and re-build the muscle damage, the muscle fills with water to flush out the by-products of exercise. This swelling can add to the heaviness described above.

4. A lack of sharpness during workouts as heart rate falls off for more than two days.

5. Eating habits are disrupted or compromised.

6. There is a decrease in your body weight.

If you have identified several of the above symptoms, and they last for three to five days or more, and if you ignore these symptoms, then you can push your body into a more severe state of fatigue called over-training.

Scheduling R&R to Avoid Over-Training

Recognize that if over-reaching crops up several times during the year this is okay. However, if you experience a bout of over-reaching and the symptoms reoccur fewer than two weeks later (or linger, as described above), you need to modify your training workload.

Recovering from over-reaching requires four steps:

1. Identify the symptoms.

2. Take two full days of rest with no exercise.

3. Take the following three days easy. No more than fifty minutes of exercise in one session. Do not attempt more than two of these easy sessions

in one day.

4. After this five-day period you can resume your normal training program. However, note that the symptoms of over-reaching should dramatically reduce during the three easy days. If they do not, then you may be on the verge of over-training. If your sleep pattern, exercise load or frequency of racing all dramatically increase and the ability to rebound diminishes, look out for over-training.

The symptoms of over-training can closely parallel over-reaching; however, without adequate recovery an over-trained athlete will quite often advance to a much deeper valley of fatigue. Over-trained athletes quite often have signs of improper hormone function, such as persistent colds, lack of sleep and muscular aches for several weeks. In addition, repeated hard sessions with little or no rest can lead to chronic low levels of amino acids in the blood. As intensity increases amino acids are released to control muscle breakdown. Additionally, if the intake of carbohydrates and protein is low, particularly after exercise, then the rate of repair and protein synthesis can be delayed. This delay can, in turn, prevent the body from rebounding. Quite simply, the body never catches up to the ongoing demands placed upon it.

Over-training requires an extended recovery period of six to twelve weeks, and, in some cases, it may take several months to regain your prior fitness level. Here are the four key steps to help you recover from a bout of over-training:

1. See a sports-medicine specialist. The protocol for evaluation will be determined by the specialist and should include a complete blood panel, muscle enzyme and hormone review.

2. Rest. This may be total rest for several weeks or light activity as determined by your specialist, coach and yourself.

3. Sleep. Increase the amount of sleep you get each night to ensure you rest for between seven and nine hours.

4. Plot out a logical step-by-step increase in your training routine after a second evaluation. This gradual increase in your desired fitness level may take anywhere from six weeks to six months.

Over-reaching and over-training can be controlled by recognizing the early symptoms and required patterns of recovery. During a recovery day or week, you need to ensure your body is given enough time to rebuild. Never compromise proper recovery for another hard training session.

The key to improving is progression, overload and recovery. Use all three forms of training to maximize your training and racing potential. Recovery is not an excuse; it is a necessity.

Summary

For your first triathlon, stay true to your original goal and just enjoy yourself. Do your best but not to the point where you feel defeated or crushed. You want to look forward to the next one so you can work out your first-time mistakes and keep getting better. If you set unrealistic or unattainable goals you'll only be setting yourself up for failure.

Keep the right mind-set. As you start your first triathlon, think of yourself as a triathlete, not a swimmer, or runner or cyclist. The best triathlete is a triathlete. The sooner you start thinking of yourself as one, the sooner you will become one.

ABOUT THAT WET SUIT

By now you've read about Jayne Williams's hilarious attempt at putting on her first wet suit, and swim coach Terry Laughlin explaining he prefers the feel of the water on his body while swimming to neoprene. Here's the real lowdown on wet suits from Ironman competitor Chris Gebhardt, who works for American Bicycle Group, a company that owns Quintano Roo wet suits as well as bikes and triathlon accessories. The founder of Quintana Roo, Dan Empfield, competed in the first Ironman held in Kona in 1981. In 1987 he created the world's first wet suits made especially for triathletes and named the company after his favorite biking area in the Baja region of Mexico.

Chris Gebhardt knows a thing or two about swimming and triathlon. He started swimming at age six and never stopped. He did his first triathlon while still in high school and to date has completed sixteen Ironman events, five at the World Championships in Kona. Here is what Gebhardt has to say about wet suits.

Why use a wet suit in the first place?

Many triathetes think that the primary purpose of a wet suit is to keep them warm. Not necessarily true. The real purpose of a wet suit is to make the swimmer more buoyant in the water, which in turn should make the swimmer faster. It's all about hydrodynamics. The wet suit helps keeps you buoyant in the water, a position where the body is aligned in a straight line and the hips are level with the rest of your body. A buoyant body will move through the water faster. The other reasons for wearing a wet suit are warmth and safety, kind of like a life preserver effect. Another advantage of a wet suit is it can act as body armor to cushion and protect against kicks and bruising from other swimmers in the thick of the event.

USA Triathlon has safety guidelines for not allowing wet suits if the water is over seventy-eight degrees, since there is a risk of overheating. This is why wet suits are not worn at the Hawaii Ironman.

Can I use my old surfing wet suit?

Triathlon-specific wet suits are not the same wet suits used in surfing or scuba diving. Those wet suits, which are thicker than triathlon wet suits, are designed specifically for warmth and have no flexibility to allow the wearer any range of motion for swimming. The neoprene used in triathlon-specific wet suits is more flexible, thinner and stretchy.

What type of wet suit should I buy?

There are basically two types, or styles, of wet suits: the full suit with sleeves and the sleeveless. Some manufacturers, like QR, also offer a short version, called the Quick John, which has short legs, ending just above the knee, and is sleeveless.

Sizing

Each manufacturer has a different sizing chart so make sure to check out the chart before purchasing. The suit should be snug but not so tight that you feel restricted in movement and breathe.

What will a new wet suit cost?

A new wet suit, regardless of manufacturers, will cost in the range of $160 to $500, based on technology and flexibility. The less expensive wet suits are actually warmer because they are thicker and less flexible.

How do I get the darn thing on?

Here are some of my patented tips for putting on a wet suit. I usually demonstrate this at my clinics, so just try and visualize as I go through the procedure.

Rub BodyGlide, a lubricating ointment, on the parts of your skin where the wet suit ends. This would include your neck, wrists and ankles (shoulders if it is a sleeveless). Do not use products like Pam or Vaseline, as their lubricating ingredients tend to dry out the wet suit, and it will crack in two or three seasons (and also void warranties).

Wear socks when putting on the wet suit so any grass or sand doesn't get picked up and trapped inside, which could cause skin irritation.

Make sure the zipper is in the back, not front. A reported mistake for some first-time users.

Step into the wet suit like you would a pair of pants and pull up like tights, rolling the suit up over the ankles and up the legs. The material is delicate, so do not grab it by your fingernails or it could rip and tear. If your suit has arms, put them on one at a time, using the rolling method.

First-time users may want to enlist the help of a friend or fellow triathlete to zip up the back of the suit.

Once it is on, run your hands over it to smooth it into place on your body.

How do I get it off?

The best way—and place—to start peeling off the suit is right out of the water. As soon as your feet hit dry land start peeling off the wet suit, arms first and one at a time. Roll the suit down to your waist as you are making your way to transition. When you get back to your bike, pull it down to your knees and then lift your knees one at a time to help get it down and over your ankles and off.

How do I take care of it?

The most important thing to do with the wet suit is rinse it off immediately after the event, especially if you swam in salt water. Shampoo a few times a year with wet suit shampoo or soapy water. Always fold and store your wet suit on a shelf, never hang it, as it will stretch over time.

For information on Quintana Roo wet suits check out www.rooworld.com

TRIATHLON NUTRITION

Nutrition has been called the fourth leg of a triathlon. Following a balanced and distance-specific nutrition plan will nsure you don't bonk, hit the wall, faint, hallucinate, or whatever else can happen when the body gets depleted of its energy source, or glycogen. Not being adequately fueled for an endurance event, which is usually defined as over two hours, can have serious, even life-threatening consequences. Much has been written about sports nutrition, such as the importance of staying hydrated and loading up on carbohydrates, but this information is generally geared to the weekend warrior. When the athlete crosses over to longer distances and longer durations of competition and is training two hours a day, six days a week, nutrition needs enter a whole new level—and unfortunately many nutritionists are not knowledgeable in this field. They receive no formal training in endurance nutrition.

That's why I turned to New York City-based Sports Dietitian Lauren Antonucci, MS, RD, CDE, and CDN. Besides being a nutritionist to top athletes, she is also an avid runner and triathlete who has completed eight marathons and numerous triathlons at all distances, including Ironman USA Lake Placid and Ironman Utah and Wisconsin. She knows from firsthand experience what it takes to fuel the body for an endurance sport, or even your first sprint triathlon. If you doubt the role nutrition plays in sports, just watch a video of the 1997 Hawaii Ironman. Canadian Heather Fuhr crosses the finish line for her first Hawaii win looking cool, calm, and as if she could keep going. In contrast, the fourth- and fifth-place women, Sian Welch and Wendy Ingraham, who are dehydrated and completely void of any sustenance, fall down yards from the finish line and have to crawl to the end, delirious, cramping, and in need of emergency medical attention. Six-time winner Paula Newby-Fraser, an Ironman veteran, also succumbed to poor nutrition in her 1995 event, DNFing during the marathon.

Since every athlete has individual nutritional needs based on their body weight, muscle mass, and hours of daily and weekly training, Antonucci will discuss nutritional needs for triathletes in general.

The first question I am usually asked when I am dealing with an athlete is, "What should I eat the night before my event?" The answer is, it's too late to be worrying about nutrition needs the night before. I tell them to take a step back and review not only what their nutritional needs are, but also what they've been eating on a daily basis. This will give them a better picture of how they are doing nutritionally and help them determine whether they have enough total calories, protein, and carbohydrates to continue training and racing as they wish. Many athletes make the mistake of thinking they only need to fuel for the event when they should be fueling and taking in the necessary nutrition all through training. You fuel with food. If you want to train you have to give your body what it needs: good healthy food. Consuming adequate total calories and total carbohydrate on a daily basis will ensure you have enough glycogen (energy our body stores in our muscles and liver) to meet your training and racing nutritional needs If you give it a bit of thought, all foods can fit into a healthy lifestyle and meal plan, including fresh fruit, carrots, grilled chicken, whole grains, ice cream, chocolate, and your favorite treats.

Caloric Needs

The general rule of thumb to figure out your estimated desirable body weight for women is to start with one hundred pounds for the first five feet, then add five pounds for each inch of height you are over five feet. Therefore a five-foot-four woman might want to weigh about 120 pounds, plus or minus 10 percent depending on body size and body composition.

For men, it is 6 pounds per inch after an initial 106 pounds for the first five feet. For a triathlete training for an event, the number of calories needing to be consumed on average can range from 2,000 to 5,000 calories a day just to maintain body weight. During an Ironman event athletes can consume up to 9,000 calories just to stay healthy and focused on the day of competition.

And it's not just any calorie that will do. In general, our diet should be made up of 60 to 65 percent carbohydrates, 15 to 20 percent protein, and 20 to 25 percent fat.

Let's Address the Carbs

Carbohydrates are extremely important for everyone, especially athletes. They provide us with the energy we need to think, work, and play our sport. A daily intake 60 to 65 percent of carbs should do the trick, and prevent glycogen depletion . . . as long as you are also meeting your daily total calorie needs. Some carbohydrate choices are better than others. The best choices include low-fat dairy, whole-grain breads and cereals, wheat pasta, brown rice, beans, lentils, and other whole grains. However, all carbohydrates will provide the energy needed to play your sport.

Athletes should always eat some form of carbohydrate before any practice, game, match, or race to provide the energy needed to perform. Here is a list of pre-game carbohydrate sources:

Oatmeal
Cereal
Pancakes with fruit/yogurt
Applesauce
Bagels
Rice, noodles
Fig bars
Ensure, Boost
Energy bars
Bread and jam
Pasta
English muffins
Yogurt
Mashed potatoes
Soup
Graham crackers
Sports drinks
Energy gels

To maintain your energy and ability to keep moving forward during an endurance event—one lasting more than one and a half to two hours, you will want to take in 0.5 gram of carbs per pound of body weight per hour during your activity. In order to get this into your system and not get sick or lose it all on the run, so to speak, you should practice eating and drinking fluids during training.

Protein Needs and Intake
Protein plays a different role than carbohydrate, but just as important.

Protein is necessary to build and repair muscle tissue, maintain your immune system, and replace red blood cells. Excess protein is converted and stored as glycogen or fat. It is important for all athletes, and especially those restricting their calories in order to achieve a desired weight loss, to consume adequate protein each day.

In the general population, most people need about 0.4 to 0.5 gram of protein per day per pound of body weight. This means a 160-pound person would require 65 to 70 grams of protein a day. Athletes require additional protein based on their total training volume and nutritional/weight goals. Your daily protein needs may reach 0.6 to 0.8 gram per pound of body weight per day. A registered dietitian can help you determine your specific protein needs, and the following chart can help you get a general idea as to whether you are eating enough protein each day to sustain your muscle mass and support your activity:

Source	Grams of Protein	Serving Size
Egg	7	1 whole egg
Egg, white only	3.5	1
Milk, low-fat	8	8 oz.
Cheese*	7	1 oz. or 1 slice
Chicken, white meat	23	3 oz.
Tuna*	20	3 oz.
Beef, lean	21	3 oz.
Almonds	3	12 nuts
Peanut butter	8	2 Tbs.
Kidney beans	6	½ cup
Tofu	15	3 oz.
Lentils	18	1 cup, cooked

*Choose mostly low-fat or nonfat milk and cheese, lean beef and chicken, and fish without skin.

Fats: The Good and Bad

Whether you like it or not, some body fat is an essential part of the body. The layer of fat just below the skin protects us from the cold. It also cushions and protects many vital organs and is part of the nerve, spinal cord, brain, and cell membranes. Fat gets its bad reputation mostly from people who eat too much of the wrong kind of fats, such as saturated and trans fats and rich, gooey desserts. But the right kind of fats can be an athlete's best friend. Fats and carbohydrates work together to give the body its energy needs. The body burns both carbs and fat during exercise. For an endurance athlete especially, this is important. Here's a list of some good fats that athletes should incorporate into their daily meals or snacks:

Nuts, preferably raw almonds and walnuts

Avocados

Flaxseed

Fish and/or fish oils

Olive oil or olives

The Importance of Hydration

Adequate fluid intake is essential for all life functions. It prevents dehydration, replaces fluids lost in sweat (which dissipates heat through the skin), and regulates body temperature. It also helps muscles recover from exercise by flushing out waste products. It is imperative that athletes begin each exercise session well hydrated, consume adequate fluids before and during workouts and continue drinking afterward to keep up with perspiration loss while exercising. Here are my guidelines for hydrating during an event:

—Drink 16 to 24 ounces one hour prior to the event

—Drink 4 to 8 ounces ten minutes before the event starts

—Drink 6 to 10 ounces every fifteen to twenty minutes during the event

—Include sports drinks with electrolytes if it is especially hot or if the event will last over one hour.

—Adjust fluid intake to match your sweat rate.

Speaking of sweat, which is water mixed with sodium and many other important electrolytes, it is the body's way of cooling down, an important and essential tool. During hard exercise, if you didn't sweat you'd overheat and cook to death. At the least, you'll develop headaches and cramping. When the body loses too much sodium, which maintains fluid balance around the cells, it causes a metabolic imbalance. Marathoners and other endurance athletes tend to experience muscle cramping and may even crave salt when they do not adequately replace that which is lost in their sweat. To avoid this they carry bags of salted foods like pretzels and other salty snacks with them on the bike and run. Chicken soup is served along the Hawaii Ironman course just for this purpose. Even at the half Ironman distance, salt tablets are highly recommended (once you have practiced in training and developed a well-thought-out plan of when and how many to take) to maintain the sodium balance. And don't try to wait as long as you can before drinking while training and racing. Your body needs continual fluids, so listen to your body and thirst and drink earlier rather than later.

Recovery

Having a recovery dietary plan is just as important as the pre-event dietary plan. Recovery nutrition not only replenishes what you have just burned off, but also helps your muscles repair and prepare for your next training session or race. Without it, your training efforts may very well be wasted. During training muscle fibers are broken down and must be repaired. A combination of carbohydrate and protein helps facilitate this process, so the ideal post-event meal contains both of these nutrients. The general rule of thumb is to start eating and or drinking recovery foods or beverages within half an hour of the event or workout.

A Few Words About:

Alcohol: Many of my clients ask about having alcohol the night before an event. The general guideline for alcohol consumption is up to one six-ounce glass of wine a day for women, and two for men. Anything above that is considered less than ideal. And in case you are wondering, you shouldn't "save" the entire count for the weekend and consume three or five glasses a night and think you have stayed within the health guidelines. One glass of wine the night before an event isn't generally going to affect your performance as long as you remain well hydrated. In fact, if an athlete is nervous and anxious the night before an event, and is used to drinking one glass of wine, it may help relax them. In moderation, alcohol can certainly have a place in a healthy athlete's diet and lifestyle, provided there is no medical reason to abstain. Do keep in mind that alcohol really is empty calories with no nutritional value. It's also a diuretic, which means it increases the body's fluid losses and can cause dehydration. That's not exactly what you're looking for right before a triathlon. Mixed alcoholic drinks can also add hundreds of additional empty calories and seem to go hand in hand with consumption of high-fat, high-calorie snacks like chips and dips.

Supplements: I would rather see my clients get their nutritional needs from healthy foods first, but if you are unsure you're eating a proper diet, than a multivitamin with mineral supplement may be a worthwhile "insurance policy".

The right time to eat: I get a lot of questions about the right time to eat. It doesn't really matter exactly what time you eat dinner, or if your biggest meal of the day is at noon or night. More important is that you do fuel throughout your day, and are sure to consume adequate fuel before *and after* your training sessions. Skipping dinner after your 8 P.M. run because you "don't eat after 8 P.M." is a much worse decision than eating a small but healthy balanced meal when you return home your your workout regardless of the time on the clock. However, studies have shown that people who skip meals during the day and eat later in the evening tend to eat more. Maybe they're hungrier because it's been awhile since their last meal. For athletes, a very heavy late-night meal the night before a big race can cause havoc on race day if the food has not had enough time to process through the GI system. So be sure to eat dinner a bit on the earlier side the night before your big events. And as a general rule, your mother was right: Breakfast is the most important meal of the day.

Test it first: The major rule of thumb for any addition, change, or deletion of food or fluids is to test it first. Sample new energy bars, gels, or drinks during training, never on race day.

TRIATHLON DIVISIONS

Youth

As the sport of triathlon grows, there has been a steady increase in the youth division. According to USA Triathlon (USAT), increase in youth one-day licenses sold has increased to more than 15,000 in 2005 from 6,000 in 2001. USAT considers the youth division to be ages 7 to 15. Age categories are generally broken down into 7-8, 9-10, 11-12, and 13-15. Rather than emphasizing competition at this age, kids, parents, and coaches should focus on enjoyment and learning proper skills and healthy exercise habits that will last a lifetime. USAT sanctions over one hundred youth races across the country, either in conjunction with an adult event or as a stand-alone.

USAT recommends two different sets of distances for youths: for ages seven through ten: 100m swim / 5K bike / 1K run, for ages eleven through fifteen: 200m swim / 10K bike / 2K run. At triathlon events that are not sanctioned by USAT, race directors are at liberty to set the age and distances. Alan Ley, coaching education manager for USA Triathlon, says their recommendations and guidelines are based on a combination of recommendations from the US Olympic Committee, other youth sports programs, and common sense. The Sara Lee IronKids Youth Triathlon series (www.ironkids.com), started in 1985, has seen more than forty thousand kids go through their highly competitive program. Some of their graduates have gone on to become quite famous. Lance Armstrong is an IronKid graduate and was runner-up at the 1985 IronKids National Championship.

At the SoBe Mini Mossman Youth Triathlon in Norwalk, Connecticut, children ages seven through fourteen have the opportunity to experience a real triathlon designed for their abilities on the same course as the adults. The youth triathlon was first offered in 2004, with sixty kids signing up. In 2006 more than 150 signed up, many of them first-timers. According to Paul Butcher, founder of Trifitness, organizers of the event, as the adult division of triathlons grow more popular, kids want their own event. "The youth division is definitely a growing segment of the triathlon market. Most of the kids who sign up have done one of three sports, usually swimming or running. This is a chance for them to experience all three. They do it for fun and really seem to enjoy themselves. Every finisher gets a medal." The SoBe Mossman Youth Triathlon is a USA Triathlon sanctioned event with the following distances: seven- through ten-year-olds swim 75 yards, bike 2 miles, and run 0.5 mile. The eleven- through fourteen-year-olds swim 150 yards, bike 4 miles, and run 1 mile. Trifitness also sponsors a USAT Youth Elite and Junior Elite National Championship, which is very competitive.

Meredith Jones is a typical example of the youth division in triathlons. A competitive high school track star who is ranked twenty-fourth in the state for cross country, she did her first triathlon in 2004 when she was fifteen. Soccer and running were her favorite sports as a kid and both her parents are runners. Inspired by some friends who had done a triathlon, she signed up for her first triathlon without any prior biking or swimming background. "I thought it would be fun," says Jones, from Ridgewood New Jersey. "I had no expectations except to finish."

For Jones, the appeal was do to a sport that didn't count, where she wouldn't be timed or her results analyzed by a coach and her peers. "I loved the fact that there wasn't any pressure on me to perform," she says.

She found the experience scary, intimidating, fun, and particularly enjoyed seeing all the different age divisions on the course. But it was a long day and she was exhausted at the finish, proclaiming she'd never do another one. She went back in 2005 and took first place in her age division.

Jones is off to Smith College, where she will continue her running career. She'd love to do more triathlons but coaches don't necessarily encourage participation in other sports that take away training time. In actuality, triathlon is the perfect cross-trainer for someone like Jones. "I get really upset if I don't PR at my meets but I love the freedom of competing in a triathlon just for myself," she says. It gives her a mental break from the pressures of competing, a refreshing change of pace.

One of the benefits of a sports program for youths is learning how to set and achieve goals. Participating on a team teaches them about cooperation, interaction, and the encouraging camaraderie of being a team player. Participating as an individual teaches them to rely on their own determination and be responsible for their own actions. Sports can also lead to a healthier lifestyle with a focus on better nutrition and improved fitness.

Tom Begg already has his two kids participating in youth triathlons. Caitlin, eleven, and TJ, eight, have done the West Point Kids Triathlon, the SoBe Mossman Youth Triathlon, and are gearing up for their first sprint-distance triathlon. They've been swimming since they were seven. Caitlin has done the one-mile division of Swim Across America, a fund-raiser that has participants swimming across Long Island Sound from New York to Connecticut in distances from one to six miles. As Begg sees it, "For five dollars a child can register with USAT and get an official card and key chain. It's great way to get involved at a young age."

To train for their triathlons they bike and run with friends in the neighborhood and also participate in other sports like lacrosse and swimming. Begg doesn't push them to do triathlons, but he supports their interest. His daughter was recently featured in *Discovery Girls Magazine,* where she was interviewed about doing triathlons. Based on comments from her interview in the July issue, she's already ahead of the game when it comes to her self-esteem and the importance of goal setting. According to Caitlin, "I like my determination to meet my goals."

Relay Teams

There is more than one way to enter a triathlon. If you don't want to do it as an individual entrant completing all three legs yourself, you can join a relay team and do one or two of the legs.

Ron Beinstock, of Fair Lawn, New Jersey, got into triathlons when he started dating Lisa Swain, a triathlete. A runner first, he took up cycling so he could spend more time with her. Now married to Lisa for more than fifteen years, he does the biking relay at triathlons while Lisa competes in the individual category. An intellectual property and entertainment lawyer as well as a musician with his band, the Suits, Beinstock finds it easier to train for one sport. "Between my work, my family, and my band I don't have a lot of time to train for all three events," says Beinstock, fifty. "I find I can get in more quality time training on the bike than I can with running and I've never been a swimmer. And I'm not really fast enough to do the run." He rides all year long and puts in an average of 150 miles a week on his bike, participating in time trials and cyclo-cross events in the winter.

The technical aspect of cycling also appeals to him. A self-described gear geek, he loves waxing poetic about all the minutiae of the sport. A discussion on carbon fiber versus titanium will get him going for hours.

He and Lisa also compete as a two-member relay team: Lisa swims and runs and Ron bikes. They work well together, beating out three-member relay teams.

He's also done triathlons in the individual category and prefers the relay. "The biggest advantage is that by the time I am getting ready to compete there are no lines at the bathroom," says Beinstock with his trademark humor.

The runner in a relay has the longest wait of the day, having to show up with everyone else in the beginning for registration and body marking, and then wait through the swim and the bike before competing.

Rick Pingitore, of Fair Lawn, New Jersey, is an elite masters runner with a five-mile PR of 26:40. He's been participating in triathlon relays for four years. In 1989 he did a triathlon as an individual and found it very tough, as he isn't a swimmer or biker. "I prefer the relay since I don't have the time to train for the swim and bike," says Pingitore, forty-seven. "This way I get to participate and do what I do best." He also likes the diversion from racing for himself. "Almost every weekend I participate in road races, a singular activity. A relay allows me to be part of a team and I enjoy that. I like the camaraderie." He doesn't mind showing up at the crack of dawn and waiting up to two hours for his leg of the race. "It's an exciting sport and I get to watch the top of the field come out of the water and get on their bikes long before anyone else. I also get to cheer for my team and at the end they are there for me at the finish line. The triathlon community is very tight and very friendly. I really enjoy being a part of it and a relay team is the perfect venue for someone like me."

One downside of relay teams is that there aren't age division categories. At fifty, Beinstock is sometimes the oldest participant in the relay, competing against much younger cyclists. According to him, "There's a lot of pressure on me to go up against younger riders. Some relay teams solicit the top athletes and their teams are stocked with semi-pros and even sponsored athletes."

Weight-Class Divisions

If you think you can't compete against the leaner, faster athletes, you can enter in a weight classification. For men, it is the Team Clydesdale competition open to any male athlete over 200 pounds; and Team Athena competition is open to any female athlete over 150 pounds.

In his youth, Urban Olsson was ranked in the top ten for swimmers seventeen and under in his native country of Sweden. He trained every day, sometimes twice a day, and was very serious and very competitive. But it got to be too much for him and he burned out at eighteen. Now forty-six and living in Little Falls, New Jersey, he competes in triathlons as a Clydesdale. His comfort weight is 190, though at times he peaks to 210. But he can still swim like a pro, clocking twelve minutes for a half-mile swim.

Olsson has always been attracted to the sporting life. In 1985 he took fifteen months off to sail from Sweden to New Zealand. He's run twenty marathons with a PR of 3:02 in 1997. Since picking up triathlons he's competed in distances up to the half Ironman. "If I didn't have to work and spend time with my family, I'd train for an Ironman," he says.

Bored with the marathon, he switched to triathlons for a new experience. With a strong swimming and running background, he only had to contend with biking. "I hate being passed on the bike. That's my weak link. I need to put in more training time or by a faster bike," laughs Olsson. "What I love about the triathlon is that there is always room for improvement. It's always a challenge."

According to Olsson, "Being a Clydesdale was not a conscious decision. I got on the scale one day and was over two hundred pounds. It just crept up on me. Sure I'd like to get back under two hundred pounds but I'm happy. It doesn't bother me. Being a Clydesdale actually helps me to stay in shape because my goal entering a triathlon is *not* to be a Clydesdale. I try to get in the best shape I can but can't seem to knock off the last ten pounds. I always have good intentions!"

THE ART OF SPECTATING

It isn't easy for family and friends to attend triathlons. Who wants to get up before dawn and stand in one place for hours scanning the crowd of hundreds or thousands of competitors trying to catch a glimpse of their loved one or friend as they enter the water en masse only to disappear into the frenzy of the swim? Then you have to check every same-colored swim cap as they emerge and try and find them running past frantically peeling off a wet suit. For a brief moment you may catch them as they charge off on their bikes with nary a wave or air kiss. Hours later they return only to go out again on a run. Finally, after still more hours of waiting, they cross the finish line and expect you to be there at the perfect spot, waiting with the camera and hugs and kisses and unlimited admiration and praise.

Is this how we athletes reward our supporters after months of being obsessive-compulsive about a training schedule taped to the refrigerator door? Getting grouchy when we're overtired or hungry? Going to bed early and rising early? Abstaining from weekend diversions because we have to get in a forty-miler Saturday morning? Is it fair to ask them to have the same interest and passion in the sport as we leave tri gear lying around the house? Constantly complain about aches and pains? Constantly agonize over whether we'll finish or perhaps drown in the swim? No. But we do it because we need them to validate what we do.

At my first triathlon, my husband agreed to wake up at 4:30 to accompany me. He didn't want to, but he's supportive and knew this was important to me. There wasn't much for him to do as I busied myself setting up transition, getting marked, and fighting my way into my wet suit. He brought the *New York Times* and a big mug of coffee.

I was feeling confident as we walked down to the water. I had put in hours of training and felt prepared and excited. But something happened when I saw the lake and all the swimmers and the crowd of over a hundred women in my wave. I panicked. I walked away from the water's edge, found my husband, and said I wanted to go home, that I wasn't going through with it.

We've been married over thirty years, so he knows me well. He gently grabbed my shoulders and told me he wasn't taking me home, I came here to do a triathlon, and get back in the water and do it. I started to cry, held him tightly, and pleaded with him to take me home. He said if I gave in to my fears and went home I would regret it all day and every day till I did one so I might as well do it now that I was here, suited up, and ready to go.

Reluctantly I headed back to the water, started the swim, had a panic attack, and tried to swim back to shore but was faced with the thirty- to forty-year-old men swimming toward me. I made it through the swim and ran back to transition, only to forget where my bike was racked. My husband was there for me on the sidelines, directing me to my bike.

I remember seeing him as I started the run, sitting in the shade reading the newspaper. I didn't disturb him. He had earned that siesta.

When I finished, he was there to hug me and congratulate and wipe away my tears. Driving home he had to listen to my minute-by-minute recap. That was the first and last event he attended and that's fine with me. He was there when I needed him the most.

Alyson Llerandi, wife of Ironman Mike Llerandi, knows a thing or two about spectating. Being the wife of an Ironman isn't easy, especially when you are also a triathlete. She layers that with other more important priorities like their three kids and being a part-time accountant. But her most serious sport is spectating at Mike's events. When he doesn't appear at the designated spots along the course her heart races and her mind fills with horrific images of him drowning, crashing his bike, or DNFing on the run.

"When Mike was competing in Panama City, it was a very stormy day. The swim didn't go along the shoreline, but out and back into the open water. It was very choppy and the swimmers were having a really difficult time. There were seven buoys to mark the course but the swells were so high the competitors kept missing the marks and turning back before circling the last two. I was standing on the beach in the storm, pregnant again, waiting for Mike to come out of the water, and he never appeared. I kept running back and forth to transition thinking I'd missed him, but I knew what his time should have been and even taking into consideration the storm, he should have been out of the water. I was convinced he'd drowned. That's a horrible feeling and I was panicking and crying when he finally appeared. Turns out Mike was the only swimmer who circled all the buoys."

There usually isn't room in a typical household, especially with three kids, for both partners to be Ironman competitors. Alyson feels it is her job to take care of all the day to day stuff so Mike can train and perform at the top of his ability and on race day herd their three kids along the route and hope to see Mike on the course. The art of spectating has its rewards, like trips to Hawaii where the kids can run their dad in at the finish and be a part of the celebration, or trips to Lake Placid where they have photos of the kids standing on the actual Olympic podiums. Spectating also has its downside.

According to Alyson, "He's fallen off his bike many times and had to be treated in the hospital for gravel embedded in his skin. He's broken all sorts of bones. At Lake Placid one year, a particularly windy and rain-swept day, I was busy herding the kids along the course and missed him. Again, I was sure he had fallen off his bike and was lying in the hospital but one of our friends who was also competing happened to pass by and said he was way ahead of his time and having a great day. That's great for Mike but I have to deal with the kids and the panic attacks and wondering if he is all right. I can never relax until I know he is off the bike. At the finish, I broke down crying more for relief that he was alive than for the great time he had."

Homemade signs, banners, balloons, and as many friends and family members as can line a course are always more than welcome. For parents, watching their child compete can be a thrill. Amy Shigo's mom wouldn't have missed going to IM Canada for the world. No one who watched the Destin, Florida, triathlon of Wendy Ellis and her niece will ever forget that day. What made tumor survivor Stacie Switzer's come-back triathlon so rewarding was seeing her daughter Maddie at the finish line.

Maybe it all boils down to a symbiotic relationship. The competitor and the spectator need each other.

Tips for Spectators:

Plan to get up early. Heck, maybe never go to bed!

Stay patient and calm as your athlete gets nervous and anxious.

Don't take anything personally or out of context. Tempers may flare due to stress levels. It's your job to stay focused and be supportive.

Bring lots of reading material, plenty of liquids, and sunscreen.

Take along a folding chair. It's going to be a long day.

Make a least one sign. If you hold it up at the beginning and the end, you've done your job.

Have the cool-down clothes ready: a clean shirt, shorts, sandals, or flip-flops.

Have the camera ready at all times. There are three legs of the race to capture. The best places for action shots are right at the water's edge before the start, coming out of the water, heading out of T1 on the bike, and heading out of T2 for the run, and of course the finish line.

Be patient on the way home as you endure—with a smile—a total recall of the entire event.

Next year, plan to be a participant and let someone else do the spectating.

BEST ATHLETE?

The first Ironman competition was held to answer a question posed by Commander John Collins: Which athletes are more fit, runners or swimmers? An article in *Sports Illustrated* magazine had declared that Eddy Merckx, the great Belgian cyclist, had the highest recorded oxygen uptake of any athlete ever measured, so perhaps cyclists were more fit than anyone. Collins disagreed with the article and formed the three-sport event to settle the question. The winner, Gordon Haller, was a runner. Even though he was a very well-rounded athlete who biked and swam, Haller was first and foremost a runner. Today, he would be called a multi-sport athlete.

I posed the same question to the athletes interviewed for this book to see if twenty-eight years later runners are still the fittest athletes and hold an advantage in the Ironman over swimmers and cyclists. Their specialty comes last and they finally get to show off their sport. Anyone who runs marathons knows the importance of pacing, how to fuel, and how to dig deep—all necessary tools during the last leg of the event when participants are into their tenth hour or more, of competition.

The answers were surprising on many fronts, and at the same time not surprising at all. Swimmers think they have the advantage and are the most fit; so do runners. Here's the swimmers' logic, stated most clearly by Karen Smyers, a swimmer: "Swimmers start the competition relaxed and with a level of comfort that runners and cyclists can't expect to have. We don't waste nervous energy at the start of the race." She explains further that the swim is the biggest challenge for everyone, even swimmers, but once through it the bike and run are less daunting. "You can't stop in the water. But you can coast on a bike and walk during a run." She makes a strong argument. When Haller and Collins and the rest of the original crew were discussing in what order to place the events, they decided to put the swim first because it had the most potential for serious injury. According to Haller, "We decided to make the swim first because everyone would be fresh and strong and the risk of injury or drowning would be minimized." However, as a pro, Smyers feels she can't have any weaknesses at all and works just as hard on her bike and run workouts.

Maggie Stovickova, the swimmer from Slovakia, feels the same way. "Swimming is second nature to me. I don't even have to think about it," she says. "I start the event fresh and relaxed and ready to go." She can also pick out the nonswimmers at events. "They are the ones with fear in their eyes. That's a terrible way to start a race."

Mike Llerandi, a swimmer-turned-runner, disagrees. "I definitely agree with the assessment that runners make the best Iron-folks, since it is so much harder than either of the other two sports. Anyone who can take the pounding of a marathon and turn in a solid performance like Haller did in the first race knows how much fun it is to pass people over the final hours."

Coach Bob Scott is in Llerandi's camp. According to Scott, "No sport-specific athlete has a big advantage in a triathlon. It's the mind-set that matters. Tour de France cyclists don't run well. Swimmers don't necessarily bike well. It takes experience to do a triathlon well. Having said that, most tri experts will agree you win the Ironman on the run. A good runner can make up quite a few minutes from the other stages."

Dave Scott agrees with Bob Scott (no relation). Dave Scott had a background in swimming but was well trained in all the events when he won his first Ironman in 1980. He doesn't think being better in one particular sport gives a competitor an edge, but he definitely feels you can win the event on the run. "You can make up more time on the run than the swim or the bike. If you break down the splits of the top twenty athletes at Ironman, there's usually a ten- to twelve-minute spread from first place to tenth during the bike leg but a thirty-minute spread in the run. It's easier to close a ten-minute gap but darn hard to close a thirty-minute one."

Swim coach Terry Laughlin uses statistics to back up his vote for the swimmers. Ninety percent of professional triathletes have a swimming background. All three women on the 2000 Olympic triathlon team came from a swimming background. "No one is intimidated by a bike or a run but nonswimmers are definitely intimidated by the swim. For nonswimmers, the swim can be their worst nightmare."

No one brought up the cyclists. They didn't even factor into the question. The main reasoning behind the lack of professional cyclists in triathlon is that professional cyclists simply don't get involved in the sport. They are purists. Of course there are exceptions like Stefani Jackenthal, a nationally ranked professional cyclist until a bad crash ended that career and she moved on to triathlon. Lance Armstrong is another exception, but backward: He was a triathlete before becoming a professional cyclist.

The biggest change in triathlon since the sport's beginning is that competitors back then were single-sport athletes. They were runners, or swimmers, or cyclists. Very few were multisport-savvy. That's changing. Although many athletes start with one sport, such as swimming, they move on to incorporate other sports even before they take up triathlon. High school athletes typically run cross-country in the fall or play soccer, join basketball in the winter, and run track or play lacrosse in the spring. Cross-training has become a popular training vehicle with coaches and running is the sport of choice. On the other hand, runners who need a break from all the pounding cross-train with biking or swimming. It's more common today to pick up many sports than just concentrate on one.

Jayne Williams, the self-described slow fat triathlete, took another approach when asked who the best athlete is. Her response: Who cares? According to Williams, unless you are a pro or are going after an age-group win for the podium, it's not an issue. "I'm just out there to have fun. I'm not particularly good at any one of them so it doesn't concern me."

And that is the point. Unless you are out to win or place, which narrows the field to a handful of participants, relax and enjoy the event. Do what Dave Scott suggests. Think of yourself as a triathlete, not a swimmer, or runner, or cyclist. The best triathlete is a triathlete. The sooner you start thinking of yourself as one, the sooner you will become one.

CONCLUSION

What I learned from all my interviews is that triathletes never look back. As sure as they yell, "never again!" as they emerge from the swim after getting pummeled in the water, or "I hate this!" as they get passed on the bike, or even "Please remind me why I am doing this?" during the run, they're already planning the next event on the way home.

They always look forward to the next event to be with friends and have fun, and perhaps attempt to shave a few seconds off the last finish time.

One appeal of the triathlon for first-timers is that it is a relatively new sport, an infant in contrast with the ancient history of the marathon, which dates back to 490 B.C. and Phidippides's famous run. Events, especially at the sprint distance, are packed with first-timers who are welcomed by all levels of athletes and race directors. At a recent sprint triathlon I attended, a group of first-timers showed up ten minutes before the start, totally unaware of the lengthy process they had to go through such as bike check, chip pickup, body markings, setting up transition, and walking half a mile down the beach to the start. Instead of being irritated, the race director just laughed, welcomed them, and hurried them through the process with the warning to arrive an hour early at their next event.

With the sport growing at such a rapid pace, it's difficult to find a small venue anymore. Just four years ago, the inaugural SoBe Mossman Sprint Triathlon in Norwalk, Connecticut, had three hundred entrants. In 2006 it had eight hundred, and it is now the largest triathlon event in Connecticut.

The engaging spirit of the triathlon community as a whole also has something to do with the growth of the sport. Newbies feel welcome, not intimidated. Pros like Mike Llerandi and Karen Smyers and coaches like Scott Willett and Bob Scott, who've been in the sport since its inception, are more than willing to give advice, lend a hand, and see to it that first-timers fall in love with triathlon. It seems to be the mission of the triathlon community to win everyone over—and they are well on their way.

I also learned that everyone dreads the swim, even the swimmers! But there is good news. A new study suggests that it's not really the subject of the bad thing (like having to do the swim leg of a triathlon) that people dread, but the time spent waiting for it to happen. Finding a distraction is the best way to cope. Maybe race directors should start a conga line at the beach complete with reggae music for the swimmers instead of having them milling around with that fear-based look in their eyes. A more practical suggestion is the use of mantras, prayers, singing, or whatever gets you through it.

People enter their first triathlon for many reasons. For some, it's to settle a bet made on a golf course, or to satisfy the nagging friends at the firehouse who won't leave you alone till you do one. For others who have survived life-threatening illnesses it is an affirmation that they are still here. Regardless of the motives, everyone finishes with a sense of accomplishment and achievement they didn't know existed. And that's why they go back for more.

COACHING CONTACTS
AND OTHER INFORMATION SOURCES

In today's world of outsourcing everything, finding a coach and triathlon information is just a keystroke away. Online coaching, once the exclusive domain of elite athletes, has opened up a new world to athletes everywhere. For a fee, online coaches design daily workout schedules that include how far, how fast, and can get as detailed as using heart rate monitors, VO_2 max indexes, nutrition, and other counseling depending on the clients interest.

The cost of personal online coaching ranges from forty to more than a thousand dollars a month depending on the range of services provided. According to Alan Ley of USA Triathlon, who manages the coaching division, there are more than fourteen hundred USA Triathlon-certified coaches, up from just eight in 1997.

Lauren Antonucci, MS, RD, CDE, CDN
Lauren@nutritionenergy.com
www.nutritionenergy.com

Chris Carmichael, Carmichael Training Systems
www.trainright.com

Terry Laughlin, Total Immersion
www.totalimmersion.net

David Pruetz, CFT
USA Triathlon-certified coach, In Training, LLC
801.573.7383
davidp@intraining.biz
www.intraining.biz

Bob Scott
Teamscott2@aol.com

Dave Scott
info@davescottinc.com
www.davescottinc.com

Overall triathlon information: www.trinewbie.com

USA Triathlon: www.usatriathlon.org

Triathlete Magazine: www.triathletemag.com

Jayne Williams' technical apparel for oversized triathletes:
www.slowfattriathlete.com

Challenged Athletes Foundation: www.challengedathletes.org
CAF was founded in 1997 with the mission to help fund disabled athletes with equipment such as handcycles, wheelchairs, and specially fitted bikes—things that are very costly but make a difference in their lives. The foundation started with one athlete—trailblazing below-knee amputee endurance racer Jim MacLaren.

At twenty-two, Yale graduate Jim MacLaren was hit by a New York City bus, thrown some eighty feet, and pronounced dead on arrival at Bellevue Hospital. His life stabilized but he lost his left leg eight inches below the knee. He went on to graduate from the Yale School of Drama and started competing in running events. He holds the Hawaii Ironman record for an amputee, with a time of 10:42. On June 6, 1993, during a triathlon in Orange County, Jim suffered a devastating second accident. He was hit by a car and thrown headfirst into a lamppost during the bike leg and was paralyzed. His first thought was what it would be like to compete in a wheelchair. His friends started raising funds for his recovery and organized the first San Diego Triathlon Challenge (SDTC)—an annual fund-raising triathlon event at La Jolla Cove. From this beginning arose CAF and their mission to make sure that people with physical challenges have the same freedom to enjoy sports that the rest of us take for granted.

GLOSSARY

Aerobic/anaerobic: *Aerobic* refers to the presence of oxygen in the bloodstream. Aerobic exercise is done at a comfortable level, not exceeding normal speed or intensity. *Anaerobic* refers to exceeding the normal speed or intensity, making the muscles use more oxygen than the body can provide. After an anaerobic exercise period, rest is required to build the oxygen in the bloodstream. Anaerobic threshold is sometimes referred to as lactate threshold.

Bonk: A biking term that refers to extreme exhaustion caused by the depletion of glycogen in the muscles. Also referred to as hitting the wall in distance running.

Brick workout: Training in two disciplines one right after the other, such as swim/bike, or bike/run.

Cadence: Revolutions or cycles per minute of the pedal stroke. The term can also be applied to swim stroke and running stride.

Carbohydrate Loading: Consuming enough carbohydrates to store adequate amounts of glycogen in the muscles for an endurance event. Recommended for events lasting longer than ninety minutes.

Cool-down/warm-down: Low-intensity run, swim, or bike at the end of a race or drills. Allows the muscles to relax and release lactic acid buildup.

Cross-training: Adding varied sports to an exercise regime. Usually the sports complement one another. Swimming stretches out runners. Cycling builds different leg muscles. Cross-training allows for rest of overused muscles.

Dehydration: Not having enough fluids in the body. Can lead to impaired performance, cramps, chills, nausea, headaches, dizziness, and heatstroke.

Drafting: Biking, swimming, or running in close proximity behind others to reduce effort.

Electrolytes: Minerals such as potassium and sodium that help the body function normally during exercise. Electrolytes are lost through sweat and must be replaced during exercise.

Endorphins: Natural chemicals in the brain released during exercise that give a pleasurable feeling, sometimes referred to as a runner's high. Endorphin levels in the blood rise during prolonged exercise.

Endurance: The ability to resist fatigue.

Frequency: The number of times per week of a training routine.

Glucose: A simple sugar.

Glycogen: The principal form in which carbohydrates are stored in the muscle and liver. When glycogen stores get low, athletes feel fatigued and lightheaded.

Hammer: A fast, sustained effort.

Hamstring: The large tendon in the back of the knee and thigh.

Hydration: Maintaining and storing the proper amounts of fluid in the body. Water is the principal source of hydration and transports glucose, oxygen, and fats to working muscles and carries away by-products.

Hyperthermia: When the body temperature rises above normal due to excess heat. Can cause heatstroke.

Hypothermia: When the core body temperature drops below normal due to excessive cold.

Interval training: A system of high-intensity workouts defined by short periods of hard exercise interspersed with periods of recovery.

Iliotibial (IT) band: A thick, strong tendon that extends from the hip across the outside of the knee and below. It can become inflamed and irritated if the foot rolls too far to the outside, putting pressure on the band. This can be caused by worn-out shoes, too much mileage, or sudden increase in mileage.

Lactic acid: When muscles are pushed beyond their normal limit, they can no longer process oxygen and fuel efficiently. The result is a buildup of waste products in the muscle, primarily lactic acid. This is the cause of the burning sensation and muscle soreness after an intense workout.

Mash: A cycling term referring to pushing in a big gear.

Masters division: An age division starting at age forty. Under forty is referred to as open.

Muscle fiber: Refers to a concentration of either FT, fast twitch, or ST, slow twitch, muscle fiber. Endurance athletes have a higher percentage of ST fibers as opposed to high FT fibers in sprinters. Middle-distance athletes have an equal proportion of ST/FT fibers.

Negative split: Completing the second half of an event faster than the first.

Overreaching: Training above the normal workload.

Overtraining: Mental and physical extreme fatigue brought on from too much overreaching.

Peaking: A planned schedule of workouts designed to reach maximum training followed by reduced training allowing the athlete to reach high levels of fitness before an event.

PR: Personal record. An athlete's best time for a particular event.

Recovery: A period of training between intervals when rest is required.

Repetition: The number of times a workout task or drill is repeated.

Set: A group of repetitions.

Taper: A reduction in training volume prior to an event.

Transition: The area of a triathlon where gear is set out and bikes are racked.

T1: The transition between the swim and the bike.

T2: The transition between the bike and the run.

VO_2max: The capacity for oxygen consumption in the body during maximal exertion.

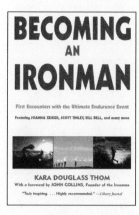

BECOMING AN IRONMAN

First Encounters with the Ultimate Endurance Event

Featuring JOANNA ZEIGER, SCOTT TINLEY, BILL BELL, and many more

KARA DOUGLASS THOM

With a foreword by JOHN COLLINS, Founder of the Ironman

"Truly inspiring. . . . Highly recommended." —*Library Journal*

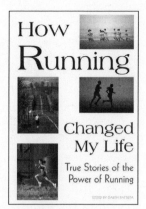

How Running Changed My Life

True Stories of the Power of Running

EDITED BY GARTH BATTISTA

THE RUNNER'S HIGH

illumination and ecstasy in motion

The Sweet Spot in Time

THE SEARCH FOR ATHLETIC PERFECTION

JOHN JEROME

Staying With It

ON BECOMING AN ATHLETE

JOHN JEROME

Staying Supple

THE BOUNTIFUL PLEASURES OF STRETCHING

JOHN JEROME

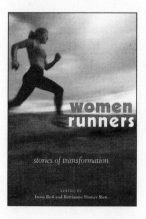

women runners

stories of transformation

EDITED BY Irene Reti and Bettianne Shoney Sien

The Spirit of the Marathon

WHAT TO EXPECT IN YOUR FIRST MARATHON AND HOW TO RUN THEM FOR THE REST OF YOUR LIFE

(A companion volume to *First Marathon*)

"Gail's stories bring the marathon to life!" —Grete Waitz

FEATURING:
Jeff Galloway
Kathrine Switzer
Ted Corbitt
Don Kardong
Gordon Bakoulis
Anne Marie Lauck
and many more!

GAIL WAESCHE KISLEVITZ
AUTHOR OF *FIRST MARATHONS*

IT'S NEVER TOO LATE!

Personal Stories of **Staying Young Through Sports**

GAIL WAESCHE KISLEVITZ
AUTHOR OF *FIRST MARATHONS*

OTHER BOOKS OF INTEREST FROM BREAKAWAY

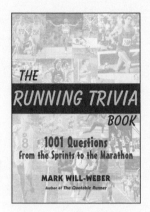

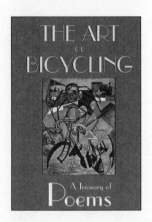

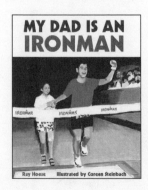